The message of Jesus may be timeless. But his life, teachings, death, and resurrection were all time-stamped. They took place in the real word at a specific time and place. In *The Forgotten Jesus*, Robby Gallaty helps us better understand the long-forgotten culture and context of Jesus's life and ministry so that we may better grasp the timeless beauty and power of his gospel.

—**Larry Osborne,** Pastor and Author,
North Coast Church, Vista, California

For many years, First Fruits of Zion has aimed to help Christians to know Jesus better by seeing Him in His Jewish context. Pastor Robby Gallaty is a pastor and Bible teacher who shares that vision. His new book *The Forgotten Jesus* will help Christians to remember the Jewish Jesus who has largely been forgotten. Read this book if you want to know and follow our Master better!

—**Boaz Michael,** Founder and Director of
First Fruits of Zion in Jerusalem, Israel

Looking for something new? Look to something old! This book is "gold" with fresh insight to the preacher in teaching God's Word and "gold" to believers in seeing new understanding into the New Testament by looking to the old—the Old Testament. Don't miss this treasure that God has revealed through Robby Gallaty.

—**Bryant Wright,** Senior Pastor of Johnson Ferry
Baptist Church, Marietta, Georgia

Robby's passion for Jesus ignites and unites the way he thinks, speaks, and acts. His design in this book is to help you do the same. To my mind, he achieves that goal. Do you crave to love God as Father the way Jesus did? Read on! And may the God of Abraham, Isaac, and Jacob grant you the desire of your heart.

—**James Whitman,** Director, Center
for Judaic-Christian Studies

I'm delighted to see Robby Gallaty's *The Forgotten Jesus* and know it will be of great benefit for anyone wanting to understand Jesus' Jewish context. As Gallaty re-situates him in his historical setting, he shows how our Rabbi brought the truth of God's Word to its greatest expression. Readers will be freshly amazed at Jesus' life and ministry when they view it in light of his first-century Jewish reality.

—**Lois Tverberg,** Author of *Walking in the Dust of Rabbi Jesus*

The Hebrew word for 'knowledge,' da'at, conveys the meaning "intimate knowledge"—a knowledge that includes love. In any relationship, constant curiosity and a desire to learn more about a person enable us to grow deeper in our understanding. And the more we learn, the more we will act in order to please the one we love. In reintroducing us to the forgotten Jesus, Pastor Robby offers us the means to ignite and rekindle our knowledge of and love for the Good Shepherd of our souls, Messiah Jesus, and for our Father in heaven. May we persevere in what my beloved, late husband, Dwight A.Pryor, called "...the great adventure of beholding the man Jesus of Nazareth, in the beauty of his humanity and the brilliance of his teaching." This book helps us do just that!

—**Keren Hannah Pryor**, Author of *A Taste of Torah*
and *A Dash of Drash* (www.ffoz.org)

This book will help you understand and appreciate the significance of the Jewish-ness of Jesus and the larger biblical narrative. I highly recommend this book!

—**Matt Carter**, Pastor, Austin Stone Community Church

THE
FORGOTTEN
JESUS

Also by Robby Gallaty

MARCS of a Disciple

Rediscovering Discipleship

Growing Up: How to Be a Disciple Who Makes Disciples

Firmly Planted: How to Cultivate a Faith Rooted in Christ

Foundations: A 260-Day Bible Reading Plan for Busy Believers

Creating an Atmosphere to Hear God Speak

THE FORGOTTEN JESUS

HOW WESTERN CHRISTIANS SHOULD FOLLOW AN EASTERN RABBI

ROBBY GALLATY

 ZONDERVAN®

ZONDERVAN

The Forgotten Jesus
Copyright © 2017 by Robert Gallaty

This title is also available as a Zondervan ebook.

Requests for information should be addressed to:
Zondervan, *3900 Sparks Drive SE, Grand Rapids, Michigan 49546*

ISBN 978-0-310-52923-1

Bible versions are listed on page 12, which hereby becomes a part of this copyright page.

Published in association with the literary agency of Mark Sweeney & Associates, Naples, Florida 34113.

Cover design: Matt Wrightson
Cover photo: Christ, by Heinrich Hofmann
Interior design: Kait Lamphere
Interior photography: Shutterstock, except page 105: © amite/istock

Printed in the United States of America

17 18 19 20 21 22 23 24 25 /DHV/ 15 14 13 12 11 10 9 8 7 6 5 4 3 2

To the late Dwight A. Pryor
Founder of Judaic-Christian Studies (jcstudies.com)
Your passion for uncovering the Jesus of
the Bible still burns in me today. I'm forever grateful for the
time we spent together in the land where Jesus lived.

Contents

Bible Versions

All Scripture quotations, unless otherwise indicated, are taken from the ESV® Bible (The Holy Bible, English Standard Version®). Copyright © 2001 by Crossway, a publishing ministry of Good News Publishers. Used by permission. All rights reserved.

Scripture quotations marked CSB are taken from the Christian Standard Bible, copyright © 2016 by Holman Christian Publishers, Nashville, Tennessee. All rights reserved.

Scripture quotations marked KJV are taken from the King James Version. Public domain.

Scripture quotations marked NIV are taken from The Holy Bible, New International Version®, NIV®. Copyright © 1973, 1978, 1984, 2011 by Biblica, Inc.® Used by permission of Zondervan. All rights reserved worldwide. www.Zondervan.com. The "NIV" and "New International Version" are trademarks registered in the United States Patent and Trademark Office by Biblica, Inc.®

Scripture quotations marked NKJV are taken from the New King James Version®. Copyright © 1982 by Thomas Nelson. Used by permission. All rights reserved.

How Have We Lost the Jewishness of Jesus?

Jesus was a Jewish man who was raised in a Jewish culture, reared by exceptionally devout Jewish parents, and lived according to the Jewish laws. He was circumcised on the eighth day of his life and was dedicated to the Lord. As he grew up, he regularly attended the synagogue on the Sabbath, participated in every biblical feast, studied and memorized the scriptures, learned a trade from his father, and started his rabbinic ministry at age thirty—all of this according to Jewish customs at the time.[1] At the age of thirty, he selected twelve Jewish men to forsake everything, learn his teachings, and carry on his mission. Consequently, prior to Jesus's death, most of his followers were Jews who professed faith in Jesus as Messiah but still kept the festivals, worshiped in the temple, and observed the Sabbath.

If we look at Christianity today and compare it to how it began, we might notice that the "Jewishness" of both its founder and its original followers has been lost.

Our journey to recover the Jewishness of Jesus will bring familiar passages to life by viewing them through a Middle Eastern lens. For example, you may have heard that at the beginning of the book of Acts the disciples were huddled in a room fearfully waiting for the filling of the Holy Spirit. But a careful reading of the text proves that this teaching is inaccurate—they were hardly in hiding, and they had *already* received the Holy Spirit. "After worshiping Him," Luke writes, "they returned to Jerusalem with great joy. And they were continually in the temple praising God" (Luke 24:52–53 CSB).

This doesn't sound like fearful disciples huddling in terror. The disciples had no reason to fear, for the first filling of the Holy Spirit they had received came in John 20 when Jesus breathed the Spirit into his followers: "After saying this, he breathed on them and said, 'Receive the Holy Spirit. If you forgive the sins of any, they are forgiven them; if you retain the sins of any, they are retained'" (20:22–23 CSB). Acts 2 is not the first time the disciples received the Holy Spirit, nor were they huddled together in one room. Very few upper rooms in Israel are large enough to accommodate 120 people.[2]

So what is the most likely explanation? When the disciples received the Holy Spirit as "tongues of fire" in Acts 2, they were in a house, but probably not the same upper room they had previously met in for Passover. The temple is commonly referred to in scripture as the "house of God,"[3] and the rushing wind accompanied with tongues of fire most likely appeared in front of thousands of worshipers in the temple complex, the same area where the early believers would worship for years to come.

This also makes sense of why 3,000 people responded to the message Peter preached on Pentecost. According to Acts 2:46–47 (CSB), "Every day they devoted themselves to meeting together in the temple, and broke bread from house to house. They ate their food with joyful and sincere hearts, praising God and enjoying the favor of all the people. Every day the Lord added to their number those who were being saved." The disciples were *openly* praising their savior, and they came to lead a movement that would reverberate through history.

The movement of early Jewish Christianity would soon extend to the Gentiles (non-Jews) as it migrated from Israel into the Roman world. These "God-fearers" were Gentiles who believed in the teachings of Yahweh, and they were often the first to convert to Christianity, as we see with Cornelius in Acts 10. The first official "ruling" of the early church is found in Acts 15. Often referred to as the Jerusalem Council, James, Jesus's half-brother, presided over the assembly.

As Jesus had prophesied, Gentiles had begun believing in the one true God and identifying themselves with the movement of Christ, and this was creating some problems and tensions between the Jewish believers and the Gentile followers of Jesus. After hearing both sides of the argument, Jesus's half-brother James declared: "Therefore, in my judgment, we should not cause difficulties for those among the Gentiles who turn to God, but instead we should write to them to abstain from things polluted by idols, from sexual immorality, from eating anything that has been strangled, and from blood" (Acts 15:19–20 CSB). From that point forward, Gentiles were given minimal prohibitions in their common fellowship with Jewish believers.

What united both of these groups was their acceptance of the gospel of Christ. Notice that Gentiles were brought *into the fold* of the Jews through the death, burial, and resurrection of Jesus. In these early days, unity was found in assimilating Gentiles into what was largely a Jewish movement.

The unity of the Jerusalem Council, unfortunately, would be short lived.

Renaming the Old Testament

A shift separating Christianity from its Jewish roots can be seen as early as the second century, with the renaming of the scriptures. The Tanak—an acronym for the Old Testament books of the *Torah* (the first five books of the Bible: Genesis, Exodus, Leviticus, Numbers, and Deuteronomy), the Nevi'im (the books of the prophets beginning with the book of Joshua), and the Ketuv'im (the writings beginning with the book of Psalms)—was renamed the Old Testament or the "books of the Old Testament" by Melito of Sardis and Clement of Alexandria.[4] Our current Protestant Bibles contain the same books of the Tanak with changes in how they are categorized. Below you can find a list of the books of the Tanak compared to the ordering of our Old Testament today.

Rejection of the Jews

The second-century work of Justin Martyr sheds further light on the growing separation of Christianity from its Jewish roots. Justin Martyr was a Christian apologist (someone who defends the faith against intellectual attacks) who waged a battle of words against Jews and Judaism in his polemical work *Dialogue with Trypho*. He argued against a Jew named Trypho that the Torah was given to the Jewish people by God as a punishment for their sinfulness.

Around that same time, Marcion, the son of a wealthy bishop, argued that the Jesus of the New Testament had overturned and replaced the God

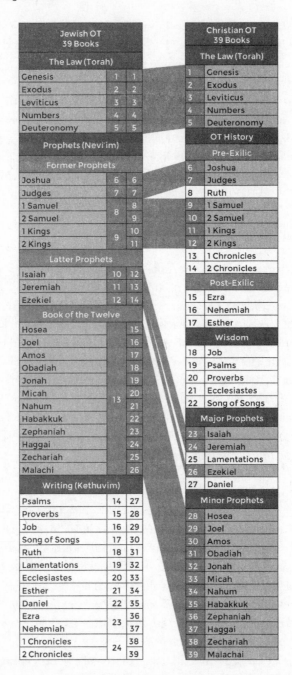

Jewish OT 39 Books			Christian OT 39 Books	
The Law (Torah)			**The Law (Torah)**	
Genesis	1	1	1	Genesis
Exodus	2	2	2	Exodus
Leviticus	3	3	3	Leviticus
Numbers	4	4	4	Numbers
Deuteronomy	5	5	5	Deuteronomy
Prophets (Nevi'im)			**OT History**	
			Pre-Exilic	
Former Prophets			6	Joshua
Joshua	6	6	7	Judges
Judges	7	7	8	Ruth
1 Samuel	8	8	9	1 Samuel
2 Samuel		9	10	2 Samuel
1 Kings	9	10	11	1 Kings
2 Kings		11	12	2 Kings
			13	1 Chronicles
Latter Prophets			14	2 Chronicles
Isaiah	10	12	**Post-Exilic**	
Jeremiah	11	13	15	Ezra
Ezekiel	12	14	16	Nehemiah
Book of the Twelve			17	Esther
Hosea		15	**Wisdom**	
Joel		16	18	Job
Amos		17	19	Psalms
Obadiah		18	20	Proverbs
Jonah		19	21	Ecclesiastes
Micah		20	22	Song of Songs
Nahum	13	21	**Major Prophets**	
Habakkuk		22	23	Isaiah
Zephaniah		23	24	Jeremiah
Haggai		24	25	Lamentations
Zechariah		25	26	Ezekiel
Malachi		26	27	Daniel
Writing (Kethuvim)			**Minor Prophets**	
Psalms	14	27	28	Hosea
Proverbs	15	28	29	Joel
Job	16	29	30	Amos
Song of Songs	17	30	31	Obadiah
Ruth	18	31	32	Jonah
Lamentations	19	32	33	Micah
Ecclesiastes	20	33	34	Nahum
Esther	21	34	35	Habakkuk
Daniel	22	35	36	Zephaniah
Ezra	23	36	37	Haggai
Nehemiah		37	38	Zechariah
1 Chronicles	24	38	39	Malachai
2 Chronicles		39		

Figure 1. Comparison of the Tanak and the Old Testament

of the Old Testament. He compiled his own version of the New Testament (now called Marcion's Bible), which included only the Gospel of Luke and ten of Paul's epistles. The remaining fifteen books were rejected because he believed they had Hebraic undertones and Jewish corruptions.[5] Even though the Roman church later labeled Marcion a heretic, his teaching and his view of the Old Testament influenced the hearts of many, further widening the ever-growing chasm between Jews and Gentiles.

Christian teachers and theologians also began to advocate a teaching we know today as "replacement theology." This is the belief that the New Testament church has replaced the Old Testament saints, assuming all of the blessings and promises bestowed upon Israel. Ironically, while the blessings are welcomed with open arms, those who advocate this view tend to avoid talking about the curses that God promises for disobedience.

Emperor Constantine drove the proverbial nail in the coffin, cementing the divide between Jew and Gentile, with his renunciation of Jews at the Council of Nicaea in 325 A.D., saying "Let us have nothing in common with the detestable Jewish rabble."[6] Some preachers, like the popular John Chrysostom, adopted this attitude of hatred toward the Jews as well, and for much of the next thousand years the Roman church was united in seeing the Jewish people as the enemies of the Christian faith. There was little to no interest in understanding the Bible from a Jewish perspective or in seeing Jesus as a Jewish rabbi and understanding him in his Jewish context.

And while we might have hoped for some change in this perspective during the time of the Protestant Reformation, when many biblical doctrines were recovered, this was not to be. In the sixteenth century, the great German reformer Martin Luther was critical of the book of James for its Jewish undertones, calling it an "Epistle of straw."

Early in his ministry, Luther shared the gospel with Jews in hopes of converting them to Christianity, but his compassion for them waned over time. Even worse, later in life he became a fierce opponent of the Jews and was very critical of them.[7] Luther and the other reformers continued to advocate the idea that the church had replaced Israel and that God had no further purposes for the Jewish people, and all of this perpetuated the separation of Jesus from his original Jewish context.

Fulfill, Not Replace

Earlier, I mentioned the problem with "replacement theology," the understanding that all of God's purposes and plans for Israel are replaced in the church. Is this a biblical way of understanding the relationship between the church and Israel? Jesus gives us a hint of how we should see this relationship when he speaks about the Hebrew scriptures (our Old Testament) in the Sermon on the Mount, "Don't think that I came to abolish the Law or the Prophets. I did not come to abolish but to fulfill" (Matt. 5:17 CSB).

Notice that Jesus uses the terms "the Law and the Prophets." This is a common Jewish way of describing the totality of the Old Testament. Instead of abolishing or destroying the Old Testament scriptures or setting them aside, Jesus says that he has come to "fulfill" them. This means he has come to properly establish, correctly interpret, and complete their intended purpose.

When I was a teenager, I wanted to be an artist, so my parents reluctantly enrolled me in art lessons. I learned a technique for painting whereby I sketched the picture in pencil as a foreshadowing of the finished product—all before applying any paint to the canvas. After I had completed the outline in pencil, I would then fill in the drawing with paint.

In many ways, the Old Testament commandments can be understood as the pencil sketch of God's purposes, and that makes Jesus the proverbial paint.[8] The full picture of who God was and what he was doing was not complete when God gave the Jewish people the Law and established his relationship with them in the Old Testament. It isn't until we get to Jesus that God begins to fill in the colors between the roughly sketched lines. Jesus fulfills the portrait we begin to see in the Old Testament. He brings the image into high definition.

Jesus fulfilled the Torah and the Prophets through his obedience to the Law of Moses, as the one who inherits the Old Testament promises to God's people, and through the fulfillment of Old Testament prophecy. As a devout, first-century Jew, Jesus faithfully observed the Law of Moses. As John Philips explains, "The Jews counted 613 separate edicts in the Mosaic law and there never was a single moment when the Lord Jesus did not absolutely fulfill in every detail every commandment."[9] Through his obedience to God in his life and teachings, Jesus fulfilled the Old

Testament by bringing God and God's purposes into clearer focus. The ancient promises, long concealed in mystery, finally make sense.

The Journey Begins

Throughout our study of Jesus in this book, you will learn that Jesus and his teachings, beliefs, and ways of acting were, in the words of D. Thomas Lancaster, "patently Jewish." As Lancaster goes on to say, "Any attempt at church reformation—any attempt to return to the original New Testament church—falls short as long as it refuses to acknowledge the essential Jewishness of our faith."[10] So the first three chapters of this book are foundational, giving you an introduction to the first-century world in which Jesus lived.

Chapter one illustrates the difference between Western and Middle Eastern thinking. Cultural systems like Hellenism (the thinking of the Greeks) and Romanism (the thinking of the Romans) have influenced our modern, Western approach to understanding the Bible far more than the Jewish or Hebrew way of thinking. We are, after all, products of our own culture. Chapter two connects Jesus with prominent Old Testament figures such as Abraham, Joseph, and Moses. Each of these figures paints a picture for us of the coming Messiah. Chapter three focuses on the 400-year intertestamental period between the writings of the final prophet of the Old Testament, Malachi, and the words of the first prophet to break the silence, John the Baptist.

Additionally, we will take a look at the significance of the temple in Jerusalem to shed light on the time period when Jesus of Nazareth is born. Chapter four describes the cultural background of Jesus's upbringing and his early ministry. We learn why Joseph was probably a stonemason and not a wood carpenter, what it means for Jesus to be called the "shoot of Jesse," why Jesus was raised in Nazareth, and how he was received when he preached his first sermon there.

Chapter five explains how Jewish believers in Jesus read the New Testament through the lens of the Old Testament by highlighting over-looked *keshers*, or textual connections between the parts of the Bible. Our lack of biblical knowledge often causes us to skip over these important links. Familiar passages such as Jesus eating at Zacchaeus's house, the

Mount of Transfiguration, and the Last Supper will come alive. The sixth chapter chronicles more of these allusions and *keshers* in Jesus's ministry as we watch him speak at the Feast of Tabernacles, heal a woman with a twelve-year blood discharge, and teach Nicodemus about how the kingdom of God is a present reality and not just a future promise.

We'll also see how God's witness in Jewish culture over the past 2,000 years continues to point to Jesus as the Jewish Messiah. According to Jewish tradition, the ministry of the coming Messiah will be recognized when he performs three messianic miracles. Chapter seven uncovers how Jesus fulfilled every one of these. The triumphal entrance into Jerusalem presents Jesus as the Passover Lamb to be tested from the tenth day of the month until the fourteenth. Chapter eight looks at the four groups who questioned or tested Jesus to determine if he truly was the spotless, sinless Passover Lamb of God. We will look at the Last Supper from a Hebraic perspective to point out some errors many Christians have believed through the years. And I'll explain how Leonardo da Vinci hijacked the Passover with his culturally inaccurate painting of a Middle Eastern festival.

Chapter nine will examine the trial, arrest, and death of Jesus, and we'll look at how Pilate presented the crowd with a choice of two Jesuses. I'll also make the case for why there was likely not a literal rooster crowing in the courtyard as Peter denied Jesus, and I will show from scripture why Jesus's words on the cross about God forsaking him may have deeper meaning than we realize. The final chapter will offer you some next steps for continuing your study as a disciple of Jesus.

How Much Does Scripture Weigh?

Let me offer one final word before we begin. While all scripture is God-breathed, not all scripture carries the same emphasis. This understanding should not minimize the impact of the truths I will be sharing with you in this book. For example, the Jews taught that among their Hebrew scriptures, the Nevi'im or the Prophets (Jeremiah, Isaiah, and Ezekiel) carry more weight than the Ketuv'im, the writings of Psalms, Proverbs, and Ecclesiastes. And the Torah—the five books of Genesis, Exodus, Leviticus, Numbers, and Deuteronomy—are the weightiest of them all.

Even in the Torah itself, one section is believed to be more central and authoritative than the rest: Deuteronomy 6:4–9.

If we study the teachings of Jesus in the New Testament, we find that he quoted from the book of Deuteronomy more than any other book of the Torah.[11] When he was tempted by Satan in Matthew 4, he responds all three times with verses from Deuteronomy ("Man does not live on bread alone but on every word that comes from the mouth of the LORD," Deut. 8:3 NIV; "Do not test the LORD your God," Deut. 6:16 CSB; and "Worship the Lord your God and serve only Him," Deut. 6:13, my paraphrase). And within the book of Deuteronomy, Jesus spoke several times about Deuteronomy 6:4–9. Jewish people refer to this passage by the first word of the section, pronounced *Shema* in Hebrew. We would translate it as the word *hear*.

The first scripture a Jewish boy or girl learns when they are able to speak is the Shema. And the final scripture on their lips before dying is the Shema. Observant Jews recite the Shema every morning when they rise and every evening before they retire to bed. There is no reason to believe that Jesus would not have done the same. At one point, Jesus responds to one man's inquiry about the most important scripture by reciting the Shema for him (see Luke 10:27). In Hebrew it reads:

> Shema Israel, Adonai Elohenu—Adonai Echad,
> Ve'ahavta Et Adonai Eloheikah,
> B'khol Levavkah,
> Uve'khol Naphshekah,
> Uve'khol M'odekah.

> Hear O Israel, The Lord is our God—The Lord Alone,
> Love the Lord your God
> with all your Heart,
> with all your Soul,
> and with all your Might.

Sadly, today you will find Bibles printed that do not contain the Old Testament. And even when our Bibles do include the Old Testament, it is not always read and studied. We often think of the Old Testament as inferior to the New. I have been guilty of this myself.

But we should not forget that the Old Testament is the Bible Jesus read. It informed his teachings, and everything he said or did or taught was related to these writings in some way. It is far from irrelevant! Jesus said that the scriptures testified about him—and he was speaking of our Old Testament. He quoted from the Old Testament to correct and rebuke people, and he interpreted it to give his disciples guidance. He quoted verses from Deuteronomy to defeat the devil in head-to-head spiritual warfare. His first recorded words after his baptism are quotations from the Torah, and his last utterance from the cross was a quotation from the Psalms.

Additionally, the New Testament itself is showered with passages from the Old Testament. One out of every twenty-two verses in the New Testament contains quotations from the Old Testament, and including allusions to the Old Testament make that ratio jump even higher. For the first-century Christian, the Old Testament was the *only* Testament.

So keep that in mind as you read and study. My hope and prayer is that if you've tried reading and studying the Old Testament and have found it confusing and difficult, you will be encouraged to give it another try as you read this book. It is the Word of God, and when we read and study it, we not only gain a better understanding of how God worked in the past; we also see the beauty of his unfolding plan culminating in the person and work of Jesus and then continuing to unfold today.

Our journey to uncover the forgotten Jesus of the first century begins now with a basic lesson about the differences between Eastern and Western thought. So grab a highlighter and your Bible, and let's rediscover the Jewish Jesus of the first century.

CHAPTER 1

Why We Need to Rediscover the Forgotten Jesus

I'll never forget the day I bought a high-definition television. Movies that I had seen many times before appeared new. Soft edges became precisely defined, flat colors became vivid and alive, chase scenes became more intense, love stories stirred new emotions, and dramatic tensions were heightened. My entire entertainment experience was enhanced instantly by this new technology.

Even more exciting than seeing a favorite movie in hi-def has been the experience of learning to apply a Hebraic hermeneutic to the Bible. I've found that as I've learned to read the Bible through a Jewish lens, it has enhanced both my understanding of and appreciation for God's Word. The Bible is like a multifaceted diamond that glitters more brightly with every minute turn. Martin Luther championed the notion that any born-again believer filled with the Spirit of God can read and understand the Bible for himself or herself without the need for extrabiblical books. And while this is certainly true, it is also true that some texts take on new shades of depth when we have a deeper understanding of the culture and context in which they were written.

Let me be clear here at the start: The purpose of this book is not to discount or distort anything you've been taught through the years. I'm not saying that what the church has believed and taught as true for 2,000 years is wrong and we need new doctrines. The core beliefs of the Christian faith are clear, and this book won't be revising them. Instead, this book is meant to bring a deeper appreciation and love for the scriptures. It's meant to enhance and bring to life familiar passages you've heard all of your life.

I do offer a warning before we begin our journey together: You may not agree with everything in this book, and that is perfectly acceptable. As a rule, you should never accept anything unless you search it out for yourself anyway. Whenever a source outside the Bible is introduced, even if that source is a trusted one, it should not carry the same weight as scripture. Never forget that the ultimate source of truth and the guiding authority for our life is the Bible alone.

Resources That Will Shed Light

So the purpose of this book is not to introduce you to a radically new doctrine or a strange teaching. It is to bring you closer to the Jesus of the Bible by placing him back into the first-century world in which he lived. The more we know him, the more our love for him will grow, and as we love him more, he will manifest more of himself to us (see John 17:3, Col. 3:1–2, and Mark 12:30). Our love grows with a deeper knowledge of God's Word.

In seminary, I was introduced to a method of studying the Bible called the historical-grammatical method. The idea behind the historical-grammatical method is that to properly interpret the meaning of a written text, we must first take into account both the original grammar of the text and the historical setting in which the text was written. This method places the biblical words within the culture of the ancient world. Since languages contain nuances of meaning and integral cultural information, the biblical reader must look at the broader context to determine meaning. Here is a simple example: The English word *fly* can signify soaring through the air, it can refer to a buzzing insect that hangs around our food, or it can mean the zipper on one's pants. The context plays a crucial part in understanding the meaning.

But how do we determine the cultural understanding of words and concepts that are over 2,000 years old? We can't travel through time, so we examine both biblical references and some extrabiblical accounts written during that period of time. Because they lacked the litany of thought-logging tools that we have at our disposal today, the ancient followers of God committed themselves to *memorizing* teachings of the sages and words of scripture and then passing them on to the next generations. Interpretations of the Hebrew Bible were passed along orally as part of the discipleship process. This was not something developed by Jesus—it was already part of the Jewish culture. "As the Mishnah demonstrates," Lancaster writes, "discipleship already existed as a well-established institution within Judaism long before the appearance of Yeshua (Jesus) and his followers."[1]

In much the same way that commentators wrestle with the meaning of scripture today, Jewish sages searched for hidden meanings, allusions, and foreshadowings of the coming Messiah. They also tried to reconcile apparently contradictory passages as best they could. A *midrash*—translated as "something that is searched out"—is a particular teaching by a Jewish teacher on a passage of scripture. The word can also refer to a collection of rabbinic teachings gathered together in a single book or oral explanations of the text that were collected and passed down through the years.

Many of these oral sayings (*midrashim*) were eventually compiled into what is called the Mishnah. The Mishnah wasn't compiled until the second century by Rabbi Yehuda, but many of the sayings contained within it were circulating in Jesus's day.[2] *Mishnah* is the Hebrew word for *repetition*, and it contains the rabbinical oral traditions and teachings on legal matters dating from around 50 BC to AD 200. Brant Pitre, commenting on the Mishnah, writes: "For rabbinic Judaism, outside the Bible, the Mishnah remains the most authoritative witness to Jewish tradition."[3] Because it circulated orally in Jesus's day, the Mishnah is often identified as the "oral law" or the "oral torah."

When reading the New Testament, it's important to recognize that Jesus never disregarded the written law, the Hebrew scriptures. When he rejected a teaching, it was always a teaching of the oral law, the extrabiblical rules and interpretations of the rabbis.

As we would find with any commentary on the Bible, the Mishnah received scrutiny over the years from different Jewish teachers. Some of them had differing perspectives on scripture from the rabbis who preceded them, and the "parables, amusing anecdotes, pieces of oral law, rabbinic proverbs, customs, midrashim folklore, and superstition"[4] they created in commenting on the Mishnah were collated into a separate commentary called the Gemara. *Gemara* means *completion* in Hebrew. Jewish scholars compiled the Mishnah along with the Gemara into a larger resource called the Talmud, which means *study*.

In addition to the Jewish writings contained in the Talmud, we can also find cultural background on the New Testament and the life of Jesus from Josephus, a first-century Jewish historian employed by the Romans. No other first-century writer provides as much commentary on the early church and the life of Jesus outside the Bible. Still, it's important to note that extrabiblical sources do not carry the same authority as the Bible. These resources do, however, shed light on the mindset of those living at that time. When we read them, we should view them as we might read a modern commentary on scripture. They can provide helpful insights, but rarely dogmatic truths.

In order to understand the mind of Jesus in his Jewish context, we should follow the advice of Pilate when he presented Jesus to the crowd: "Behold the man." Our goal is to get an accurate picture of the man and the type of ministry he modeled. We do this because we want to grow as his disciples. The Bible tells us that believers grow in their spiritual journeys as they, "with unveiled faces, are looking as in a mirror at the glory of the Lord and are being transformed into the same image from glory to glory; this is from the Lord who is the Spirit" (2 Cor. 3:18 CSB).

To begin our journey, we'll learn what it means to adopt an Eastern mindset when we read the New Testament. Remember, Jesus thought and communicated as a Middle Eastern man. His worldview and culture were quite different from the culture of most American evangelicals.

Thinking Like a Hebrew

The first step in understanding Jesus as a Jewish rabbi is to take a closer look at the Hebrew language and thought. The Hebrew language tends to be characterized as dynamic, impassioned, and explosive, in contrast to the more abstract and systematic Greek language that has influenced much of our Western culture. In his book *Hebrew Thought Compared with Greek*, Thorleif Boman writes: "Greek mental activity appears harmonious, prudent, moderate and peaceful; to the person to whom the Greek kind of thinking occurs plainly as ideal, Hebrew thinking and its manner of expression appear exaggerated, immoderate, discordant, and in bad taste."[5] Adopting a Hebraic mindset forces the reader to think with two hands simultaneously: on the one hand and on the other hand. "[Apparent] contradictions and inconsistencies," cites Hebrew theologian Brad Young, "are part and parcel of God and his mysteries."[6]

One immediate implication of the Hebrew way of thinking is in the cultural approach to learning. As Brad Young puts it, the Middle Eastern mind "learns by doing." Young summarizes this mindset:

The Eastern mind loves riddles and is fond of mystery. On the contrary, the Western theologian explains much and understands little. The Eastern mindset of Jewish theology reveres God and wonders at his unexplainable mysteries. All attempts to systematize God fall short. If we are to understand God like an Eastern Jew would have, we must stand in amazement. We should wonder in awe. Jesus is like that. He never wrote a creed. He did not occupy himself with systematic theology. But He is a profound theologian even if He would feel uncomfortable with this Western designation. He is a theologian, but his theology is Jewish to the core, being rooted in Torah-faithful Judaism. He stressed action more than belief [see John 6:28–29]. His theology emerges in the metaphor of parable and a holy reverence for life.[7]

Sometimes this way of thinking is called "dialectical thinking." James Fleming, Jewish scholar and author, describes it as keeping opposite and even opposing concepts in mind. He compares this Eastern way of thinking to our common Western perspective: "In Western thought, A + B = C. There is a one statement conclusion for A + B. In Middle Eastern thought and in the biblical mind, there is dialectical thinking. The diagram for this is A + B = AB. There can be more than one statement. The answer is yes, yes, or AB. Many of the difficult sayings of Jesus are examples of dialectical thinking."[8]

This ability to hold multiple options in tension may be why many Western readers of the Bible struggle with paradoxical concepts. We long to have a single answer to a question or a problem, and we apply this approach to doctrines such as divine sovereignty vs. free will, the kingdom of God being future vs. present, and election vs. man's responsibility. But these seemingly contradictory doctrines may be congruent in the Jewish cultural framework that gave birth to Christianity. If you ask a Jewish man, "Did God choose you or did you choose God?" he will likely say, "Yes."

What Does God Do, Not What Is God Like

When an American Christian desires to know more about God, he or she typically asks, "What is God like?" And what is the expected answer? A list of attributes or a definition of characteristics. A first-century Jewish disciple, however, might pose the question this way: "What does God do?" In other words, if you want to learn about someone, you watch and observe rather than learn a collection of facts about them. Imitation was more important than mere information.

A great example of a New Testament book that exemplifies this dynamic is James. This apostle writes, "But someone will say, 'You have faith and I have works.' Show me your faith apart from your works, and I will show you my faith by my works" (James 2:18). Who is the audience for this letter? James tells us that he is writing to Jewish readers, the twelve tribes of the dispersion, Jews who have been displaced from Palestine, and as cultural Jews they would have immediately understood what James was saying: Following God involves both words and concrete actions.

In general, biblical Jews didn't think primarily in the abstract; they looked for concrete examples to imitate. They worked to translate the abstract into the concrete—something doable and repeatable. As modern Western followers of Jesus, we often have a tendency to move in the opposite direction—taking something simple and making it more complex. Consider some of the biblical jargon we toss around without explanation: Since your *inner man* has been *blinded* by the *god of this world*, ask God to *cleanse you* from the *stains of sin* and *wash you clean* with his *blood from*

Calvary so you may be *justified* in his eyes. A person raised in a church might understand some of the terms in this sentence, but it would take some effort to translate this into everyday life.

Abstract vs. Dynamic

So what is the primary difference between abstract understanding and dynamic understanding? A good way to see the difference between the two is to look at how a person examines something. A person with a more dynamic way of thinking will often approach something differently from a person who takes the abstract approach. For example, let's assume a representative of each cultural view is in the same biology class. The abstract thinker would likely pin the frog to the table and reach for the scalpel to make an incision. By opening the frog up, he will be able to examine the organs, the muscles, and the skin through a microscope. He will be able to learn a great deal about the frog by studying it this way, but he will not gain much direct knowledge of how the frog lived—its birth patterns, breeding practices, and the tone of its croak. A dynamic approach would likely start by studying the frog in its habitat. In its environment, he can gain insight into the way that it lived its life.

While the analogy isn't perfect, it illustrates a key difference between the two approaches. The dynamic thinker is more interested in how the frog lives than in simply gaining information about the animal by studying samples of its liver tissue.

When we say that the Hebrew mindset tends toward dynamic under-standing, that's not to suggest that Hebrews do not value theories or complex ideas. It's simply to point out the broad cultural difference that came from living in a culture that trained them to learn and to experience the world—and thus, God—differently from ours. Boman says,

> God revealed himself to the Israelites in history, and not in ideas; he revealed himself when he acted and created. His being was not learned through propositions but known in actions. The majority of the Old Testament books are historical, and those that are not (Song of Solomon, Proverbs, Job, Ecclesiastes, for example) have concrete human life as their subject; they are not systematic presentation.[9]

When God chose to teach us about himself, he didn't just drop a book of ideas from heaven. He sent his son in the form of a man. I wrote about this way of thinking in *Rediscovering Discipleship*:

> It's popular to say that Hebrews think with two hands. This means learning to balance seemingly contradictory ideas. For example, on one hand we have the idea that God selected his chosen people before he created the world. On the other hand, there is the idea that we must choose him. Or consider prayer. God knows what you are going to say before we ask, but still he commands us to pray.
>
> The Hebraic way of thinking is more comfortable holding these concepts in tension because they tend to prefer word pictures, stories, poetry, imagery, and symbolism to the "Western" or "Greek" preference for words, ideas, definitions, outlines, lists, and bullet points. The goal is not to simply resolve a problem or arrive at a conclusion. When a rabbi tells a story, he speaks to the heart first and the head second. Traditionally, Western ways of thinking tend to speak to the head first and the heart second. Since the majority of the Bible was written by Hebrews to Hebrews, those who read it from a Westerner's frame of mind tend to overlook many of the nuggets of wisdom buried throughout.[10]

A Purpose Is Worth a Thousand Words

Another way to clarify the difference between the more dynamic way of thinking of Hebrew culture and our more abstract approach today is to say that Hebrews focused not simply on how a thing looks but on describing its purpose—how it is used. We witness this when we read the accounts recorded in the Bible. The Bible rarely describes people, places, or things visually, like we are used to doing in our cultural context in the West. The Jews were not interested in "photographic appearances of things or persons. In the entire Old Testament, we do not find a single description of an objective photographic appearance. The Israelites give us their impressions of the thing that is perceived."[11]

When God instructed Noah to construct the ark, he outlined detailed dimensions of the vessel, but he never described the finished product.

Notice the description in Genesis 6:14–15 (CSB): "Make yourself an ark of gopher wood. Make rooms in the ark, and cover it with pitch inside and outside. This is how you are to make it: The ark will be 450 feet long, 75 feet wide, and 45 feet high." Hebrews are concerned with how something is created and developed and the purpose that it serves. Usefulness trumps aesthetics.

Similarly, the plan for the traveling tabernacle in the wilderness consisted of painstaking details in constructing the altar, curtains, and veil, yet from those details, we are left clueless as to what it actually looked like. Exodus 25:10–11 (CSB) provides the outline: "They are to make an ark of acacia wood, forty-five inches long, twenty-seven inches wide, and twenty-seven inches high. Overlay it with pure gold; overlay it both inside and out. Also make a gold molding all around it."

The physical appearance of the structure appears simply not to be a priority to the Israelites. Boman describes the thought process of a Hebrew as he or she views a structure:

> When an Israelite sees an edifice, his consciousness is at once concerned with the idea of how it was erected, somewhat like a housewife who cannot be satisfied with the taste of a cake but is particularly interested in what its ingredients are and how it was made. . . . The Israelite also, when he confronts other objects such as buildings, is interested in them not for their appearance but first for their use; they are for him tools or implements of human or divine actions. . . .[12]

Descriptions are provided to help readers understand what purpose something serves and how it fits with other objects, not to recreate it visually.

Years ago I heard author and teacher Ray Vander Laan illustrate the juxtaposition between dynamic (Hebraic) thought and abstract (Western) thought by asking a simple question: "What is God?"[13] If you were to go to an American seminary and ask the students there this question, you would likely hear answers like this: "God is righteous; God is holy; God is love; God is wise." You would certainly hear several references to his omnipotence, omnipresence, and omniscience. If, on the other hand, you traveled to Jerusalem to pose the same question to students at a Yeshiva, an Orthodox Jewish Seminary for learning in Jerusalem, the students would answer that same question quite differently. Their response would be something like this: "God is a rock," "God is living water," "God is an eagle's wing," or "God is freshly baked bread."

The point is not that one description is better than another. The Bible describes in both ways, of course. My point is that we have cultural habits and patterns that predispose us toward one way of thinking, and we may need a corrective to grasp aspects of God that we have missed or neglected. The benefit is that these biblical truths can help us grow in our faith. Just picture in your mind what you think of when you hear words like love, holy, wise, omnipotent, omnipresent, and omniscient. If you're like me, your mind's eye pictures the words or the letters.

Now picture the responses given by students from the Yeshiva: living water, a rock, an eagle's wing, and freshly baked bread. What do you see? Or maybe a better question is, what do you feel? If you linger long enough, you may be able to smell the bread coming from that hot stone oven. Hebraic culture embraces this more dynamic understanding and concrete, descriptive language.[14]

One for All, Not One Alone

Another key cultural difference between the East and the West is in our conception of our place in society. Jewish people didn't primarily think of themselves as individuals, at least not in the way that we do today. In that culture, the individual was part of a larger, corporate body. The individual was only as strong as the family unit and was identified with the group he belonged to (family, tribe, or nation).[15] The corporate identity—your place in the larger group—was primary. And this is something we often miss in our identity as Christian believers today. The Bible teaches us that we are created and called by God to live more like one of the Three Musketeers, not the Lone Ranger. The motto of the Three Musketeers sums up the Christian's life well: "One for all, and all for one." We were created to live in harmony with other believers as members of the body of Christ.

Dietrich Bonhoeffer, German theologian and reformer, gives a vivid description of how sin festers when a person is isolated from the community:

Sin demands to have a man by himself. It withdraws him from the community. The more isolated a person is, the more destructive will be the power of sin over him, and the more deeply he becomes involved in it, the more disastrous is his isolation. Sin wants to remain unknown. It shuns the light. In the darkness of the unexpressed, it poisons the whole being of a person.[16]

The cultural values of community over individualism found in Hebrew culture were useful in addressing individual sin. Each person understood that his or her choices did not simply affect his or her own life but also had implications for his or her family and nation.

Bloated Christian Syndrome

In years past, some churches may have wrongly judged a person's spiritual maturity by how many services or Bible studies they attended. They might have selected deacons based on how often they showed up at church. Yet, as we all know, frequent church attendance does not equal spiritual maturity. You can read a book and understand each of the words in it, but that does not mean you understand the concepts or can put what you have read into practice in your life.

Understanding what a book says goes deeper than reciting the words or even abstractly grasping the concepts. There is a deeper level of understanding where you grasp what the author is trying to say, the motivations of the characters, and what makes the plot move forward. In the same way, learning biblical information doesn't automatically produce spiritual growth. Having the right information is necessary, but it is insufficient. True growth must also involve repetition and reiteration of deep spiritual truths and their application to one's own life.

Some churches have a problem we can call "Bloated Christian Syndrome." In this syndrome, members are fed lots of great information every week. If you were to add up all of the facts and data that some people have accumulated from attending church services over several decades, it would surpass the level of a biblical scholar. And yet many people emerge from this experience having retained almost nothing of what they have heard. Why?

Let's pretend that you are heading to a typical American church this Sunday morning. You hear some music followed by a forty-minute message about a topic. Perhaps you also head to Sunday school where you hear another lesson from the Sunday school curriculum. By doubling the amount of content you've heard, you've now cut the impact of the message roughly in half. You return that evening after lunch and your Sunday nap to hear the pastor's next topic as he works through a book you've been studying together. Now you've cut the impact of the morning message by four. On Wednesday night you come back to church to have a prayer meeting and you hear a devotional that one of the members prepared throughout the week, cutting the impact of that message by eight. Maybe you wake up early on Tuesday or Thursday to attend a Bible-study group you've joined, where you study something entirely different. This is all in addition to your daily Bible reading, scripture memory, and discipleship group, since you're one of the faithful ones.

Can you see where there might be a problem? By the time you get around to Sunday again, you won't be able to recall a single point from the previous week's sermon, let alone remember all of the biblical truth you've been exposed to that week! Am I saying that too much Bible is bad for you? No. The Bible is God's Word, and it is life and nourishment for a hungry soul.

The problem is in how we engage the Bible. We have bought into the fallacy that we grow by the introduction of new information alone. We focus on new teachings and more information, rather than allowing a single teaching to saturate our minds by meditating on it and applying it to our lives. Jewish rabbis taught much differently. They believed that rehearsing older lessons was just as important as, if not more important than, learning new ones. Jews read through the Torah day after day, year after year, repeating the words of God throughout their lives. They were in their Bibles all the time, but their goals were typically different than ours.

In the Shema (Deut. 6:4–9), parents are instructed to "repeat them [the Word of God] to your children." The word *repeat* is another word for *honing*, as in sharpening a knife with repeated strokes of a stone or leather strop. One rabbi is quoted as saying, "One who repeats his lesson a hundred times is not like him who repeats it a hundred and one."[17] Professor Shumel Safrai describes this rabbinical method of information transformation:

Individual and group study of the Bible, repetition of the passages, etc., were often done by chanting them aloud. There is the frequent expression "the chirping of children," which was heard by people passing close by a synagogue as the children were reciting a verse. Adults too, in individual and in group study, often read aloud; for it was frequently advised not to learn in a whisper, but aloud. This was the only way to overcome the danger of forgetting.[18]

First-century students in a Jewish school would rely on repetition and recitation for understanding, and it was common for students, by the time of their thirteenth birthday, to have most of the Torah committed entirely to memory. This capacity for memory was made possible by constant repetition. The Jewish Talmud also emphasizes the importance of reviewing information frequently: "He who studies the Torah and does not review is like one who plants and does not harvest."[19]

So where did our Western cultural focus on learning new things and acquiring new information come from? The Greeks. In contrast to the Jews, the Greeks were famous for loving learning new ideas, often without coming to any conclusions about them. Today, we would call them "information junkies." In the New Testament we read that Paul was welcomed at Mars Hill because the scholars enjoyed discussing new ideas—as many as they could find. They loved to hear anything new and interesting, eager to listen before moving on to the next new idea.

Hebrews, on the other hand, were taught to treasure and remember old truths, to rehearse stories of the past, to compare everything they heard against the standard of the Word of God. Moses stood on the shoulders of the patriarchs; the prophets emerged from the judges; and Paul would preach no one else but Christ. All of this was built upon the revelation God had given to the prior generation. In fact, it is interesting to note that the religious leaders of Jesus's day accused him of nullifying old truths by proposing new ones. In response, Jesus stated, "Do not think that I have come to abolish the Law or the Prophets; I have not come to abolish them but to fulfill them" (Matt. 5:17 NIV). Jesus was clear that he wasn't bringing something radically new—he was bringing about the fulfillment of all that God had revealed before his coming.

In *Reaching Out Without Dumbing Down: A Theology of Worship for the Turn-of-the-Century Culture*, Marva J. Dawn states that "television has habituated its watchers to a low information-action ratio, that people are accustomed to 'learning' good ideas (even from sermons) and then doing nothing about them."[20] This illustrates one of the problems with modern Christianity: It is not that we lack knowledge, for we know an awful lot about a lot of different things. The gap is between what we know and what we *obey*. *We have educated ourselves beyond our obedience.*[21]

But here is the biblical model for growth: "The more you know Him, the more you love Him. The more you love Him, the more you obey Him. The more you obey Him, the more He manifests Himself to you." You start with the information about God that you currently have, you put as much faith as you have in as much of Jesus as you know, and he will take it from there as you yield your life in obedience to him.

Words with a Deeper Meaning

When Jewish scholars seek to understand the meaning of a word, they examine the first occurrence of the word in the Hebrew Bible, where it first appears in our Old Testament. The first usage shapes the meaning of the word for the rest of scripture. Scholars refer to this as the "interpretive rule of first usage." For example, the word *love* is first used in Genesis 22 when God asked Abraham to take his son, his only son whom he loved, Isaac, and offer him in sacrifice to God. Isaac, the one and only son, is a picture of God's coming son, Jesus: "For God loved the world in this way: He gave his one and only Son, so that everyone who believes in him will not perish but have eternal life" (John 3:16 CSB).

Genesis 22 also contains the first occurrence of the word *worship* in the Bible. In the language of the Old Testament, worship normally implies bowing down or becoming prostrate as a sign of submission. However, in this case, worship is described by the actions that Abraham takes in faithful obedience to God.

Let's examine another common word found in the Bible, the word *faith*. We typically translate this word as *believe* or *trust*. But where is the word (in Hebrew) first found in the Bible? You might guess that it's found in Genesis 12 or 15 with the calling of Abraham.[22] Unfortunately, if you are relying on your modern English Bible, you might miss the first usage because it is actually found in Exodus 17. Exodus 17:11–13 states,

> Whenever Moses held up his hand, Israel prevailed, and whenever he lowered his hand, Amalek prevailed. But Moses' hands grew weary, so they took a stone and put it under him, and he sat on it, while Aaron and Hur held up his hands, one on one side, and the other on the other side. So his hands were steady until the going down of the sun. And Joshua overwhelmed Amalek and his people with the sword.

The Hebrew word for faith is *emunah,* and in the passage quoted the ESV renders the word as *steady.* It can also be translated as *faithfulness* or *steadfastness.* Jeremiah 5:3 (CSB) uses the same word: "LORD, don't Your eyes look for faithfulness?" And James 2:26 states, "For as the body apart from the spirit is dead, so also faith [faithfulness] apart from works is dead." In Romans 1:17 Paul quotes Habakkuk 2:4, "The righteous will live by faith [faithfulness]."

What does this suggest? One way of saying it is that the opposite of Hebrew faith is not unbelief, as we might typically think. The opposite of faith is understood as a matter of faithfulness, in the context of a covenantal relationship. The opposite of faith is disobedience or disloyalty. Hebrews 11 is not called the "Hall of Belief," it's called the "Hall of Faith"—or better yet, the "Hall of Faithfulness." Faith is not just believing facts despite contrary evidence. It is obeying someone in spite of consequences. It's faithfulness.

Faith is demonstrated by imitating God. Jews devoted time to *studying God in order to imitate him.* They opened the scriptures and took a close look at what God did. He *created* in Genesis; therefore, we should be creative. He *rested* after creation; therefore, we should rest. He *visited* the sick with Abraham, he *cared* for his flock, he *rescued* his people, etc. Or consider what Jesus did in gathering and teaching his disciples. He said repeatedly, "Follow Me," "Do what I do," "Talk like I talk," "Live as I live," and "Love as I love." The next time you read the Bible, don't just look at what God said, but observe what he did and think about what it means to faithfully imitate him.

I hope this first chapter has given you a taste of some of the cultural differences between our Western way of understanding the Bible and the Hebraic way of thinking. In the chapters that follow, we will look even more closely at the person of Jesus, but not as an intellectual exercise or as ammunition to win an argument with an unbeliever. Instead, we will seek to know him better so that we can follow him more completely and with more faith than we ever thought possible. My hope is that you will rediscover a person many of us have forgotten.

CHAPTER 2

Uncovering Christ in the Old Testament

As we saw in the previous chapter, biblical faith is best expressed through faithful action, not just intellectual understanding. Again, my point is not to downplay the importance of the intellect or to suggest that facts don't matter. Instead, I hope to correct an imbalance that is common in our culture.

Our modern American culture has been heavily influenced by Greek and Roman culture in ways in which we are often unaware. For example, when a Greek or Roman individual wanted to communicate a concept, he or she would typically write a theological treatise or lay out a rhetorical argument or speech about the topic. When a Hebrew teacher would seek to communicate something, he would often convey the message through a story. Much of the Bible unfolds through narrative. One reason Jesus was such an effective communicator was because he was a masterful storyteller. He told stories about sowers and seeds, a prodigal son, a lost coin, and a lost sheep, illustrating his points by using the landscape around him (see

Mark 4; Luke 15). His purpose in telling stories was to communicate truth about God by providing believers with pictures they could concretely comprehend.

We will never be able to fully understand the ministry of Jesus without understanding the culture in which he lived and the Bible he read. Over three quarters of our Bible is devoted to the Old Testament, yet many believers today spend the majority of their time reading through the New Testament. I'm all for studying the New Testament, but much of the meaning of the New must be understood in light of the Old. Our faith is fortified when we understand that God's plan for sending his son to the world began long before the sending of Moses, before the salvation of Joseph, and even before the calling of Abraham.

Abraham: A Picture of Sacrifice

To see this, let's look more closely at one of the first demonstrations of faith recorded for us in scripture. Earlier, we looked back on the life of Abraham as a portrait of faithfulness to God, but prior to this act of obedient faith, Abraham himself experienced a picture of what God's faithfulness looks like. In Genesis 12, we see God making a covenant with Abraham, saying to him, "I will make you into a great nation, I will bless you, I will make your name great, and you will be a blessing" (v. 2 CSB). Then, in chapter 15, God reiterates that covenant: "And he brought [Abraham] outside and said, 'Look toward heaven, and number the stars, if you are able to number them.' Then he said to him, 'So shall your offspring be.' And he believed the Lord, and he counted it to him as righteousness" (vv. 5–6).

Whether or not Abraham believed that God would do what he said is not up for debate. He clearly believed God at his word. Still, notice what Abraham says in verse 8 (CSB). He asks for something tangible to help him visualize the promise God has made, to hold him up during his twenty-five year wait before seeing it fulfilled. Abraham says to God, "Lord God, how can I know that I will possess it?"

Most Christians probably have a basic understanding of a biblical covenant. It is a formal contract between two parties in which they both promise to accept the terms and conditions of an agreement. We sign contracts all the time in our culture when we sign up for email or Facebook accounts, make a purchase on iTunes, or update our computers to the latest software version. We agree to the line that says "I have read and agree to these terms and conditions." This holds us and the entity we are signing up with to certain legal obligations.

While we may have a casual approach to making contracts today, in the ancient world the contractual obligations of making a covenant were not taken as casually. (How many of us have read every set of terms and conditions we agree to?) Covenants were relational agreements often struck between friends. On more than one occasion Abraham is called God's friend. James, quoting Genesis 15:6, states in his epistle, "[T]he Scripture was fulfilled that says, 'Abraham believed God, and it was counted to him as righteousness'—and he was called a *friend* of God" (2:22–23, emphasis mine).

People typically employed four kinds of covenants in the ancient world to bind themselves to an agreement: a salt covenant (2 Chronicles 13:5), a shoe covenant (Ruth 4:7), a hand covenant, and a blood covenant. The most serious of the four was the blood covenant, which is what we will see God committing himself to in Genesis 15.[1]

In a blood covenant, a greater party and a lesser party entered into an agreement.[2] The lesser party would contribute sacrificial animals as a sign of that agreement; the blood from the animals they provided was a symbol of their own commitment to keep their end of the bargain. They would slaughter their animals, cut them in half, and arrange them on either side of the path formed by the flowing blood. Next, both of the participants would walk through that path of blood as a symbol that they were contributing their own blood to the agreement. The greater party walked through it first and the lesser party followed, surrounded by the slaughtered animals, which served as a visible statement of their commitment to their agreements. In essence, they were saying, "If I do not hold up my end of the bargain, make me like these animals."

A blood covenant was serious business. The consequences of breaking an agreement are mentioned in Jeremiah 34:18 (CSB): "As for those who disobeyed my covenant, not keeping the terms of the covenant they made before me, I will treat them like the calf they cut in two in order to pass between its pieces."

Cutting a Covenant

Ray Vander Laan, founder of That the World May Know ministries, helpfully sheds additional light on the significance of the covenant God made with Abraham in Genesis 15. (For teachings on various topics from a Hebraic perspective visit www.followtherabbi.com.) Ray points out that in Genesis 15 we see God instructing Abraham, the lesser party, to gather five animals for the covenant ceremony: "He said to him, 'Bring me a heifer three years old, a female goat three years old, a ram three years old, a turtledove, and a young pigeon.' And he brought him all these, cut them in half, and laid each half over against the other. But he did not cut the birds in half. And when birds of prey came down on the carcasses, Abram drove them away" (vv. 9–11).

God's instructions to Abraham were specific both in number—five—and in the way that Abraham was to slaughter them—the beasts were to be killed and halved; the birds were to be killed and left whole.[3] God made Abraham do all of this to impress upon him the seriousness of the agreement.

Traditionally, after the preparation for the ceremony was finished, each party would step into the aisle of blood and say aloud, "May what was done to these animals be done to me if I do not keep this covenant."[4] Abraham may have realized that this commitment presented him with an impossible choice. Abraham knew that God would uphold his end of the bargain because he is God, but the only way Abraham could uphold his end, according to the Vander Laan,[5] was to be sinless—a requirement he couldn't fulfill.

For most of us, coming from a Western cultural perspective, this passage sounds ancient, bloody, and foreign to our twenty-first-century ears. But when you look at what God is doing in light of the original cultural context, it comes alive. Verse 12 sets the stage for what is about to take place: "As the sun was going down, a deep sleep fell on Abram. And behold, dreadful and great darkness fell upon him."

By putting Abraham to sleep, God reveals his sovereign control over the situation. The passage says that God puts a "dreadful and great darkness" on Abraham. This particular phrase is a Hebrew colloquialism for death—signifying that Abraham was in no way responsible for the things to come. God in his sovereignty was making a deal with man he knew would stand no chance of fulfilling under his own power. The covenant made will not depend on Abraham. God himself will be solely responsible for keeping its obligations.

The rest of the passage shows us how this unfolds: "When the sun had gone down and it was dark, behold, a smoking fire pot and a flaming torch passed between these pieces. On that day the Lord made a covenant with Abram, saying, 'To your offspring I give this land, from the river of Egypt to the great river, the river Euphrates, the land of the Kenites, the Kenizzites, the Kadmonites, the Hittites, the Perizzites, the Rephaim, the Amorites, the Canaanites, the Girgashites and the Jebusites'" (Gen. 15:17–21).

Still in a dream-like state after the sun had gone down, Abraham witnesses two specific items pass through the cut-up animals on the ground, one of which is "a smoking fire pot." According to M. G. Easton, this smoking fire pot "was a large pot, narrowing towards the top. When it was heated by a fire made within, the dough was spread over the heated surface, and thus was baked."[6]

What is the significance of this fire pot? Throughout scripture, God is constantly associated with smoke from a fire. On Mount Sinai, God would meet Moses on a mountain enveloped with smoke and fire. Isaiah 30:27 says, "Behold, the name of the LORD comes from afar, burning with his anger, and in thick rising smoke; his lips are full of fury, and his tongue is like a devouring fire." And Psalm 18:8 says, "Smoke went up from his nostrils, and devouring fire from his mouth; glowing coals flamed forth from him." Each time God would enter the tabernacle or the temple, it would be consumed with smoke (Isaiah 6:4). Scripture repeatedly uses smoke and fire to indicate the presence of God.

The second item that passed through the animals was a flaming torch. The flaming torch was "a light carried in the hand consisting of combustible substance such as a stick of resinous wood or bundle of tow."[7] Like the smoke from the pot, fire is an image frequently associated with God. God summoned Moses through a flaming bush in the desert. He led the Israelites through the wilderness with a pillar of fire. Deuteronomy

4:24 calls God a "consuming fire." When the Holy Spirit comes on the believers at Pentecost in Acts 2, the text tells us that "divided tongues as of fire appeared to them and rested on each one of them" (v. 3).

Fire is never used in the Bible in reference to a human being; it is always a reference to God. *Easton's Bible Dictionary* states that both of these elements—smoke and fire—are "symbolic of the presence of the Almighty."[8] Rabbi Rashi, author of the extensive commentary on the Tanak and the Talmud, confirms this symbolic understanding of these objects in his commentary on Genesis 15:

> Because God was cutting a covenant with Abraham to keep His promise to give to his children the land as an inheritance, as it is written [in Genesis 15:18], "On that day the LORD made a covenant with Abram, saying, 'To your descendants I have given this land,'" and it was the custom of those cutting a covenant to divide an animal to pass between its parts, just as it says [in Jeremiah 34:19], "all the people of the land who passed between the parts of the calf." So too it says [in Genesis 15:17] "a smoking oven and a flaming torch which passed between these pieces."[9]

By having these three images come together—Abraham's deep sleep, the smoking pot, and the flaming torch—God shows that he will be the one responsible to keep both sides of the agreement. God kept his promise and later sent Abraham a son named Isaac. But "the promise of a son for Abraham," according to D. Thomas Lancaster, "did not refer only to Isaac, Abraham's natural son. It referred to his seed as numerous as the stars; that is, the Jewish people. More than that, according to Paul's interpretation, it refers to a special son of Abraham who will one day have universal sway over all the nations."[10]

Paul offers us his commentary on God's promise in Galatians 3: "Now the promises were made to Abraham and to his offspring. It does not say, 'And to offsprings,' referring to many, but referring to one, 'And to your offspring,' who is Christ" (v. 16). The grave and serious nature of the ritual covenant between God and Abraham is, according to Pseudo-Philo in the second-century work *Biblical Antiquities,* God's way of telling Abraham,

"This night will be a witness between us that I will not go against my words."[11] God designed every piece of the ritual to be something that Abraham could look back on in the years to come as a reminder of what God promised him.

The Promise Keeper

In remembrance of the covenant with Abraham, Jewish priests sacrificed animals twice a day in the temple: at 9:00 a.m. (the third hour) and 3:00 p.m. (the ninth hour).[12] The sacrifices, called the perpetual sacrifices, or *Tamid* in Hebrew, were offered on behalf of the nation as a reminder for God and the people to keep the promises that had been made to Abraham and were prescribed in the Torah (see Num. 28:1–8; Exod. 29:38–42).[13] Innocent animals were slain every weekday, every weekend, and every feast day. The offerings were made in the rain, in the cold, during sandstorms, and in the heat. This practice continued in the temple for hundreds of years until the time of Jesus.

During these ritual sacrifices a priest would stand with a *shofar* (ram's horn) in hand in a niche of the temple, the right corner overlooking the city. He would blow the horn to announce to the city and the priests that it was time for the offering. Standing below him, another priest waited with a knife to the neck of an innocent lamb for the echo of the horn to die out. When the sound faded, he would slice the throat of the lamb, and all who could hear the horn would think to themselves, *God, don't forget about the promise you gave our father Abraham. Remember the covenant you made. Save us!*

In our culture today, we may be guilty of minimizing sin or down-playing its significance. But if you ever wanted to know how much God hates sin, try to picture the hundreds of years' worth of blood that ran in the temple courts twice a day. Now place yourself eighteen hundred years after the sealing of the covenant with Abraham in Genesis 15. On this day, thousands of people are gathered in Jerusalem for the largest festival of the year: Passover. This festival is going to be unlike any that have come before it. As the priest assumes his position in the niche of the temple, as he has twice a day for more years than anybody can remember, a man is being led out of the city. He is bloody and beaten by Roman whips and Jewish fists and can barely carry his cross to the place of crucifixion before he is thrown down upon it. Nails penetrate his wrists, and the shofar rings out from the temple.

Notice that we've been talking about the Tamid, the perpetual sacrifices that happened every day as reminders of God's covenant with Abraham. But there were additional sacrifices that were required on certain days, too—Passover being one of the more famous. The perpetual sacrifices should not be confused with the Passover sacrifices that took place between 3:00 p.m. (the ninth hour) and 5:00 p.m. (the eleventh hour), according to Jewish historian Josephus.[14] Josephus writes, "These High Priests, upon the coming of their feast which is called the Passover, when they slay their sacrifices, from the ninth hour [about 3 p.m.] to the eleventh [about 5 p.m.]."[15]

The Mishnah, written years later, supports Josephus's account when it says that the Passover sacrifices could not occur before 1:30 p.m.[16] So on this particular day there would have been more sacrifices than normal: the perpetual sacrifices at 9 a.m. and 3 p.m., and the Passover sacrifices between 3 p.m. and 5 p.m.

With this in mind, let's take a closer look at what Jesus did on that day.

At that moment when the nails are driven into Jesus's hands, we know that a shofar would have blown. How? Because Mark documents the exact hour when Jesus is mounted to the cross. "And they brought him to the place called Golgotha (which means Place of a Skull). And they offered him wine mixed with myrrh, but he did not take it. And they crucified him and divided his garments among them, casting lots for them, to decide what each should take. And it was the third hour when they crucified him" (15:22–25). The third hour is 9 a.m. It is the time of the first of the perpetual sacrifices.

Jesus hangs on the cross for six long, agonizing hours. Mark once again documents the times of different events that day: "When it was noon, darkness came over the whole land until three in the afternoon" (Mark 15:33 CSB). As 3 p.m. approaches, the man hanging in the middle of three crosses appears to be drawing his last breath. At the same time, a priest is climbing to the niche of the temple with a shofar in his hand, and another priest is preparing to cut a spotless lamb's throat.

Then, at 3 p.m., the ninth hour of the day, a shofar blows as the Passover lambs are ritually slaughtered, and Jesus, the Passover Lamb who takes away the sin of the world, lifts up his head and shouts: "It is finished!"

All of these sacrifices, all the offerings, all the bloodshed, all the innocent slaughter, and the entire sacrificial system finds fulfillment in Christ. His death means that sin's grip on our lives is finished. The devil is finished. Our bondage from sin is broken, and the grave can no longer hold us. Aren't you glad it's finished?

The Anguish of a Loving Father

Each Gospel account mentions a detail about Jesus's death: the curtain in the temple tearing. Luke tells us, "It was now about noon, and darkness came over the whole land until three, because the sun's light failed. The curtain of the sanctuary was split down the middle" (Luke 23:44–45 CSB).

Keep in mind that this piece of sacred cloth was massive. It was nearly 60 feet tall, 20 feet wide, and 4 inches thick.[17] The curtain had to be massive because of what it did. It separated the glory of God in the Holy of Holies from the people outside of it, a constant reminder of the division between God and man. Only one man, the high priest, was allowed to enter into God's presence to atone for the sins of the nation, and he could only enter it one time a year. The death of Jesus not only ended the sacrificial system once and for all, but also ripped the divide, ending the separation between God and man and providing access to God for everyone who believes.

The torn veil may also depict another significant reality as well. As Jesus died, the veil in the temple was torn in two from top to bottom (Matt. 27:51), symbolizing that man did not tear the veil. God ripped it. When we read about torn garments in scripture, we should be reminded of the numerous times when people tear their clothes in anguish over lost loved ones. When Jacob was given Joseph's multicolored coat drenched with what he believed to be his son's blood, he ripped his garments apart. Likewise, David tore his clothes when he heard of the death of King Saul.

Again, David ripped his clothes after hearing that "Absalom has struck down all the king's sons" (2 Sam. 13:30).

It was not uncommon to see a piece of torn fabric pinned to the jacket or shirt of someone attending a Jewish funeral.[18] One Jewish resource site explains what happens at a funeral and the significance of the fabric: "Kriah [ripping] is performed by the child, parent, spouse, and sibling of the deceased. It is usually done at the funeral home before the funeral service begins. If a black ribbon is used, it is provided by the funeral director."[19]

The torn ribbon is a sign of agony and distress. When a Jewish man or woman reads the account of God tearing the temple veil, they not only observe the truth that the barrier between God and man has been destroyed; they also hear the hint of grief—a loving father in anguish over the death of his one and only son. The Bible tells us that in the death of Jesus, God offered up his one and only Son as the sinless, spotless lamb of God to take away the sins of the world.

Faith in Action

In the Tanak (what we call the Old Testament), God foreshadowed the coming of his Son in the account of Abraham's offering of his son Isaac. Earlier, we read about the covenant Abraham entered into with God. He was seventy-five years old when this happened. After entering into that covenant with God, Abraham endured nine tests of his faith before God directed him to offer up his son.

1. The Call to Leave His Country, Family, and Home
2. Famine in Canaan
3. Abduction of Sarah
4. War with the Four Kings
5. Long Wait for a Son and Marriage to Hagar
6. The Command to Circumcise Himself
7. Abduction of Sarah by Abimelech
8. The Exile of Hagar after She Gave Birth
9. The Exile of Ishmael
10. The Sacrifice of Isaac

Warren Wiersbe describes this period of testing:

> Abraham had his share of tests right from the beginning. First was the "family test," when he had to leave his loved ones and step out by faith to go to a new land. This was followed by the "famine test," which Abraham failed because he doubted God and went down to Egypt for help. Once back in the land, Abraham passed the "fellowship test" when he gave Lot first choice in using the pastureland. He also passed the "fight test" when he defeated the kings and the "fortune test" when he said no to Sodom's wealth. But he failed the "fatherhood test" when Sarah got impatient with God and suggested that Abraham have a child by Hagar. When the time came to send Ishmael away, Abraham passed the "farewell test" even though it broke his heart.[20]

Genesis 22:1–2 (CSB) presents to us the final test of the ten: "After these things God tested Abraham and said to him, 'Abraham!' 'Here I am,' he answered. 'Take your son,' he said, 'your only son Isaac, whom you love, go to the land of Moriah, and offer him there as a burnt offering on one of the mountains I will tell you about.'" Each of the previous nine tests of his faith have brought Abraham to the place of knowing that God does not test his children without reason. He has learned to discern the voice and direction of God.

The expression used here, "your only son," cuts Abraham to the heart because he had just sent his son Ishmael away. Abraham understands that if God doesn't intervene, he will be known as the guy who sent one of his sons away and slaughtered the other one. Still, Abraham obeys God: "So Abraham got up early in the morning, saddled his donkey, and took with him two of his young men and his son Isaac. He split wood for a burnt offering and set out to go to the place God had told him about. On the third day Abraham looked up and saw the place in the distance" (Gen. 22:3–4 CSB). He doesn't spend days in prayer or time fasting about the decision. He doesn't inquire about Sarah's opinion or poll a friend for insight. He obeys without question.

Abraham has learned that, in God's eyes, both partial obedience and delayed obedience are disobedience.

Shouldering Wood up a Mountain

When Abraham and Isaac arrive at the mountain, we are told that, "Abraham took the wood for the burnt offering and laid it on his son Isaac. In his hand he took the fire and the knife, and the two of them walked on together" (Gen. 22:6 CSB). *Genesis Rabbah*, a pre-Christian Jewish midrash, connected Isaac walking with the wood on his back to a condemned man carrying his own cross.[21] These early rabbis, without realizing it, painted a prophetic image of Jesus "bearing his own cross, to the place called The Place of a Skull" (John 19:17).

After the father and son arrived at the top of the mountain, Abraham constructed an altar, laid out the wood, and tied up his son. Then, he placed him on the altar and reached for the knife to slay him. At this point, I want to point out something you may not have considered. *Abraham is not forcing Isaac to do any of this.* Abraham could not have offered Isaac without his consent. How can I say that? Because at this time Abraham was over one hundred years old, and Isaac was somewhere in his late twenties or early thirties.

Many commentators have misinterpreted Isaac to be a young child because of the word "lad" or "boy." Yet the term does not prescribe a determinate age. The first-century Jewish historian Josephus suggested that "Isaac was 25 years old,"[22] and some place him at thirty-seven years old because of Sarah's immediate death in Genesis 23. (Those who back this theory assume she may have died from shock when she got word Abraham was going to sacrifice Isaac.)

What we do know is that Isaac was what we would consider an adult. We also know this by considering the size of the offering he carried up the mountain. Lois Tverberg and Ann Spangler, in their book *Walking in the Dust of Rabbi Jesus*, explain how the offering would have taken "several hours to burn over a full fire. The large logs needed for fuel would require the strength of a full-grown man to carry them."[23] There was no way the elderly Abraham could lift them (remember, he was one hundred already when Isaac was born), so he carried the knife while Isaac carried the wood.

So while we can't give a firm age, we can assume that Isaac was at least somewhere in his late twenties, too old to be forced by his father to do anything. And the reason why this matters is that it means that Isaac *willingly* offered up his life to his father in accord with God's command. Jesus communicated virtually the same truth about this own life and death: "No one takes it from me, but I lay it down on my own. I have the right to lay it down, and I have the right to take it up again. I have received this command from my Father" (John 10:18 CSB).

As we know in the story, God provided an animal sacrifice in place of Abraham's firstborn son. Later, in a similar way, God would direct the Israelites to offer a lamb on Passover to protect their firstborn sons. Donald Barnhouse explains the significance of these sacrifices: "God was instilling a reflex in the minds of His people so that every time they thought of sin they would think of death, for sin means death. It means the death of the sinner or the death of the Savior."[24]

More Parallels on the Mountain

Abraham's journey up and down the mountain also provides us with a picture of worship. After the young man, Isaac, gathers the wood, he asks his father, "Behold, the fire and the wood, but where is the lamb for a burnt offering?" Abraham responds, "God will provide for himself the lamb for a burnt offering, my son" (Gen. 22:7–8).

Interestingly, both Isaac's question and Abraham's answer contain just six Hebrew words. In a manner of speaking, we could say that Abraham's answer matches Isaac's question, suggesting that the sacrifice God will provide is exactly sufficient to cover what he requires.

Another insight comes from the manner in which Abraham's response is structured. Normally in Hebrew, the verb precedes the noun. In English we would say, "Robby ran to the store," but in Hebrew it would be similar to this: "Ran Robby to the store." Genesis 22:8 reverses the usual construction by having the subject precede the verb: "God himself will provide the lamb." The language emphasizes God's initiative in providing the sacrifice, something he will repeat thousands of years later when he provides for the sins of mankind by sending his only son to die.

These are just a few examples that show how this instance in Abraham's life gives us clues of the Savior to come. There are other similarities we can note as well. Both Isaac and Jesus were miraculously conceived. Both sons were unique and beloved by their fathers. They were roughly the same age at the time of the offering. A donkey was used to ascend the mountain to sacrifice Isaac. Similarly, Jesus rode a donkey into Jerusalem to be the sacrifice for us, a connection to Solomon being anointed king in 1 Kings 1:38–40.

Abraham and Isaac ascended the mountain on the third day, and Jesus rose from the grave on the third day. The writer of Hebrews may have had this in mind when he writes about Abraham's son in Hebrews 11: "By faith Abraham, when he was tested, offered up Isaac, and he who had received the promises was in the act of offering up his only son, of whom it was said, 'Through Isaac shall your offspring be named.' He considered that God was able even to raise him from the dead, from which, figuratively speaking, he did receive him back" (Heb. 11:17–19). Early Christians read the account of Abraham's sacrifice of Isaac figuratively through the lens of Christ.

Mount Calvary

The location of Isaac's sacrifice is also significant. God directed Abraham to the uninhabited mountain of Moriah instead of settling for Beersheba or some other location along the way, but his command was not arbitrary. Moriah is a name derived from the word *yarah* in Hebrew, which means "to teach." Isaiah 2:3 uses this same word, saying "Come, let us go up to the mountain of the Lord, to the house of the God of Jacob, that he may *teach* us his ways and that we may walk in his paths" (emphasis mine). It suggests that God was going to use Mount Moriah to *teach* a lesson that would reverberate throughout history.

Mount Moriah is the exact location where God directed Solomon to construct his temple. We know this because 2 Chronicles 3:1 reads, "Then Solomon began to build the house of the Lord in Jerusalem on Mount Moriah, where the Lord had appeared to David his father." That ridge where Isaac was bound would eventually be the spot where thousands and thousands of perpetual sacrificial lambs would be offered up daily in the temple. Years later, it would also be the site of another sacrifice, the death of God's Son, Jesus of Nazareth.

Some have wondered why God would ask a man like Abraham to sacrifice his only son. Remember that when God asked this of Abraham, God did not expect anything he wasn't going to do himself. James Montgomery Boice points out that

> Abraham was only *asked* to sacrifice his son; he did not actually have to do it. Even if he had, there was only a physical death involved. But when the time came for God, the heavenly Father, to sacrifice his Son, it was not a mere physical death; it was a spiritual death, one that achieved redemption for sinners. When God's hand was raised at Calvary, there was no one to call out, "Stay your hand. Do not harm the boy." When God offered up his sacrifice, the hand that was poised above Christ fell. Jesus died. Through that death, God brought life to all who trust in Christ's sacrifice. Hallelujah![25]

John 3:16 drives this home: "For God so loved the world that he gave his one and only Son, that whoever believes in him shall not perish but have everlasting life" (NIV). God used one man's life and testing—the life of Abraham—to give us a living portrait of what his own faithfulness looks like. When we feel lost or forgotten, we can look to the story of Abraham and be reminded of God's commitment to us and the lengths he is willing to go to save us from our sin. Every aspect of the encounter on the mountain points us to the coming Christ.

Joseph: A Portrait of Salvation

Similar to what we have seen in the life of Abraham, we find hints and shadows of Jesus in the life of Joseph as well. Joseph's life gives us a picture of things to come, foreshadowing Christ. In rabbinic literature, the suffering Messiah spoken of in the prophets is often referred to as "the son of Joseph" because of Joseph's rejection by his brothers.[26] In the New Testament, Philip used that same term to describe Jesus to Nathanael in John 1: "We have found the one Moses wrote about in the law (and so did the prophets): Jesus *the son of Joseph*, from Nazareth" (John 1:45 CSB, emphasis mine). Let's take a closer look at how Joseph was a picture of the Savior.

A New Testament passage mentioning Jesus's death in connection with Joseph is found in Acts 7:9–10. It reads: "And the patriarchs, jealous of Joseph, sold him into Egypt; but God was with him and rescued him out of all his afflictions and gave him favor and wisdom before Pharaoh, king of Egypt, who made him ruler over Egypt and over all his household." When we first meet Joseph in Genesis, we see him as a shepherd: "Joseph, being seventeen years old, was pasturing the flock with his brothers" (Gen. 37:2). The role of shepherd was common in referring to Israel's leaders, and Jesus would one day refer to himself as the "Good Shepherd" (John 10:11).

Joseph's father was named Jacob, but Jacob's name had earlier been changed by God. God had renamed Jacob "Israel," the name by which God's people would later come to be identified. All those who came after Israel and belonged to Israel were held in special regard by God. Jacob is also the last in the traditional list of Israel's forefathers, and God regularly is called "The God of Abraham, Isaac, and Jacob."

These three men, three generations called by God, point us down the line of their lineage toward the Messiah. How? We see a hint of this in the genealogy of Matthew's Gospel. The Joseph of Genesis is not the only Joseph to be born of a man named Jacob. In fact, there is one other instance of this recorded for us in scripture at the beginning of Matthew's Gospel. Matthew records a genealogy from Abraham to Jesus, but our attention should be grabbed by Matthew 1:16, where Matthew writes, "Jacob the father of Joseph the husband of Mary, of whom Jesus was born, who is called Christ."

Carmen Tripp, in her book *Joseph, Jesus, and the Jewish People,* points out that there are many similarities between the two Josephs of the Bible: "Not only did God place those two men so strategically, but He gave us other parallel details to catch our attention: God communicated with both Josephs in dreams, sent them both to Egypt, sent them both there for the purpose of rescue, and to rescue Israel in both cases."[27] Jesus is a child of Joseph, son of Jacob. Like the Joseph of Genesis, his life continues the promises of Israel, and his name would become the new name under which God's people identify and belong.

Joseph's life also gives us a picture of mercy and forgiveness. Joseph moves from a pit to a prison before he is eventually exalted to a palace as the right-hand man to Pharaoh. Ultimately, he would forgive the brothers who had sold him into slavery. After the young shepherd boy is appointed to a position of power, Pharaoh gives him a new name: Zaphnath-paaneah, which means "revealer of secrets."[28] Josephus translated the name with some additional nuance, suggesting that it could also mean "finder of mysteries."[29]

The similarities don't end there, however. Both Joseph and Jesus were firstborn sons. And both were removed from their homeland into Egypt to escape death (Hos. 11:1; Matt. 2:15), though both men were eventually brought back to Canaan—Joseph after his death, and Christ as a child. Both men had brothers who didn't respect their righteousness and devotion to God. Both Joseph and Jesus were rejected and condemned (Gen. 37:18; Luke 23:21). Joseph was known for his righteousness in resisting temptation from Potiphar's wife; likewise, Jesus was tempted like us in every way, yet also resisted and was without sin (Gen. 39:7–12; Heb. 4:15). Joseph suffered rejection and was stripped of his elaborate coat before his trial of suffering began. Jesus, in a similar manner, was stripped and then mocked by the soldiers as they placed a purple robe upon him, symbolizing kingship, before his scourging began (Ps. 22:7–8; Matt. 27:39–40). Both men were given authority for their ministry around the age of thirty (Gen. 41:46; Luke 3:23). Joseph was sold by his brothers for a slave's price, twenty pieces of silver. Jesus was sold out by one of his disciples for thirty pieces of silver (Zech. 11:12; Matt. 26:15).[30]

As Joseph was in prison, he encountered two people: a butler and a baker. The butler was saved from death, while the baker was condemned (Genesis 40). Again, we see a parallel as Jesus hung on the cross with two criminals flanking him on either side. One man mocked him and remained condemned, but the other man asked for forgiveness and was promised a place in paradise (Luke 23:43). Finally, we see similarities in their death. Joseph was declared dead by his family, but would eventually "come back to life," reappearing to redeem his family and the world from the famine. Jesus was literally resurrected from death and raised to life on the third day after dying on the cross to redeem mankind from sin.[31]

These kinds of connections confirm that Joseph is what is referred to as a "type" of Christ. Joseph possessed qualities and did things that would foreshadow the Christ to come. But he was not the only type we find in the Old Testament. Another example, foreshadowing the life of Christ, was Moses.

Moses: A Prophet of Separation

The Jews believed that the Messiah would be a Moses-like redeemer, and the pages of the New Testament are littered with clues pointing to this. Jesus establishes a connection to Moses early in his ministry when he quotes from one of the books of Moses, Deuteronomy. During his initial temptation in the desert, Jesus responds to the devil by quoting Moses, saying, "Man shall not live by bread alone, but by every word that comes from the mouth of God."

Jesus also knew that the hope of Israel had been shaped for hundreds of years to the words of Deuteronomy 18:15 and 18, which says, "The Lord your God will raise up for you a prophet like me from among you, from your brothers—it is to him you shall listen. I will raise up for them a prophet like you from among their brothers. And I will put my words in his mouth, and he shall speak to them all that I command him." In fact, we read in John 6 that after Jesus feeds the 5,000 men (15,000 with women and children), the people make the connection to Moses and exclaim, "This is indeed *the* Prophet who is to come into the world!" (John 6:14, emphasis mine).[32]

Peter also affirmed the connection to Moses. We read in Acts 3 as Peter quotes Moses: "Moses said, 'The Lord God will raise up for you a prophet like me from your brothers. You shall listen to him in whatever he tells you. And it shall be that every soul who does not listen to that prophet shall be destroyed from the people.' And all the prophets who have spoken, from Samuel and those who came after him, also proclaimed these days" (Acts 3:22–26).

There are several obvious comparisons between Jesus and Moses. Here are a few of them to consider:

- Moses was a shepherd.
- Jesus was a shepherd.
- Moses was chosen to lead the people of Israel out of the bondage of the Egyptians.
- Jesus was God's chosen Son to lead the people from the bondage of sin.

- Moses hid in Egypt as a child.
- Jesus hid in Egypt as a child.

- Moses fasted for forty days.
- Jesus fasted for forty days.

- Moses selected and sent out twelve spies into the land (one for each tribe).
- Jesus selected and sent out twelve disciples into the world.

- Moses' first plague was turning the water into blood.
- Jesus's first miracle was turning the water into wine.

One of the more striking parallels between Moses and Jesus is seen at the cross. To understand this connection, we first need to have some understanding of the Jewish holy days. Leviticus 23 informs us of the dates and times of the holy days and feasts of the Jewish calendar. The most important day of the year was Passover—the first major holy day mentioned in the chapter.

Passover was a time when the people celebrated God's mercy in passing over them, sparing their children and killing the firstborn sons of Egypt, and eventually allowing them to escape from slavery. There were a number of feasts to eat and practices to engage in during this time, and the next major celebration occurred seven weeks from Passover: Shavuot, the Feast of Weeks, which we know as Pentecost. This feast was a celebration of the next major event to happen in the Israelite's exodus from Egypt: the giving of the Law at Sinai.

Notice the timeline here. When the Israelites left Egypt, it was because God had killed the male firstborn throughout the land of Egypt (Passover), which convinced Pharaoh to let them leave. Moses led the people for two months through the desert, arriving at the base of Sinai roughly shy of fifty days after this. Moses ascended the mountain and received the Law from God. This is the celebration mentioned earlier called Shavuot, or the Feast of Weeks.

If you know the story, when Moses began coming down the mountain after having been in the presence of God, he saw the Israelites worshiping a golden calf that they had forged out of their jewelry. He was exceedingly angry and delivered a word from God to them: "This is what the Lord, the God of Israel, says, 'Every man fasten his sword to his side; go back and forth through the camp from entrance to entrance, and each of you kill his brother, his friend, and his neighbor.'" The text then tells us that *"about three thousand* men fell dead that day among the people" (Exod. 32:27–28 CSB, emphasis mine).

Here is a graphic to help you grasp the timeline:

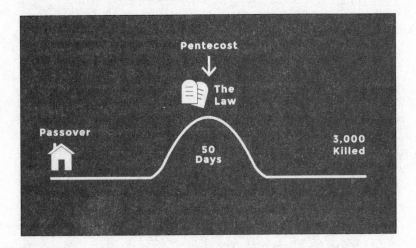

So what is the connection to the life and ministry of Jesus? If we look closely at the events that transpired during the crucifixion of Jesus and the following weeks, we see a connection between the events of the exodus and the death and ascension of Christ. At Passover, Jesus was led outside of Jerusalem and up a mountain to be crucified. He was the Passover lamb who was sacrificed, then he was buried and rose again three days later. For the next forty days we know that he "presented himself alive to [his disciples] after suffering by many proofs, appearing to them during *forty days* and speaking about the kingdom of God" (Acts 1:3, emphasis mine). He then ascended to heaven, commanding his disciples "not to leave Jerusalem, but to wait for the Father's promise" (1:4 CSB).

At this point, the disciples were forty days removed from his crucifixion. The Bible tells us that the disciples were together a week after that until the day of Pentecost—a total of fifty days after the Passover. On that day, the book of Acts tells us that the apostles were filled with the Holy Spirit and immediately began speaking the gospel to all of the Jews who had come to Jerusalem to celebrate the festival of Shavuot. After Peter preached his famous sermon in Acts 2, something remarkable happened: "Those who accepted his message were baptized, and *about three thousand* were added to their number that day" (Acts 2:41 NIV, emphasis mine).

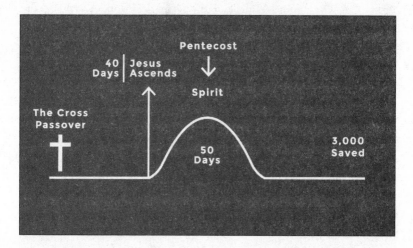

The parallels are striking and instructive. While the original Passover spared the nation of Israel, it could not change their hearts, so they fell back into idolatry. The giving of God's commandments was accompanied by disobedience and death. But the true Passover lamb died to remove sin and its effects, to give God's people a new heart and a new Spirit. At Pentecost, the law was written on the heart through the gift of the Spirit. The reversal of the effects of death can be seen in the number of people who got saved. It's no coincidence that 3,000 moved from life to death on the same day. Jesus came to fulfill or "fill with fullness" the festivals the Jews had been celebrating for a millennium.

Jesus is presented as a parallel to Moses so that the contrast between them is clear and obvious. Jesus proves to be the savior that Moses was incapable of being. Notice that both men are posed with the dilemma of hungry people seeking food in the wilderness (Exod. 16; John 6), and both provide manna or heavenly bread for the people. But where Moses called upon God to provide the manna, Jesus created the bread himself. The recipients of the massive dinner Jesus served on the northern shore of the sea of Galilee would have realized that Jesus had done what Moses could not. Only God can create something from nothing, as Jesus had done with the bread and fish.

The comparisons between Moses and Jesus are numerous, and we look at several more in the pages that follow. The key point is clear: The life and ministry of Moses points us ahead to the person and work of Jesus Christ.

Shepherds in the Old Testament

Joseph and Moses were both shepherds, but they were not the only prominent shepherd leaders of the Old Testament. There are six significant shepherds mentioned in the Old Testament, and each of them provide us with a picture of the ministry of the coming Messiah.

The first one we meet is Abel. Genesis 4:2 tells us that Abel was a keeper of sheep. Abel prefigures Jesus Christ because he is a picture of the faithful and innocent shepherd slain by his wicked brother Cain. His life points us to the obedient shepherd, Jesus, whose sacrifices, like those of Abel, are acceptable to God. The second shepherd we meet is Jacob. Genesis 30:31 (CSB) reads, "And Jacob said, 'You don't need to give me anything. If you do this one thing for me, I will continue to shepherd and keep your flock.'" Jacob is a picture of one who cares for his sheep. The third shepherd, as we've seen already, is Joseph. Joseph represents the shepherd who is faithful to feed the flock, providing for them when they are hungry and in need.

The fourth shepherd is Moses, and he performed three duties: He watered, protected, and guided the sheep. We see these connections in Exodus 2:16 and Exodus 3:1, respectively: "Now the priest of Midian had seven daughters, and they came and drew water and filled the troughs to water their father's flock. The shepherds came and drove them away, but Moses stood up and saved them, and watered their flock" and, "Now Moses was keeping the flock of his father-in-law, Jethro, the priest of Midian, and he led his flock to the west side of the wilderness and came to Horeb, the mountain of God." Like Moses, Jesus is a good shepherd who protects and guides those who follow him.

Then we meet David, the fifth shepherd found in the Old Testament. David risked his life for the sheep, as we read in 1 Samuel 17:34–35: "But David said to Saul, 'Your servant used to keep sheep for his father. And when there came a lion, or a bear, and took a lamb from the flock, I went after him and struck him and delivered it out of his mouth. And if he arose against me, I caught him by his beard and struck him and killed him.'"

Amos was the sixth shepherd mentioned in the Bible. He was from Tekoa in Judah, a village roughly ten miles south of Jerusalem. His profession can be roughly translated as "sheepbreeder," as one who watches over the flock, as seen in 2 Kings 3:4. Some have speculated that the word used here meant that he was in charge of "(royal) herds [since] one text refers to the chief of the priests and the chief of the shepherds as the same person."[33] We can't know his role for sure, but we do know that he cared for sheep, even as he spoke God's Word to the people.

There is also a ruthless and worthless shepherd mentioned in the Old Testament, one not commonly associated alongside the good shepherds we have mentioned. He is spoken of by the prophet Zechariah and described as a false shepherd who deceives the flock during the last days. In Zechariah 11:16–17 we read:

> For behold, I am raising up in the land a shepherd who does not care for those being destroyed, or seek the young or heal the maimed or nourish the healthy, but devours the flesh of the fat ones, tearing off even their hoofs. "Woe to my worthless shepherd, who deserts the flock! May the sword strike his arm and his right eye! Let his arm be wholly withered, his right eye utterly blinded!"

Sometimes we can best understand what something *should* look like by seeing what it *shouldn't* look like.

The New Testament speaks of a seventh and final shepherd of God's people: Jesus. As number seven in the lineage of good shepherds, he is the perfect good shepherd (seven is frequently used in scripture to symbolize wholeness or perfection). Jesus calls himself the "good shepherd," and Peter calls him the "great shepherd." Jesus embodies all of the characteristics of the shepherds who came before him, and he stands opposed to the worthless shepherd prophesied in Zechariah, the anti-Christ. Jesus knows his own sheep, and his sheep know him. He cares, guides, directs, and provides for his sheep, even laying his life down for them (see John 10:14–15).

Why Study Something Old?

A missionary once lamented that the Old Testament wasn't very helpful in his work. "I don't find the Old Testament much help. So I seldom read it and have never really studied it. My call from the Lord was to take Jesus to the people of this country who have never heard of Him."[34] Today we live in a culture where we are fascinated with the new, and anything old or outdated is relegated to an antique store. Old versions of software are useless and need to be upgraded. Why bother with the old when you can have something new and fresh?

Sadly, many Christians take a similar approach to their interaction with the Old Testament. Perhaps by calling it the Old Testament, we have made a mistake, assuming that the old is somehow less important than the new. In reality, nothing could be further from the truth. The Old Testament was not old to Jesus. It was his story. It was his Bible. And it tells his story.

God's plans did not begin with the life of Jesus of Nazareth. According to Peter, they predated the creation of the world: "He [Christ] was foreknown before the foundation of the world but was revealed in these last times for you. Through him you believe in God, who raised him from the dead and gave him glory, so that your faith and hope are in God" (1 Peter 1:20–21 CSB).

God sent his Son into the world at a particular time, to a particular people, and during a particular era for a reason. And to understand that reason, we need to know the story before the story, the story that prepares for the arrival of God, showing us why he came and what he came to accomplish. In the next chapter, we'll take a closer look at how God arranged the events of history for this momentous event, using pagan rulers and religious leaders to prepare the way for the coming of Jesus.

CHAPTER 3

Preparing the Way
for the Messiah

By the first century BC, the priesthood of the Israelites had become so corrupt that a group of priests chose to leave their positions in Jerusalem in an attempt to escape the moral corruption. They became known as the Essenes. Each priest relocated from Jerusalem to the wilderness area around to the Dead Sea, an area called Qumram. They did this in an attempt to separate themselves from the decaying culture.

We should first note that wilderness in Israel does not look anything like the wilderness we often picture in America. Most Americans think of mountains with trees and streams, places of rolling hills and lush vegetation. The Hebrew word for wilderness is *midbar*, which the original translators of the KJV translated as *wilderness*. But if we want an accurate match to the original landscape, the correct translation should be *desert*.

The desert wilderness of Israel is an arid region with very few water sources and minimal rainfall. Only two to three inches of rain fall during the dry season, making it difficult for crops or vegetation to grow. Typically, there was just enough water and vegetation for the animals to graze and survive.

The desert wilderness, as it is mentioned in the scriptures, presents us with both positive *and* negative connotations. On the one hand, the desert was a symbol of emptiness and chaos, a place where God matured his people through trials of despair and isolation. On the other hand, the wilderness was also a place of hope, a symbol of rebirth and renewal, bringing to mind images of God's promise, provision, and dependability.

According to the prophet Isaiah, God would one day use the desert as the backdrop for the arrival of his Messiah. This was the hope of the Essenes as they looked in despair at the moral corruption of the nation of Israel. They took the words of Isaiah 40:3–5 quite literally:

> A voice cries: "In the wilderness prepare the way of the LORD; make straight in the desert a highway for our God. Every valley shall be lifted up, and every mountain and hill be made low; the uneven ground shall become level, and the rough places a plain. And the glory of the LORD shall be revealed, and all flesh shall see it together, for the mouth of the LORD has spoken."

The Essenes left behind the comforts of indoor plumbing, choice foods, and relatively comfortable living conditions—luxuries enjoyed by the priests—to endure 100+ degree temperatures, sand storms, and isolation. They "prepared the way of the Lord" with their lives by fasting twice a week and praying fervently for God to come.

Along with separating themselves from the outside world and retreating into the desert, they dedicated themselves to studying the scriptures, hoping that this would prepare a way for the Lord. They meticulously copied the Old Testament scrolls, devoting enormous amounts of time to ensuring every brushstroke of a Hebrew letter was accurately reproduced. Tradition tells us that there would have typically been four men working on one scroll at a time. One man would read the first word, while another watched over his shoulder to ensure the word was pronounced perfectly. One of the men at the writing table would write that word, and the final man would watch over his shoulder, checking his work. When the reader called out the name of God, Yahweh, the man would place his pen down, walk toward the *mikvah*, a ceremonial pool for cleansing, and submerge himself before returning to his desk to write God's name.

Scrolls like that of the prophet Jeremiah contain over seven hundred mentions of God's name and took considerable time to translate. The men doing this work had a high view of God's word as sacred, inerrant, and infallible, and we are indebted to them for faithfully preserving multiple copies of the Hebrew scriptures that we use to this day in translating our English Bibles.

Mikvah in Jericho[1]

Was John the Baptist an Essene?

Several scholars have suggested that John the Baptist was influenced by the Essenes. There are certainly similarities between them, especially their devotion to the wilderness lifestyle and to the practice of baptism. Some have also suggested that John was adopted into the Essene community, since his parents Zechariah and Elizabeth were older and could have possibly died when John was very young.[2] The Essenes were known for adopting orphans into their priestly family, and this may explain why John began his preaching ministry near the Qumran region.

Like the Essenes, John the Baptist chose to separate himself from the rest of society by living and preaching in the wilderness. John's father was a priest, so John could have claimed a place to work and serve in the temple. Instead, he battled the harsh conditions of the wilderness to preach righteousness and call people to repent. The Essenes were also known for their practice of ritual baptisms—something that John came to be identified with as well. In order to maintain their cleanliness and ritual holiness before the Lord, the Essenes baptized themselves in a *mikvah* (see picture). A washing was necessary for the induction of a new member, and people would self-administer their own baptisms by going into the water three times with their arms folded across their chests.

Still, even though there are some similarities between John the Baptist and the Essenes, there are also several differences we should note. First, although John separated himself from society, he eventually emerged from the desert. The Essenes, on the other hand, remained in the desert until the Roman military massacred them in AD 68. John also baptized for different reasons. The Essenes baptized themselves continuously, at least three times a day: before they ate, worshiped, prayed, or copied literature. John's baptism was more than a ritual act of cleanliness; it was a sign of repentance and turning away from a life of sin. In this way, John prepared the way for the Lord who would do this same work, baptizing (immersing) people in the Holy Spirit. Finally, and most important, John the Baptist recognized Jesus as the Messiah, whereas the Essene community awaited the resurrection and return of their "Teacher of Righteousness" and died still waiting for him to come. They never put faith in Jesus as the promised Son of God.

Preparing the Way for the Messiah

God selected John the Baptist as his prophet, and in doing so he broke four hundred years of silence. We first meet John the Baptist in Matthew 3, where he is described in this way: "Now John wore a garment of camel's hair and a leather belt around his waist, and his food was locusts and wild honey. Then Jerusalem and all Judea and all the region about the Jordan were going out to him, and they were baptized by him in the river Jordan, confessing their sins. But when he saw many of the Pharisees and Sadducees coming for baptism, he said to them, 'You brood of vipers! Who warned you to flee from the wrath to come?'" (Matt. 3:4–7). This description tells us a few things worth noting about John.

1. John was an unusual dresser.

We might find John's attire a bit strange, but camel's hair clothes and a leather belt were not uncommon. They were the attire of a poor person, and were an outward indication of John's humble choice to live a lifestyle of poverty. Even more significant than John's obvious humility, though, is the connection between John's clothes and the Old Testament prophet Elijah.

We read about Elijah's dress in 2 Kings 1:8, and John's clothes directly link him to Elijah. This connection is prophesied in the last words written by Micah, just before the four hundred year period of silence when God ceased speaking through his prophets: "Behold, I will send you Elijah the prophet before the great and awesome day the Lord comes. And he will turn the hearts of fathers to their children and the hearts of children to their fathers, lest I come and strike the land with a decree of utter destruction" (Mal. 4:5–6). John's dress and his prophetic message identify him with Elijah, the prophet who comes as the forerunner of the Messiah before the day of the Lord.

2. John had an unusual appetite.

John's diet consisted of locusts and wild honey. These are also parallels to Elijah (e.g., 1 Kings 8:37; 14:3) and signs of John's humble existence. The word for "locusts" here is *akrides*, meaning that they are the large insects—not the fruit of the locust tree, as some have suggested. Locusts are still eaten in the Middle East today. They are a good source of protein and allowable within the guidelines of Jewish dietary laws.

3. John spoke with unusual authority.

John was raised by righteous parents, and his father was a priest who had the privilege of serving in the temple (see Luke 1:5–25). But John did not worry about offending people. He did not hesitate to rebuke the religious leaders of his day. Though he may have lacked formal religious training, John's message carried weight and authority as he revealed the corruption in the priesthood and other religious sects.

A Divine Meeting in the Holy Place

The priesthood of Israel consisted of twenty-four divisions of men who were appointed to their role through birth. You couldn't earn your way into the priesthood, nor could you bargain, buy, or barter your way into it. It was something you were born into. Each division was assigned two rotations of service every year. Some activities garnered more respect and appreciation than others. For example, preparing an offering for sacrifice or loading salt into the storage room was not as honorable as burning incense on the altar. Choice jobs, such as burning incense, were only engaged in once in a lifetime. Lots were drawn to decide who could participate in these jobs, and once an act of service was complete, you were excluded from performing that job again.

Luke begins his Gospel with a description of Zechariah's service in the temple on the day his lot was cast for burning incense. Zechariah and his wife, Elizabeth, had been praying for some time about having children, but they were old, far past the age of conceiving. We get the sense that this was a repeated prayer, a constant burden on both of their hearts.

Elizabeth's barrenness calls to mind other Old Testament women who played crucial roles in the story of the coming Messiah: Sarah, Rebekah, Rachel, Samson's mother, and Hannah. Thomas Lancaster writes that "when the Bible tells the story of a child miraculously conceived in a barren womb, it does so to emphasize that the child's destiny is ordained by God for some great purpose."[3] If we look at Abraham's wife, Sarah, we are reminded that God answered her prayer for a son by sending them Isaac. God also answered Elkanah and Hannah's prayers for a son by sending Samuel, the one who prepared the way for King David. It is interesting to note that Abraham and Sarah's account is found in the Law, and Elkanah's and Hannah's account is found in the Prophets, a reminder that both the Law and the Prophets paved the way for the Messiah.

J. C. Ryle also points out the significance of Elizabeth's barrenness by connecting it with the wilderness where John would come to preach and minister. Ryle writes, "The wilderness is a prophetical and figurative description of the spiritual barrenness of Israel."[4] Just as John had been born to a barren woman, his ministry would bear fruit in a barren place, both representing hope for a spiritually barren nation. The ritualism and legalism of God's people had overshadowed their love for God. So instead of preaching to them from the temple steps or meeting people where they were, John positioned himself in the middle of nowhere and waited for the people to come to him. As a priest, he would have been welcome on the steps of the temple, but John intentionally left that option behind and followed God's call to preach in the wilderness a message of repentance that ran counter to the formulaic religious practices of the day.

The location where John chose to prepare the way for the Messiah was no accident. Many biblical encounters with God happened in close proximity to this location. Moses called the nation to covenant with God, and he preached his farewell discourse to them near this spot. Joshua circumcised the men of Israel, led the nation into the Promised Land, and built a monument of remembrance for crossing the river at or around that location. Elijah parted the waters of the Jordan and ascended into heaven on a fiery chariot around the same area. Like those before him, John selected a preaching platform rich in biblical history, possibly choosing to set up his ministry at the stones erected by Joshua as the Israelites crossed the Jordan many years before.

John (the Gospel writer) tells us that John the Baptist knew that he was the one spoken about in Isaiah. John 1:23 reads: "He [John the Baptist] said, 'I am the voice of one crying out in the wilderness, "Make straight the way of the Lord," as the prophet Isaiah said.'" John the Baptist saw himself as a herald, one designated to prepare for a king's arrival by announcing it to the community. Townspeople would form an entourage trailing behind the herald and removing obstacles, clearing the streets, and smoothing the roads for the king's arrival. The messenger's role was not to draw attention to himself. It was to direct the people to prepare for the one coming behind him.

Preaching in the Desert

As already noted, the Jewish priesthood had spiritually and morally declined through cultural compromise and political coercion. As Rome expanded its empire throughout Judea and Jerusalem, the office of high priest—a lifelong position as the spiritual leader of God's people—was bought and sold. "The Romans sold the office of high priest to the highest bidder and awarded it only to loyal Roman sympathizers among the priesthood."[5] To represent the people's need for moral and spiritual regeneration, John prepared the way for Jesus by calling people to repentance.

This was outwardly signified by the practice of baptism. People would ask John, "'[W]hy are you baptizing, if you are neither the Christ, nor

Elijah, nor the Prophet?' John answered them, "'I baptize with water, but among you stands one you do not know, even he who comes after me, the strap of whose sandal I am not worthy to untie.'" These things took place in Bethany across the Jordan, where John was baptizing (John 1:25–28).

Baptism in the first century was somewhat different from the practice we have today in most churches. The root word for baptize means "to dip fully, to plunge, or immerse."[6] Before entering the temple or synagogue, people would submerge themselves in the living water of a *mikvah* for ritual purification. Most baptisms in the first century were self-administered, and contrary to tradition, it is most likely that this is what happened in John's ministry as well: "John did not baptise people. In Judaism, the person undergoing immersion immerses himself or herself. The one desiring immersion enters the water to at least chest-depth and then bends at the knees to submerge his head beneath the water. He then repeats the immersion two more times. John supervised the immersion process."[7] People would cross their arms over their chest before immersing themselves three times.

So John is not dunking anyone. Instead, the people are engaging in baptism as a response to his preaching. John's preaching pricked the hearts of people, helping them to recognize that they had strayed from God's ways, and many would follow through on their conviction by baptizing themselves. So did John "dunk" Jesus? A first-century fresco depicts John the Baptist, not in the water, but standing on the bank helping Jesus out of the water after his baptism. (To see a picture of this fresco visit http://www.jerusalemperspective.com/6137.)

What we need to know about John is that he was a unique individual, born to do something incredible, and that he did his job with humility. John never wavered in his devotion to the message of God. And yet this man who was willing to die for the Messiah still found it necessary to ask Jesus whether he was the one they should be looking for or not. Was it possible that John had doubts? Let's take a closer look at why John asked Jesus these questions.

Are You the Messiah, or Should We Find Someone Else?

Jesus once said of John, "Truly, I say to you, among those born of women there has arisen no one greater than John the Baptist" (Matt. 11:11). And yet the Gospels record that the man who warranted such praise questioned the ministry of Jesus near the end of his earthly life. Matthew records, "When Jesus had finished instructing his twelve disciples, he went on from there to teach and preach in their cities. Now when John heard in prison about the deeds of the Christ, he sent word by his disciples and said to him, 'Are you the one who is to come, or shall we look for another?'" (Matt. 11:1–3).

We have the benefit of knowing the full story, but we still wonder, how could John ask this? Did he have doubts that Jesus was the Messiah? We might say to him: "John, by your own admission, you are the Elijah-like figure spoken about in Malachi, the voice of one crying in the wilderness spoken of by Isaiah. You've already declared, 'Behold the Lamb of God who takes away the sins of the world.' You testified that you saw the Spirit descend from heaven like a dove, and it remained on him. You experienced the Holy Spirit descending like a dove upon Jesus as he rose from the waters. How could you have any questions about Jesus's identity?"

I've been puzzled by John's question, as we all should be. But when we put the verse into its proper context, the passage makes sense and comes alive in a fresh way. First, we need to back up the story a few months and uncover why John is in prison in the first place.

The Bible tells us that John called Herod out, rebuking him for his affair with his brother's wife, Herodias. So Herod had John arrested. It may have been that Herod intended to eventually release John, but that was not to be, for Herodias was not happy with John either. In fact, she was so upset by John's rebuke of Herod that she instructed her daughter to seek revenge. On Herod's birthday, she sent her young daughter to dance for Herod (Matt. 14). Herod feels a perverted pleasure from this dance and is so captured by the young girl that he offers her one request—anything that she desires. She consults with her mother, who is still bitter about John's audacity, and then makes her request to Herod: "Give me the head of John the Baptist here on a platter" (Matt. 14:8).

This is where we find John at the time of his question to Jesus. He is caught between prison and a platter. Read through a Western lens, we interpret this as a situation of desperation, and we expect that Jesus will respond by coming to John's rescue.

But that is not how Jesus responds. He has a different answer for John, one that would have given John hope in his discouragement.

The "Coming One"

The key to understanding John's question and the response of Jesus is found in the concept of a *kesher*. We will unpack this idea in more detail in chapter 5, but the basic idea of a *kesher* is that it is a connection, quote, or allusion to a passage in the Old Testament. In Hebrew, John is asking Jesus: "Are you the 'coming one'?"

When John asks this of Jesus, he is referencing two Old Testament passages. Malachi 3:1–2 states: "Behold, I send my messenger, and he will prepare the way before me. And the Lord whom you seek will suddenly *come* to his temple; and the messenger of the covenant in whom you delight, behold, he is *coming*, says the Lord of hosts. But who can endure the day of his *coming*, and who can stand when he appears?" Zechariah 9:9 says, "Rejoice greatly, O daughter of Zion! Shout aloud, O daughter of Jerusalem! Behold, your king is *coming* to you; righteous and having salvation is he, humble and mounted on a donkey, on a colt, the foal of a donkey" (emphasis mine).[8]

What is the significance of John using a phrase that calls to mind these passages? First, it means that John's question is not about Jesus's *identity* as much as his *ministry*. John is not questioning *who* Jesus is; he is asking when he will do what he is expected to do. Israelites believed that the Messianic age would bring with it the judgment of the wicked and the trampling of Israel's enemies. The wrath of God would finally be poured out upon those who had persecuted God's people.

John wasn't asking simply for his own sake; he was trying to prod Jesus along. According to Richard Hays, "John was probably inquiring whether Jesus meant to assume the role of conquering royal Davidic Messiah."[9] It's as if John were saying to Jesus, "When I look around, I still see evil men prospering and wicked men sinning blatantly. What are you waiting for, Jesus? Let's get this Messianic agenda started! I want to see the Holy Spirit poured out on God's people. I want to witness fire from heaven poured out on the wicked." Dwight Pryor sums up John's request this way: "He is not doubting Jesus's messianic identity. He's challenging Jesus's messianic agenda."[10]

How does Jesus respond? Let's look at Jesus's response as recorded for us in Matthew 11:

"Go and tell John what you hear and see: the blind receive their sight and the lame walk, lepers are cleansed and the deaf hear, and the dead are raised up, and the poor have good news preached to them. And blessed is the one who is not offended by me" (vv. 4–6).

Jesus responds to John's question, asking if he was the "coming" one, by quoting from Isaiah 35:3–6. Additionally, Jesus is alluding to Isaiah 61, the text he reads in the Nazareth synagogue (see Luke 4:16ff.). We might interpret Jesus's response as an attempt to inspire John by strengthening his faith, but there is a problem with this line of reasoning—John already knew that Jesus was doing these amazing miracles. Matthew begins this episode by saying, "When John *heard in prison what Jesus was doing*, he sent his disciples to ask him . . ." (Matt. 11:2–3, emphasis mine). So John already knows that Jesus is doing these miracles. How does the response from Jesus help John if it is simply confirming what John already knows?

The answer is that Jesus was not speaking to John's doubts about his identity. He was telling John that his agenda might differ from what John had expected from the Messiah. Using the reference to Isaiah, Jesus says to John, "John, I'm fulfilling the expectations of Isaiah. I've protected and spared others. I'm doing miracles. But I'm not coming to get you. I have chosen a different path for you. Hang in there. Stay strong. Don't fall away because of me." In essence, Jesus is telling John that his present imprisonment was part of God's providential plan.

And that is a message we all need to hear. Often, when circumstances don't align with the agenda we think God should have for our lives, we doubt Jesus and his identity. But Jesus's message to John is a reminder to us that Jesus is who he said he was. He is the Messiah, the coming one, but that doesn't mean his mission is always our immediate deliverance from pain and suffering.

Those who trust in God know that there are no accidents in the economy of God. Jesus knows our future better than we know our own past. If you are struggling in the Christian life, you can probably relate to John's question—"Are you going to deliver me from these circumstances?" And sometimes the answer is no, and we learn that God has a reason, and he is working all things together for his glory and our ultimate good. Joni

Eareckson Tada describes it this way, "Sometimes God permits what He hates to accomplish that which He loves!"[11]

The more that we understand the life of Jesus as a first-century Jewish rabbi, the more we realize that there is more going on than we might see at first. If we focus on Jesus's ministry hoping to get temporal benefits from it, we will likely miss the bigger picture of what Jesus came to do. Jesus came to bear witness to the truth about God and to accomplish the cosmic purposes of God's plan of salvation and redemption (see John 18:37). Seeing him as a first-century rabbi, speaking and teaching with these rabbinic methods, helps us to better understand his message.

CHAPTER 4

Growing in Wisdom and Stature

The incarnation of Christ is a beautiful picture of God's desire to be present with his people. The Bible begins in a garden, as God walks with Adam, and it ends in a garden-city where God once again abides with his people. "He will be with them . . ." (Rev. 21:3).

Every encounter in between these two events explains and unpacks God's desire to dwell with us. He communicates and reveals himself to us, leads his people through the wilderness, outlines plans for a dwelling place to reside among them, and speaks to them through burning bushes, animals, and elements of the atmosphere. But none of this can compare to the day he comes in person as Jesus of Nazareth. God wraps himself in human flesh, entering time and space in order to redeem mankind. The infinite, eternal God enters the temporal, finite universe at a specific time for a specific purpose. D. Thomas Lancaster illustrates the power and purpose of the incarnation this way:

An author is writing a novel. He creates the settings, situations, stories, and plotlines, and populates his novel with characters. He likes the characters he created so much that he wants to interact with them but he cannot because the novel is his creation. It's just a story. The characters in the book cannot hear the author; they cannot see him; they cannot experience him because the author completely transcends the words written on a page. What does the author do? He writes himself into the novel as one of the characters, creating a written story-version of himself with which the characters can interact. The written ink-and-paper version of the author accurately expresses the author's person. It is not disconnected from the author, but neither is it really the author in his total transcendence outside the book.[1]

This is what God has done. The divine storywriter has written himself into his own documentary as the "word becoming flesh and dwelling among us" (John 1:14). The word translated as "dwelt" in John 1:14 can be translated as "tabernacled" or "pitched a tent." This is a clear allusion to the Old Testament passage Exodus 25:8, which states, "And let them make me a sanctuary, that I may dwell in their midst." Jesus's human body is the final tabernacle, the true and lasting dwelling place of God. Jesus is where God takes up permanent residence to live in his creation and among his people.

Our Holy God Is a Humble God

If I asked you to describe God in one or two words, what words would you choose? Some might say that God is wise, and that would be true. According to Job 37:16, he is the one "who is perfect in knowledge." God is also holy, and according to Revelation 4:8, the angels constantly declare his moral purity and transcendent perfection: "Holy, Holy, Holy is the Lord God Almighty." Or we might say that God is loving. According to 1 John 4:8 (NIV), "Whoever does not love does not know God, because God is love." A rather uncommon answer would be to say that God is humble. But as we look closely at the events surrounding the birth of Christ, we see this truth clearly revealed and find ourselves comforted and filled with joy as we meet our humble God.

Luke records the baby Jesus entering the world in Luke 2: "In the same region, shepherds were staying out in the fields and keeping watch at night over their flock. Then an angel of the Lord stood before them, and the glory of the Lord shone around them, and they were terrified. But the angel said to them, 'Don't be afraid, for look, I proclaim to you good news of great joy that will be for all the people: Today in the city of David a Savior was born for you, who is the Messiah, the Lord. This will be the sign for you: You will find a baby wrapped tightly in cloth and lying in a manger'" (Luke 2:8–12 CSB).

On that dark night, as the shepherds were in the field tending their sheep, suddenly, a glorious light enveloped them. An angel came forth with an amazing announcement to the most unlikely of men. When a child is born to a member of British royalty, as we witnessed when Prince William and Princess Kate gave birth to their son, Prince George, they don't send messengers to the docks to break the news to the fishermen or the boat captains. They don't issue personal invitations to the cab drivers on the streets of London. Quite the contrary. They send golden, sealed invitations to the political leaders of the United Nations. The national media documents every moment of the birth.

But when the God of creation, the Lord of the universe, announced the arrival of his Son, he didn't inform the world with gold-leafed announcements, grand parades, or royal messengers sent to the heads of Israel. He didn't publicize his birth to the Pharisees, elders, scribes, Sadducees, or chief priests. God overlooked the upper class of society and informed the lowly shepherds of his appearance. According to biblical scholar Dwight Pryor, "Shepherds were detestable and unreliable. They sometimes couldn't testify in court. Nobody wanted to be a shepherd. Shepherds were despised by the 'good' respectable people of that day. According to the Mishnah, shepherds were under a ban. They were regarded as thieves. The only people lower than shepherds at that particular time in Jewish history were lepers."[2]

This makes sense, if you look at the biblical history. Consider David. We think of him as a mighty king, but before he was king, he was out tending sheep when the prophet Samuel came to visit his family. Why? Because he was the least of the brothers. His older siblings were out fighting battles and working for the family. David was the least important, and he had the job of tending the sheep. The shepherds weren't respected members of society. But when the God of Heaven arrived on earth, he didn't enter the courts of royalty, he was born in the caves where animals fed. He was not visited by the scholars, the scribes, and the Pharisees, but by unlearned shepherds. He was not found by the shepherds in a palace, but in a feeding trough. His attire was not a royal garment, but swaddling clothes, and his welcome was not from praises of men, but from sounds of farm animals.

Why? God was revealing something about himself, his nature, and his mission. He was teaching us a lesson through the announcement of his Son: that he is a God who cares for the lowly and those in need. He speaks to the poor in spirit, he bypasses the haughty and proud of this world, and he meets the humble. As James would later say in describing God's response to people: He opposes the proud, but gives grace to the humble. Jesus did not come to befriend the politically powerful or the social elites. He is the savior of all, especially those who most see their need for a savior. He doesn't discriminate based on age, class, intelligence, education, profession, social status, or occupation. He's the God of the Jews and the God of the Gentiles. He eats with tax collectors, welcomes prostitutes, heals Gentiles, touches lepers, and saves sinners.

Although he is the high and holy God of creation, he is also a humble God. He despises human pride because it reveals our arrogance and rebellion, and highlights our sin—our refusal to acknowledge him as king and thank him for all we have. At root, sin is the attempt to set ourselves up on the throne of God.

The Significance of Swaddling

Even though Jesus came as a baby, he wouldn't remain an infant. He grew in wisdom and stature, lived a sinless life, and was eventually condemned to die on a Roman cross for crimes he did not commit. He would be crucified and his body buried, but he would rise from the dead.

What you may not know is that his death is foreshadowed in the very clothes in which he was wrapped at birth. The angel doesn't just describe the scene to the shepherds by saying, "You will find a baby in a feeding trough in a cave." That in itself would have seemed very odd to them. But the angel adds one additional detail: "And this will be a sign for you: you will find a baby wrapped in *swaddling* cloths and lying in a manger" (Luke 2:8–12).

What are swaddling cloths? These are not just random pieces of fabric. In fact, a better translation would be swaddling bands. These were strips of linen five inches wide by five or six yards long, and according to the Mishnah, they were used to wrap lambs destined to be Passover lambs immediately after birth to protect them from injuring themselves.[3] Baby lambs would often thrash back and forth, sometimes causing harm to themselves during the first couple of hours of their lives, so shepherds would protect them by wrapping them in these swaddling bands. It's also interesting to note that the lambs used for the temple sacrifices were raised in Bethlehem.[4] So when the shepherds rushed to see the God of the universe born as a human baby, they would have recognized the type of cloth he was wrapped up in immediately.

The word for this type of cloth was also used to describe burial cloth. In fact, the same strips that protected a newborn were the ones used to prepare a body for burial. Jesus was not born in a country stable but in a cave, and as Arnold Fruchtenbaum, a Jewish theologian, points out:

> Interspersed among the caves were caves used for burial purposes. So, in these burial caves, in niches, in the walls you can still see to this day, they would store burial cloth. If a person died within the town, they would bring the body out, wrap the body up in strips of cloth from the cloth stored in the stable caves, and then take him to be buried, either in a different cave, or in a cemetery below the ground. Because he was born in a stable cave, Mary and Joseph had to make use of that which was most readily available, which was burial cloth.[5]

These insights are full of rich symbolism because they hint to us of what is yet to come in the life of this baby. On the first day of Jesus's earthly life he was wrapped up like a Passover lamb and laid in a cave, and on the day of his death he would be wrapped in the same type of cloth and laid in a cave. In his birth and in his death we find these parallels, reminding us that though we were born to live, Jesus, our Passover lamb, was born to die for us so that we could live forever.

Unusual Visitors

Every year, Christians erect nativity scenes populated by the same cast of characters: kingly men with gifts in their hands kneeling around a manger holding baby Jesus surrounded by Mary, Joseph, and a farm's worth of animals. Most people recognize the opening line from a popular song as well: "We three kings of orient are, bearing gifts we've traversed afar." Yet while the figurines and the song may be heartwarming, several of the details surrounding the birth of our savior are speculations based on misinformation, attempts to fill in the gaps of what is not mentioned. Let's examine a few insights that can enrich our understanding, deepening what we think we know about this familiar event.

The visit of the magi, the "kings" of the Christmas story, is found in Matthew 2:1–12. The first thing that we notice from this account is that several things we accept based on tradition have no basis in scripture. We are not told how many men show up. Based on the length of their journey and their profession, it is safe to assume that there were more than three of them. We are told that the gifts they brought were gold, frankincense, and myrrh, but these are simply categories of gifts. We are not told what quantity they brought with them. What is interesting is that the gifts of the magi are mentioned as a fulfillment of Old Testament prophecies from Isaiah 60 and Psalm 72:

> Caravans of camels will cover your land—young camels of Midian and Ephah—all of them will come from Sheba. They will carry *gold* and *frankincense* (Isaiah 60:6 CSB, emphasis mine).

> May he live long! May *gold* from Sheba be given to him. May prayer be offered for him continually, and may he be blessed all day long (Ps. 72:15 CSB, emphasis mine).

It is also likely that the magi arrived to visit Jesus and his family roughly two years after Jesus had been born. First we read that, upon arrival, the men entered the house (Matt. 2:11) where Jesus was staying, which contrasts with the stable where he was born. We also read that when

Herod learned he had been tricked by these men, he ordered the death of all boys two years old and younger, an indication that the child had been born within the past two years.

It is also questionable if the star we often sing about was actually a star as we define it today. Here are five reasons why the star of Jesus may have been something else:

1. The star is called "His [Jesus's] star."
2. The star rises and descends.
3. The star moves from east to west.
4. The star appears and disappears.
5. The star hovers over a single house.

It is also helpful to understand that the Greek word we translate as "star" can "indicate many different astrological phenomena, including comets, meteors, or planetary conjunctions."[6] Matthew is probably using this word as an allusion to Numbers 24:17 (NIV), which says that "a star will come out of Jacob; a scepter will rise out of Israel." Whatever this phenomena was, these men saw something extraordinary in the sky that piqued their interest so much that they traveled hundreds of miles to worship a baby they believed was born to be a king.

Do we know what the "star" was? It is difficult to draw definitive conclusions, but many have speculated. Some have argued that it may have been a "great conjunction" where the planets Jupiter and Saturn align in the night sky. German Astronomer Johannes Kepler believed three planets formed a conjunction around 7 BC that would have been visible in the constellation Pisces, which was "a sign sometimes connected in ancient astrology with the Hebrews."[7] Others have argued that it may have been a supernova, a comet, or another temporary nighttime phenomenon.

What we do know is that it was a supernatural light that revealed to these sky-watchers the Shekinah glory of God! And it is remarkable that Babylonian astrologers came to the grand conclusion that this star signified the birth of the King of the Jews. What was it that could have led them to that conclusion?

Daniel the Disciplemaker

To understand why and how these magi would have known to search the Hebrew scriptures looking for a king, we need to consider the history of the Jewish people. There is only one place in the Old Testament that dates the Messiah's arrival, and it is found in the book of Daniel. As a young boy, Daniel was exiled from the Southern Kingdom of Judah in Israel to Babylon almost 600 years before the Messiah's birth. Daniel became a well-known prophet of the East, and on several occasions he gave time limits with his prophecies. In one of them, found in Daniel 9:24, he predicted that the Messiah would come in "seventy weeks," or more specifically, "seventy sevens." Daniel didn't mean that the Messiah would arrive in seventy weeks; he was saying that seventy sabbatical cycles or 490 years (a sabbatical cycle was seven years) would have to pass before the Christ would appear.

Daniel wrote his prophecy at a time when the Israelites were in captivity[8] in the city of Babylon. Babylon, in many prophetic writings, is simply referred to as "the East." Since the ancient city of Babylon existed in the heart of modern-day Iraq, that places it due east from Israel. Both Babylon and Persia are associated with the term "East" in the thread of Israel's history, and both of these lands have a rich history of prophecies. What we learn from Matthew 2:1 is that these wise men came from "the East." Babylon would be one of the most likely places for them to come from.

It's also interesting to note that not only did Daniel write from his captivity in Babylon, but he was directly connected with astrologers five times in his book. We are told that Daniel was in charge of them. How he came to this position is providential. The book of Daniel tells us that Nebuchadnezzar had been plagued with bad dreams and was looking for help from his "wise men," all of whom were unable to interpret the dreams for him. He became angry with all of the wise men who claimed the ability to interpret dreams, and he put out a decree that all the wise men of Babylon be destroyed (Dan. 2:12). Daniel approached the king and, through God's wisdom, told Nebuchadnezzar what his dream had been and interpreted it for him. His work literally spared the wise men's lives.

Because of this, Daniel was made the overseer of the wise men of Babylon—essentially becoming the headmaster of the Babylonian School of Astrology. Daniel 2:48 (CSB) says it this way: "Then the king promoted Daniel and gave him many generous gifts. He made him ruler over the entire province of Babylon and chief governor over all the wise men of Babylon." And it is from this school of prophecy, so to speak, that Daniel's later writings about the coming Messiah would come. Since Daniel was in charge of overseeing the education of the Babylonian wise men, he likely had some influence over what they were taught. Since he was a devout Jew living in exile, he would have taught his followers one thing: the writings of the Hebrew Bible.

A Star Has Risen

So how does all of this connect to Daniel's prophecy about the Messiah? Daniel's prophetic timeline was the final piece in a centuries-long puzzle about the coming of the Messiah. In the course of their learning, Daniel and his disciples would have studied the Torah and learned about a man named Balaam, a prophet who had come from a town called Pethor. More than a millennium before the birth of Christ, Balaam had been hired by an enemy of Israel to curse the people of Israel. As we read in Numbers, God's design was that Balaam's curse would be turned to blessing instead. We read one of Balaam's curses-turned-blessings in Numbers 24:17, where he speaks about the Messiah: "I see him, but not now; I perceive him, but not near. A *star* will come from Jacob, and a *scepter* will arise from Israel. He will smash the forehead of Moab and strike down all the Shethites" (CSB, emphasis mine).

According to Numbers 22, Balaam was an astrologer from Pethor, a city that eventually became a part of the Babylonian empire during the reign of Nebuchadnezzar. It is even possible that Balaam himself may have once associated with the ancient Babylonian school of astrology. Daniel and his disciples may have also had access to the writings of a prophet who had lived a hundred years before the Babylonian captivity, a man named Micah. In Micah 5:2, this prophet wrote of a little town called Bethlehem: "But you, O Bethlehem Ephrathah, who are too little to be among the clans of Judah, from you shall come forth for me one who is to be ruler in Israel, whose coming forth is from of old, from ancient days."

Now let's bring these prophecies together. Balaam, speaking hundreds of years earlier, had revealed that Israel would produce a king worthy of being announced by the heavens. Then, just a hundred years earlier, Micah had said that this king would come from a humble city called Bethlehem. Finally, Daniel predicted when all of this would happen.

Daniel's disciples, the magi he oversaw in Babylon during Israel's captivity, would have probably passed these insights down to their own disciples. After all, these were prophetic teachings taught to them by the man who had saved their lives, so it would not be surprising if they had carefully taught those who came after them as well. If they did this, they would have known that the King of Israel would be born in Bethlehem, at least 490 years in the future, and that he would be identified by a star over Judah. Over the next 500 years these teachings were passed down, and when the time came and these observant magi noticed what was happening in the heavens, these Gentile Babylonian wise men set off on a six-hundred-mile journey of faith to meet the King of the Jews. Over the course of two months they wandered through the desert—expending their time, resources, and precious gifts—all while the devout, Jewish religious leaders didn't bother travelling six miles to welcome their king.

Do we know for certain that this is who the magi were and why they came? No. But it is likely that these were men who had spent time studying the Hebrew Bible and had some familiarity with its prophecies. I believe the most likely reason for this is that they were from Babylon, descendants of the magi of Daniel from the time of Israel's captivity.

Growing in Wisdom and Stature

With the exception of the visit from the magi, which made for a rather atypical event, the rest of Jesus's upbringing was, by all accounts, fairly normal. If it was comparable to that of other Jewish boys of that time, we can piece together an approximate picture of what it would have looked like from what we know of ancient Jewish culture.

The only thing we are told explicitly about Jesus's upbringing is that at an early age he is found in the temple studying the scriptures with the sages of Israel. For the Jews, study was encouraged and expected. Jewish philosopher Moses Maimonides describes the commitment the Jews had to reading and studying the Torah:

> Every person in Israel is obligated to be engaged in Torah learning, whether one is poor or wealthy, whether one is whole in body or afflicted with suffering, whether one is young or one is old and feeble, even a poor person who is supported by charity and goes from door to door seeking benevolence, even the man supporting his wife and children—everyone is required to find a set time during the day and the night to study Torah, as it was said, "you shall go over it, again and again, day and night" (Joshua 1:8).[9]

Hebrew men and women spent time with God in prayer throughout the day, and families were encouraged to have discussions about the Torah at every meal.

The New Testament tells us that Jesus was fully human, like us in every way, yet without sin. Philippians 2 tells us that the Son of God humbled himself and didn't exercise his divine privileges while he lived on earth. We are told that he grew and developed physically, mentally, and relationally like any other human being. This means that Jesus didn't exercise his divine omniscience in a way that would have made him superhuman or seem otherworldly. To give you an example, it's safe to assume that an interaction like this probably did *not* happen:

> "Can anyone quote Psalm 119?" asks the teacher.
>
> "I can," says young Jesus, standing and reciting the entire thing.
>
> "No fair," cry the other kids. "That's easy for him to do—he wrote the book!"

While it's fun (and humorous) to imagine Jesus exploiting his divine abilities as God's Son, it's inaccurate. Jesus, as a human being, worked, studied, learned, and did all the things human beings normally do. He took the time to *learn* the scriptures. He experienced emotions and *loved* God's Word. He also *lived* God's Word, living out what he learned and living in obedience to it. Scripture flowed out of his mouth because it was hidden in his heart. The practice of memorizing scripture was common for Jewish men, and Jesus would have been no different. Saul Lieberman, in his book *Hellenism in Jewish Palestine*, states,

> There is no evidence that the Rabbis prepared special lexica of the Bible; they had no need of them. The entire rabbinic literature bears testimony to the fact that the Rabbis knew the Bible by heart. Jerome testifies that the Palestinian Jews of the fourth century were able to recite the Pentateuch and the Prophets by heart. The Jewish sages could well manipulate their explanations without the help of special vocabularies of the Bible.[10]

If Jesus was able to quote Psalm 119 by heart—as he likely was—it was not because he possessed an unfair advantage. It was because he was a faithful student who loved God's Word. When Jesus quoted the scriptures and those around him instantly understood the context and application, it was because the Jews were "people of the book." They knew and loved God's Word.

With this in mind, I'd like to paint a picture of Jesus's childhood based on what we know today of Jewish customs at that time and what we learn from later rabbinical literature. By reconstructing Jesus's upbringing, we better understand who Jesus was and what he taught. We begin by looking at his earthly adoptive father, Joseph. Joseph was a devout Jewish man, and he would have typically discipled his firstborn son in the commands of the Torah. He would have done this in obedience to Deuteronomy 6:7, probably reciting the passage twice daily. Jesus would have enrolled in Torah school at the age of five, when most boys began their education in the Hebrew scriptures. What did they learn? In my book *Rediscovering Discipleship*, I explain it this way:

> As a Torah-observant Jew, Jesus would have learned the Hebrew alphabet as an infant. Parents were instructed in the Talmud, which is a commentary on the Scriptures by famous historical rabbis, to teach their children the alphabet—or "alephbet"—before they walked. Next, Jesus would have enrolled in the "house of instruction" or "school," the local synagogue. The first use of this word is found in Sirach (Ecclesiasticus) around 180 BC. Shortly thereafter, synagogues became

the epicenter of learning, with the institution of the first district school system for youths being credited to the Pharisees around 75 BC.[11]

D. Thomas Lancaster describes life in the Jewish home as follows:

> a predictable rhythm of daily prayers, studies, Sabbaths, festivals, and other pious observances. Every Thursday was market day, and every Friday was preparation for the Sabbath. Friday nights the family welcomed the Sabbath at sunset and enjoyed a special meal serving wine, the best foods, and a double portion of bread. On Saturday morning Joseph heard the Torah read at the synagogue, and Yeshua [Jesus] watched as His father sometimes went up to read from the scroll.[12]

Every year the family would have celebrated three pilgrimage feasts: Passover, Pentecost, and Tabernacles. Luke 2:41 supports this practice: "Now his parents went to Jerusalem *every year* at the Feast of the Passover" (emphasis mine). All of this reminds us that Jesus was raised by loving, godly parents of exceptional piety.

Because of their commitment to annually celebrating the pilgrimage feasts, we get the only account of Jesus's childhood that has been preserved for us in scripture. It is found in the Gospel of Luke, and it tells the story of Mary and Joseph realizing they have lost Jesus as they are travelling on the road back home after the feast. Western readers often read this story and think, *How could they have lost him? What were they thinking?* Before we cast stones at Mary and Joseph, it helps to understand the "mass transit" systems of the first-century Jewish world.

Finding the Son in His Father's House

The simplest way to grasp the difference between then and now is to say that the Jewish people did everything as a community, including their travel. Ancient Jews traveled with a caravan of people for protection, security, and safety. Imagine a large group of people who know one another all moving together and looking out for their own children as well as their friends' and neighbors' kids. In such a system of travel it's not difficult to see how a young boy could have been easily overlooked. There were hundreds of people from Bethlehem all traveling together on this particular pilgrimage, and Joseph and Mary would have assumed that Jesus was with his friends or some other family members. Why would he stay behind in Jerusalem when everyone else was leaving town?

Jesus did stay behind, and he was not missing for more than a few days before Joseph and Mary found him "in the temple, sitting among the teachers, listening to them and asking them questions" (Luke 2:46). The normal practice of the teachers during the Sabbath and the times of the pilgrimage festivals was to sit around the courts and terraces of the temple discussing the Torah.[13] I always picture this verse as something akin to a Sunday school class. The lost boy from Bethlehem is asking questions about lessons he'd learned earlier in the week, waiting for his parents to come back and find him. But Luke 2:47 paints a very different picture for us: "And all who heard him were amazed at his understanding and his answers." So was Jesus asking the questions or answering them?

Dwight Pryor provides some additional insight when he explains the Jewish process of learning: "In advanced Jewish study of Scripture, a rabbi would engage a student by asking a question; the student would respond in kind with a related question, showing he understood what the rabbi was asking, and thereby advancing the discussion."[14] If you've read any of Jesus's teaching elsewhere in the Gospels, you likely recognize this question-and-answer approach. Remember that Jesus *constantly* responded to questions with his own questions.[15] Again, he wasn't trying to amaze the religious leaders with his supernatural understanding; he was simply proving his grasp of deep theological truths by posing well-formed questions. Yes, it would have been amazing, but at the level of a man who displayed "wisdom beyond his years."

Luke 2 also gives us Jesus's first recorded words at the age of twelve, as he speaks to his parents. He asks them: "Why were you searching for me? . . . Didn't you know that it was necessary for me to be in my Father's house?" (v. 49 CSB). It can be helpful to think of this statement more along these lines: "Did you not know that I had to be about my Father's business?" Boys would typically choose an occupation to pursue around the age of twelve or thirteen, so it is no surprise that Jesus was in the temple at this same age choosing his occupation—his Father's business.

The Jewish historian Josephus suggested that the Old Testament prophet Samuel also heard the word of God at the young age of twelve.[16] Similar to Samuel, Jesus was hearing and discussing the words of his Father, developing in four key areas: mentally (wisdom), physically (stature), spiritually (favor with God), and socially (favor with men).[17] Dann Spader describes this growth in light of what theologians call the hypostatic union—the union of Jesus person as both human and divine. He writes: "Jesus veiled His deity so that His humanity could find its full expression."[18] As disciples of Jesus, we also progress intellectually and spiritually in the same manner today. Discipleship, even for Jesus, was a matter of intentional commitment, growing out of his love for his Father and for the Word of God.

A Product of His Environment

In his book *Jesus the Jewish Theologian*, author Brad Young writes that "Jesus was unlike any person, and yet he is like every human being."[19] What Young means is that even though he was sinless at every stage and age of his life, Jesus still grew and matured like any human person. As Luke reminds us, he grew "in wisdom and stature" (Luke 2:52). His parents taught him the Torah at an early age because they were devout Jews who were careful to follow the laws and customs prescribed them.

Mary knew the scriptures, as evidenced by her proclamation of Old Testament passages during her meeting with her cousin Elizabeth. Commonly called the Magnificat, Mary's words echo Hannah's prayer of thanksgiving in 1 Samuel 2 in gratitude for conceiving her child. Both proclamations begin with almost identical words. Hannah cries out, "My heart exalts the Lord," while Mary says, "My soul magnifies the Lord." Mary also references or alludes to eighteen Old Testament passages in her song (1 Sam. 2:1; Hab. 3:18; 1 Sam. 1:11; Gen. 29:32; 30:13; Ps. 126:3; 103:17; 136:12; 89:11; 1 Sam. 2:7; Ps. 113:7; 107:9; 1 Sam. 2:5; Is. 41:8, 14; Ps. 98:3; Ex. 32:13; and Mic. 7:20). Clearly, Mary knew and understood the Hebrew scriptures. In a moment of gratitude and thanksgiving to God, the Word of God overflowed from her heart and onto her lips in praise.

As mentioned earlier, the home Jesus was raised in followed a pattern of daily study of scripture, rhythms of prayer, participation in the festivals, and weekly Sabbath observances.[20] From the Mishnah, we glean the typical roadmap for a boy in that world:

> Scripture study begins at age 5;
> Mishnah study at 10;
> Torah obligations come at 13;
> Continued rabbinical study starts at 15;
> Marriage at 18;
> Formal strength [able to teach others] 30.[21]

Like every other Jewish boy, Jesus would have begun his study of the Torah at the age of five. Remember, the Bible does not suggest that he was any different in his upbringing. So while we cannot know for certain, it is safe to speculate that Jesus began working with his father full time at the age of thirteen or fifteen. Study and work were not mutually exclusive and were, in fact, encouraged. Rabbi Gamliel described the importance of studying Torah *and* working a trade: "The study of the Torah combined together with an occupation is good, because the demands of the two of them keep sin out of one's mind, but the study of Torah that is not combined with an occupation will end in naught."[22]

A Jewish boy would have been considered an adult at the age of thirteen, which today is celebrated with a rite of passage called a bar mitzvah. The Hebrew word *bar* means *son of. Mitzvah* is the Hebrew word for commandment. Although this celebration did not formalize until centuries after the time of Jesus, the concept of a rite of passage was already in place during the first century. A young boy would receive the commandments at the age of thirteen in the synagogue, becoming a legal adult with all the responsibilities and duties that apply. Jesus's journey in Luke 2 may have been the last time he visited the temple before being recognized as a man, and this would also explain his question to his parents after they found him in the temple. "Why were you looking for me? Did you not know that I must be in my Father's house [the temple]?" (v. 49). In other words, Jesus's question would have been a statement describing his future earthly ministry to them, the profession he had chosen as an adult man.

The Time Has Come

While a Jewish boy would typically transition to adulthood at the age of twelve or thirteen, he would not immediately begin his ministry. We know that Jesus began his earthly ministry around the age of thirty, which was the time when most rabbis allowed their disciples to begin following them.[23] It is also around this time that Jesus is called "the Christ," a title that means "Anointed One." According to Jewish tradition, to be called the "Anointed One," a person must have been anointed by a prophet and possess the credibility of those in the community. Roland de Vaux writes, "Anointing is a religious rite, . . . accompanied by a coming of the Spirit."[24]

We see the precedent for this anointing in 1 Samuel 16:13, where anointing oil is used to convey God's power and presence through the outpouring of his Spirit: "Then Samuel took the horn of oil and anointed him in the midst of his brothers. And the Spirit of the Lord rushed upon David from that day forward." But there is something interesting about the anointing of Jesus. The Bible records no moment where Jesus is anointed with oil, so what prophet would have given Jesus the title of Messiah or the Annointed One? The answer is our old friend John the Baptist. John, as the greatest and final prophet of God, had announced Jesus's coming and then proceeded to anoint Jesus for ministry, much as Samuel did for David. When did this happen? At Jesus's baptism. Matthew documents what happened:

> And when Jesus was baptized, immediately he went up from the water, and behold, the heavens were opened to him, and he saw the Spirit of God descending like a dove and coming to rest on him; and behold, a voice from heaven said, "This is my beloved Son, with whom I am well pleased" (3:16–17).

How do we know that this event was a "valid" anointing? We see it by noting the clear parallels between Jesus's and David's receipt of the Holy Spirit. Again, we find a *kesher*, or connection through a key phrase mentioned in Matthew's account of the event. The phrase "the heavens were opened" is a connection to Ezekiel 1:1, which reads: "In the thirtieth year, in the fourth month, on the fifth day of the month, as I was among the exiles by the Chebar canal, the *heavens were opened*, and I saw visions of

God" (emphasis mine). Jewish sources would use this phrase to announce an apocalyptic vision from God. As Lancaster writes, pointing out the connection between this and the baptism of Jesus, "In a prophetic trance, Ezekiel saw the chariot of God descend. In a similar vision, Yeshua saw the Spirit of God descend like a dove."[25]

Shortly after emerging from the water, the Holy Spirit leads Jesus into the desert for forty days and forty nights of fasting. Why forty days and nights? The experience of Jesus in the desert wilderness, relying on God's provision to sustain him, was an echo of Israel's own forty years of wandering in the wilderness. Yet there are differences between the two. While Israel constantly proved herself unfaithful, unable to stand against temptation and repeatedly falling away in disobedience to God, Jesus endured the tests and trials of the enemy without sin. Jesus was able to accomplish what Moses and the people of Israel could not. Johan Kemper, in his commentary, notes, "Just as by the first redemption before they came to the land, they had to be vagrant and wandering in the wilderness for forty years, so it was needed that Yeshua, to accomplish the last redemption should endure fasting for forty days, one day for each year."[26]

This connection between the forty days of Jesus and Israel's forty years might seem like a stretch if it weren't for the explicit connection Jesus draws between the two. When the enemy tempted Jesus to turn stones into bread to feed his hunger, Jesus responds in Luke 4:4 by quoting from the book of Deuteronomy, saying, "It is written: Man must not live on bread alone but on every word that comes from the mouth of God." This is part of a larger quotation from Deuteronomy 8:

> "And you shall remember the whole way that the LORD your God has led you these forty years in the wilderness, that he might humble you, testing you to know what was in your heart, whether you would keep his commandments or not. And he humbled you and let you hunger and fed you with manna, which you did not know, nor did your fathers know, that he might make you know that man does not live by bread alone, but man lives by every word that comes from the mouth of the LORD" (vv. 2–3).

It is interesting to note that sages and teachers of Israel believed that the people would be able to identify the Messiah through his miraculous provision of bread. They looked at the example of Joseph, a messianic figure, and how he provided bread for Israel during a time of famine. Moses, the redeemer of Israel, also helped to sustain the people by calling upon God to provide bread in the wilderness. A Jewish commentary on the book of Ecclesiastes supports this connection as well:

> As the first redeemer was, so shall the latter Redeemer be. . . . Just as the first redeemer caused the manna to come down, as it is written [in Exod. 16:4], "Behold, I will rain bread from heaven for you," so too will the latter redeemer cause manna to come down, as it is stated [in Psalm 72:16], "May there be abundance of grain in the earth on top of the mountains."[27]

Not only did Jesus multiply bread for the people of Israel on two separate occasions in two regions;[28] he was born in a "bread factory." What do I mean? The name of the city where Jesus was born, Bethlehem, is made up of two Hebrew words: *bet* and *lechem*. *Bet* is the Hebrew word for house, and *lechem* is the word for bread. Jesus was born in the "house of bread"—what we would call today a "bread factory."

Who was Jesus as a young boy? While his birth was unusual, his early years were like those of most Jewish boys. Jesus was likely a product of his environment, careful to follow all of the customs of the culture. Jesus grew physically and spiritually, and his growth was a product of his environment.

Yet, as he grew, everything about who Jesus was cried out the fact that he was, truly, the Son of God.

"I AM WHO I AM"

Liberal religious scholars like to debate and question the divinity of Jesus. They will suggest that Jesus never claimed that he was one with God, or point out that he said, "I am God." The problem with these claims is that they are narrowly true if you read them through a Western perspective. But when we unpack how Jesus lived and spoke in his own cultural context, his words and actions tell a different story. Consider this example: If Jesus were a citizen of the United States living in our world today, perhaps he would have come out and said plainly, "I am God, and here are ten reasons why." Contrary to the claim of liberal skeptics, Jesus said virtually the exact same thing—repeatedly claiming oneness with God—but he did it in a manner that would have been understood and recognized by the people and the culture of his day. Jesus made his claims as a Jewish rabbi, not as a Western religious scholar.

Sometimes we seek to define a person by words they say, phrases that sum up their life mission and purpose. Julius Caesar is remembered best for his report of his military leadership at Gaul: *"Veni, vidi, vici"* (I came, I saw, I conquered). John F. Kennedy challenged every American to contribute in some way to the public good when he famously said, "Ask not what your country can do for you—ask what you can do for your country." Sentences like these capture the essence of a person and are gripping statements that convey some of their mission and drive. At the risk of reducing the life of Jesus to a few summary statements, I want to draw your attention to the seven "I am" statements recorded by John in his Gospel. John tells us that he has written his Gospel to introduce us to Jesus, that we might believe he is the Son of God.

These seven statements are not summary statements about what Jesus did; they are proclamations of who he was.

1. "And Jesus said to them, 'I am the bread of life. He who comes to me shall never hunger, and he who believes in me shall never thirst'" (John 6:35).
2. "Then Jesus spoke to them again, saying, 'I am the light of the world. He who follows me shall not walk in darkness, but have the light of life'" (John 8:12).
3. "I am the door. If anyone enters by me, he will be saved, and will go in and out and find pasture" (John 10:9).
4. "I am the good shepherd. The good shepherd gives his life for the sheep" (John 10:11).
5. "Jesus said to her, 'I am the resurrection and the life. He who believes in me, though he may die, he shall live'" (John 11:25).
6. "Jesus said to him, 'I am the way, the truth, and the life. No one comes to the Father except through me'" (John 14:6).
7. "I am the true vine, and my Father is the vinedresser" (John 15:1).

Why are these statements significant? God shares his name "I Am" when he first interacts with Moses through a burning bush in Exodus 3:14–15. "God said to Moses, 'I AM WHO I AM.' And he said, 'Say this to the people of Israel, "I AM has sent me to you."'" God also said to Moses, 'Say this to the people of Israel, "The Lord, the God of your fathers, the God of Abraham, the God of Isaac, and the God of Jacob, has sent me to you." This is my name forever, and thus I am to be remembered throughout all generations."

What you may not know is that the Hebrew alphabet has no vowels, and it was not until much later in the development of the Hebrew language that a system for inserting vowels became standardized. This means that whenever a word was originally written in Hebrew, the only characters that were recorded were the consonants.

This did not present much of a problem when converting old manuscripts into the new form of vowel writing, except when it came to the name for God. When the name for God is written, only four letters are represented: YHWH. Scholars have debated over the years about where to best place the vowels, but there were no oral records to consult since, out of reverence, Jews refrained from speaking God's name or even pronouncing the four consonants of his name: *Yod, Ha, Vav, Ha* (often referred to as the Tetragrammaton). Some Jews, out of reverence, refer to God with the Hebrew word *Ha Shem*, what we translate into English as *the name*.

Without the specific vowel placements, scholar Dwight Pryor has argued that the four consonants in God's name were used to form three distinct verbs in Hebrew:

- *Hayah*—I am
- *Hoveh*—I was
- *YeYah*—I will be[29]

What is the significance of this? It means that by revealing his name as Yahweh, God is identifying himself as the God who was, who is, and who will be. Jesus describes himself using this language in Revelation 1 (ESV) as "the Alpha and the Omega," the Lord God "who is and who was and who is to come, the Almighty." Jesus claims to be the God of Moses, the one speaking from the burning bush, the one revealed as Yahweh.

Because our English Bibles generally translate Yahweh in all capital letters as "The LORD," we miss some of the connections that Jesus makes to himself. By making these seven "I Am" statements recorded in John, Jesus was connecting God's divine name to his own activity. In the content of his messages (Who but God could be "the bread of life"?) and the form in which he spoke them (Who but God could claim "I Am"?) Jesus was revealing his divine identity.

Was Jesus a Carpenter or a Stonemason?

We learned earlier that at the age of thirteen a Jewish boy would typically choose a trade to enter, and Jesus was no different—he was almost certainly trained by his father Joseph in his profession. For centuries, Western Christians have associated Joseph, Jesus's earthly father, with carpentry. For many of us, we read children's Bibles that show him teaching young Jesus how to saw, hammer nails, and create wooden joints. But was this the type of work that Jesus was engaged in? Is this what he learned from his earthly father, Joseph? We have perhaps been misled over the years by faulty cultural assumptions, overshadowing much of what Jesus said, did, and fulfilled in his life and ministry.

The central misunderstanding comes from a translation issue that occurred centuries ago. It focuses on a verse in Matthew 13. After Jesus teaches in his hometown synagogue, the crowd asks, "Is not this the carpenter's son? Is not his mother called Mary?" (v. 55). The Greek word *tekton,* translated here as carpenter, is more accurately rendered as craftsman or builder. At face value, without taking the Jewish cultural background into consideration, a carpenter *could* fit that description. However, a quick survey of northern Israel's landscape reveals that the job of carpenter may not be the best fit for that Greek word.

The majority of homes in Israel, as noted by Hebraic scholar James Fleming, are constructed with stone. Fleming explains: "Jesus and Joseph would have formed and made nine out of ten projects from stone either by chiseling or carving the stone or stacking building blocks."[30] Does this mean that Jesus never worked with wood? While we can't say conclusively one way or the other, the fact is that a man attempting to make a living as a wood carpenter would have had a challenging time because trees were, and still are, relatively scarce in that region.

Another reason why it is most likely that Jesus and Joseph worked with stone and not wood is because Nazareth was only three miles from the ancient town of Zippori, or Sepphoris as it was called at the time. During the first century, Zippori was developing at a rapid rate under the reign of Herod Antipas and would eventually be called "The jewel of all Galilee" by Jewish historian Josephus. Herod's massive beautification project in Zippori would have required the help of every available and skilled *tekton* in the surrounding area, likely including Joseph. Joseph would have been in the perfect location to commute to work, for halfway between Nazareth and Zippori was an enormous rock quarry. Regardless of whether Jesus himself worked there or not (I believe he did), he definitely visited the ancient quarry and would have seen the stones being cut by his stonemason father.

If it is true that Jesus was the son of a stonemason, he would have been trained in stonemasonry, following his father's profession. With this background knowledge, it is helpful to take a fresh look at his language and that of his followers when they speak of stones in the Bible. For example, after the chief priests, scribes, and elders questioned Jesus's authority in the temple, Jesus shared the parable of the wicked tenants. Upon completion, he "looked directly at them and said, 'What then is this that is written: "The *stone* that the builders rejected has become the cornerstone?"'" (Luke 20:17–18; Ps. 118:22, emphasis mine).

Again, when defending himself before the religious leaders, Peter cites the same Old Testament passage, "This Jesus is the *stone* that was rejected by you, the builders, which has become the cornerstone. And there is salvation in no one else, for there is no other name under heaven given among men by which we must be saved" (Acts 4:11–12, emphasis mine). Peter quotes directly from Psalm 118:22, a passage where, as John Wesley explains: "The commonwealth of Israel and the church of God are here and elsewhere compared to a building, wherein, as the people are the *stone*, so the princes and rulers are the builders. And as the master builders rejected David, so their successors rejected Christ" (emphasis mine).[31] The stone mentioned here is a reference to the messianic lineage of David, and the concept of a cornerstone would have been quite familiar to those building with stone.

Or again, when selecting a concept for describing believers in the family of God, Peter writes, "[Y]ou yourselves like living *stones* are being built up as a spiritual house, to be a holy priesthood, to offer spiritual sacrifices acceptable to God through Jesus Christ" (1 Peter 2:5, emphasis mine). Notice that Peter refers to building a house with stones, an image that would have been quite familiar to those listening, and something Jesus himself may have been skilled in doing as a trained stonemason.

Whether Jesus was a carpenter working with wood or a stonemason has no bearing on his work as Savior of the world, but it does help us when we read the Bible, bringing a fresh sense of his words and their meaning. This knowledge enhances our picture of him, bringing him into sharper focus. Can you sense the loving grip of a master craftsman clutching you in his hand as he molds and shapes you into the image of Christ for his glory? Of all the professions in the world, Joseph, Jesus's earthly father, was a craftsman, a stonemason. He could have been a vineyard worker, a fisherman, or a sandal maker, but he wasn't.

Remember, Jesus learned this trade from his father, and he is still shaping his followers today, fitting them together into a spiritual house, a temple that is built to bring glory to God.

A Shoot of Jesse

Matthew's Gospel is commonly described as the most Jewish of the four Gospels. Some scholars believe it was first written in Hebrew before being translated into Greek. If this is true, then as a result of the conversion, many Hebrew idioms and colloquialism were likely lost in the shift. Matthew also includes more Old Testament references than any other Gospel, and he uses a phrase in reference to Jesus's fulfillment of Old Testament prophecy ten times: "So that what was spoken might be fulfilled. . . ." At the beginning of his Gospel, he traces a genealogy from David to Jesus that contains some valuable insights we can better understand with a little cultural background.

Hundreds of years before the birth of Jesus, the Old Testament prophet Isaiah prophesied that David's throne would fall, but that God would grow a new branch from the old stump of David's dynasty. First-century Jews read Isaiah 11 as a prediction of the coming Messiah: "There shall come forth a shoot from the stump of Jesse, and a branch from his roots shall bear fruit. And the Spirit of the Lord shall rest upon him, the Spirit of wisdom and understanding, the Spirit of counsel and might, the Spirit of knowledge and the fear of the Lord" (vv. 1–2). Notice that phrase, "there shall come forth a *shoot*. . . ."

The Hebrew word for *shoot* is *netzer*, and it is from this word that we get the English word Nazareth. Rabbi Lichtenstein makes the argument connecting the two: "All the prophets said that Messiah's name is *tzemach*, 'Branch' (Zechariah 3:8, 6:12; Jeremiah 23:5; and Isaiah 4:2). Isaiah also called him *netzer* in 11:1, since *netzer* and *tzemach* are synonyms. This hints at the name Yeshua the Nazarene (*notzri*) and that he would be called a notzri."[32] As we noted earlier, Hebrew originally lacked the vowel markings, so a wider range of pronunciations was possible. Since the words *netzer* and *notzri* are quite similar, they may have been associated together as the fulfillment of the Isaiah prophecy, something we see among the early Christians and church fathers, including Jerome and Eusebius.

A glance at Matthew's genealogy of David and at the history books written about the royal lineage reveals that a Davidic king had not occupied the throne for more than five hundred years when Jesus arrived on the scene. Because of the prophecies containing language about the shoot of Jesse and Nazareth, fanatical residents of Nazareth believed the Messiah would come from their town.

Bible teacher Ray Vander Laan speculates that at the time of Jesus the people of Nazareth may have affectionately referred to their town in a way we would translate as "shootville" or "branchtown."[33] Outsiders may have viewed the residents suspiciously because of their religious zeal for the Messiah's arrival. Notice that when Philip approaches Nathanael about finding the Messiah, Jesus of Nazareth, his response was one of doubt and disdain for Nazareth. He asks: "Can anything good come out of Nazareth?" With an estimated population of three hundred, Nazareth was fairly insignificant, so much so that early maps didn't have the city marked. The entire town was less than three acres, yet it was a hotbed for insurrectionist activity.

Jesus was referred to as a Nazarene throughout his ministry, but we should remember that he was not born there. His birthplace was also crucial to identifying him as the Messiah. As we saw when we looked at the visit of the magi, Micah the prophet predicted that the Messiah would be a descendant of the house of David and would be born in Bethlehem: "But you, O Bethlehem Ephrathah, who are too little to be among the clans of Judah, from you shall come forth for me one who is to be ruler in Israel, whose coming forth is from of old, from ancient days" (Mic. 5:2). Luke 2:4–5 confirms the fulfillment of this prophecy: "Joseph also went up from Galilee, from the town of Nazareth, to Judea, to the city of David, which is called Bethlehem, because he was of the house and lineage of David, to be registered with Mary, his betrothed, who was with child."

Amazingly, in his place of birth and in his childhood home, Jesus fulfills *both* of these prophecies. Jesus was most certainly a Nazarene, and he was also born in Bethlehem, a rare combination that he perfectly fulfills—just as it was written.

No Respect in Nazareth

Because the Jewish inhabitants of Nazareth had strong messianic expectations, they were literally ready for the Messiah to come at any time. Prayers went up daily to God beseeching him to save them from the oppression of the Romans. Every Jewish boy and girl knew Isaiah 61 by memory, a prediction of the Messiah's coming. Isaiah writes, "The Spirit of the Lord God is upon me, because the Lord has anointed me to bring good news to the poor; he has sent me to bind up the brokenhearted, to proclaim liberty to the captives, and the opening of the prison to those who are bound; to proclaim the year of the Lord's favor, and the day of vengeance of our God; to comfort all who mourn" (Isa. 61:1–2).

As Jesus began his ministry near his hometown of Nazareth, word about him spread quickly throughout the Galilean region. Here was a new Messiah-like figure, and people quickly realized that he had been reared in Nazareth. After traveling informally with six disciples (James, John, Andrew, Peter, Philip, and Nathaniel), Jesus invited the men to join him on a homecoming trip he was making to the synagogue of Nazareth. Many of the residents of the town would have likely been related in some way to Jesus. Jewish families lived in *insulas*, not suburban neighborhoods like many Americans do. When a son married, he would add on to his father's house, who had previously added on to his father's house. So it was not uncommon for one family to occupy a small village. It is very likely that when Jesus came to visit his hometown, many of Jesus's uncles, aunts, cousins, nephews, nieces, brothers, and sisters would have been there living in Nazareth as well.

Can you picture the scene? The disciples swagger into the synagogue because their rabbi is speaking. The excitement is palpable. Everyone has turned out for the big day. Anticipation fills the crowded room. "Could this be the Messiah?" "He is from Nazareth!" "This is Joseph's son." After bypassing the chief seats against the wall and locating their spots on the floor, the synagogue attendant begins the service.

"[A]s was his custom, [Jesus] went to the synagogue on the Sabbath day, and he stood up to read," Luke 4:16 tells us. Notice that it was his custom to visit the synagogue, so this occasion would not be the first time Jesus read or even spoke. Any respected teacher or traveling rabbi could deliver the Sabbath teaching, and Luke implies that he had been doing this frequently.

Jesus probably sat to speak on the same stool many times as he was growing up. So what is different about this day, this visit? What intensifies this encounter are the claims being made about Jesus outside of his hometown of Nazareth. Jesus has been identified by John the Baptist as the long-awaited Messiah. In addition, he has performed two miracles: turning the water into wine and healing the son of a local official. He has also stirred up some controversy by cleansing the temple in Jerusalem, driving the corrupt money changers away. He has spoken to two individuals: Nicodemus, a respected religious leader, and the Samaritan woman at the well. The people have heard rumors, and they want an explanation for all the clamor circling about Jesus.

Unlike modern, Western-style worship services where the Bible is read for five minutes and preached for forty minutes, in first-century Jewish culture the teacher or rabbi would read, standing along with the attendees, for forty minutes before sitting down to preach a five-or ten-minute message. The liturgy looked something like the following:

> As in the Temple, the congregation prayed the blessings before the *Shema* [Deut. 6:4–9], recited the *Shema* passages, the blessings after the *Shema*, and then prayed some early form of the standing prayer

(*Amidah*) to correspond with the Temple liturgy. . . . The Sabbath service included three elements: 1. A reading from the Torah (*parashah*); 2. A complementary reading from the Prophets (*haftarah*); 3. A teaching that expounded upon the two readings (*derashah*). The synagogues read from the Torah each Sabbath in a consecutive progression through the scroll. The weekly portion is called the *parashah*.

The *haftarah* reading from the Prophets ordinarily mirrored the language or the content of the week's reading from the Torah *parashah*. The teacher giving the *derashah* explained and expounded—though often only tangentially—on the day's Scripture readings.[34]

Following the pattern of the service, Jesus began with a reading from the Torah (the *parashah*). We read in Luke 4:16 that, as usual, he entered the synagogue on the Sabbath day and stood up to read the Torah. Then, he followed his reading of the Torah with a reading from the Prophets (the *haftarah*). Luke 4:17–19 (CSB) says:

> The scroll of the prophet Isaiah was given to him, and unrolling the scroll, he found the place where it was written: The Spirit of the Lord is on me, because he has anointed me to preach good news to the poor. He has sent me to proclaim freedom to the captives and recovery of sight to the blind, to set free the oppressed, to proclaim the year of the Lord's favor.

In his reading, Jesus employs a rabbinical technique called "stringing pearls," whereby he connects multiple passages to prove a point.[35] "Pearls" is an image that was synonymous with scripture, as used by Jesus in Matthew 7:6 when he warns against casting pearls before swine. In this case, Jesus reads from Isaiah 61:1–2 and strings a pearl by inserting a line from Isaiah 58:6, "to set the oppressed free." Amazingly, he links together the only two passages in the Old Testament that refer to the favor of the Lord (Isa. 58:5 and 61:2).[36] By making this connection, Jesus provides "two witnesses to his main message and thereby emphasizes to his listeners that the proclamation of the 'favor of the Lord' will be at the heart of his ministry as the Messiah."[37] Notably, Jesus stops short of reading the end of Isaiah 61:2: "and the day of vengeance of our God."

Finally, Jesus delivers a succinct teaching (the *derashah*). We read this in Luke 4:20–21 (CSB): "He then rolled up the scroll, gave it back to the attendant, and sat down. And the eyes of everyone in the synagogue were fixed on him." With every eye upon him, Jesus delivered the shortest sermon ever delivered by a rabbi: "Today as you listen, this Scripture has been fulfilled." It's quite clear what he is saying. Jesus is claiming to be the Messiah. Notice how the people respond in verse 22: "And all spoke well of him and marveled at the gracious words that were coming from his mouth. And they said, 'Is not this Joseph's son?'" (ESV).

The people were not questioning Jesus's claims; they were affirming his identity as Joseph's son. Everyone in the town knew that Joseph was of the lineage of David, a shoot of Jesse, and that Jesus was his son. Jesus, however, knew that these people were looking to him for their own personal gain. They had built up in their minds a picture of what the Messiah would be like according to their own expectations, and they would not be able to accept what he had come to do.

Knowing that the people wanted proof of his Messiahship through a sign, Jesus squelched their expectancy. He said to them, "No prophet is accepted in his hometown" (v. 24), before referencing two Old Testament passages where God bypassed the Jewish people to extend healing and assistance to Gentiles. His message to them was clear. In the same manner that Elijah bypassed Israel to provide for a Gentile woman and Elisha healed a Gentile leper instead of an Israelite leper, Jesus was about to relocate his messianic ministry outside of Nazareth. As you can imagine, the mood of the crowd quickly turned sour. They were outraged by his statements and attempted to throw him off a cliff.

When we approach Jesus today, we too run the risk of responding like his hometown crowd in Nazareth. When we approach Jesus, aren't we also full of our own preconceived ideas of who he is, what he does, and why he came? The response of the people of Nazareth is a warning to us that we must be careful to understand Jesus as he presents himself to us, ready to drink in every word he said with as much understanding as our minds can manage, and obey him with the strength he provides. In the chapters that follow, we will continue studying about our Messiah Jesus, but we must remember to receive everything we learn about him not as a useless nugget of information, but as coal to throw into the ever-growing fire of our faith.

CHAPTER 5

Connecting the New to the Old

Jesus was fully God, yet at the same time, he was fully man—both divine and human, united in one person. As the eternal son of God, he is one with the Father, yet he is a distinct person of the trinity (see John 10:30). The son of God was born to a woman, Mary, and this child was the historic human being, Jesus of Nazareth. Jesus, being a Hebrew, did not come out and directly prove his divinity with a ten-point Buzzfeed list, as much as we might want him to. Instead, he did it in a way that was understandable to the Jews he lived among, and in a way that fit the tradition of teaching in his culture.

When rabbis of Jesus's time would teach, instead of reciting entire chapters (chapters and verses didn't appear until the sixteenth century), they would recall a line from a verse, and the audience, knowledgeable in the scriptures, would inherently know the context. Most of them had likely committed large sections of the Hebrew Bible to memory. Sadly, we live in a world today where literate believers remain illiterate when it comes to the Bible, particularly the Old Testament. While we may all agree that we need to grow in our understanding of scripture, I am particularly interested in helping Christian believers develop a more comprehensive knowledge of the Old Testament. By knowing the Old Testament, the Bible Jesus read and studied, we are better able to identify the connections that Jesus made, identifying himself as one with God.

In earlier chapters I referred to something called a *kesher*. This is a Hebrew word that simply means a connection. I first heard the term *kesher* from Dwight Pryor at a Judaic Christian Studies Haverim Retreat (see jcstudies.com), and Dwight uses this word to talk about references in the New Testament that point readers back to particular verses and chapters from the Old Testament. Think of it as something like an ancient computer mouse hovering over a hyperlink to another webpage. Another way to describe it is as an allusion or a phrase that creates resonance with another word or passage in the Bible. These are textual connections that connect passages together, often by a simple word or phrase. In this chapter, I hope to introduce you to this concept and provide a basic framework for understanding some familiar New Testament passages in a different light—connections that further prove Jesus's divinity.

Keshers are not unique to Jewish culture. In fact, every culture has something similar. If I said to you, "'Twas the night before Christmas," you might follow my words by saying, "and all through the house, not a creature was stirring, not even a mouse." The first line of the poem brings to mind the rest of the poem and all of the associations you have with it. You might see red and green stockings in your mind's eye. You might even taste cookies and milk. It's an allusion that you readily recognize. I could do something similar with this phrase: "Our Father, who art in heaven." You would probably respond, "Hallowed be thy name." Or I can mention a line from a song: "Amazing grace, how sweet the sound." Without missing a beat, you would sing back, "That saved a wretch like me."

We frequently use a part of a larger work as a shorthand reference to call it to mind. When we do this with a written work, we call it an allusion. We may be reading in one literary work and discover a phrase that refers to another work—a song, a statement, or a famous line—and immediately we sense that the author is drawing a connection between the two.

Connecting what you were teaching or saying to something in the scriptures was a common way of communicating in the first century, and it was a method used by the early Christians as well. When we look closely, with an awareness of the Old Testament scriptures, we find that the New Testament is filled with allusions to the Old Testament, and many of them come to us from the lips of Jesus himself.

Allusions on the Mount

One of my favorite textual allusions in the Bible is found in the dialogue between the Father and the Son on the Mount of Transfiguration (Matt. 17). Many significant events happen on mountains in the Bible. We find him on a mountain sending his apostles out to preach in Mark 3, tempted on a mountain in Matthew 4, and praying on a mountain in Mark 6. Jesus taught the Sermon on the Mount in Matthew 5 through 7. He issued the Great Commission on a mountain in Matthew 28. Jesus also used mountaintop excursions as teachable moments for his core group of disciples (Peter, James, and John).

In Matthew 17, we find Jesus on a mountaintop yet again. We read that while he is praying on the mountaintop, his face shone white as he is transfigured before the disciples. While this event indicates the presence of God, the connection takes us even further. The allusion here points us back to the Old Testament, to Moses' encounter with God on the mountain in Exodus 34:29. As Jesus's face is shining, the disciples who were with him noticed two unexpected guests. The presence of these guests—Moses and Elijah—really drives the connection home. Let's see why.

Moses and Elijah

Students of the Hebrew Bible would have been aware of many similarities between Moses and Elijah. Both men met God personally on a mountain (Exod. 33:18–23; 1 Kings 19:9–18). Both witnessed God displaying his glory. Both men had memorable departures from this world. Moses was buried by God himself on Mount Nebo; Elijah was whisked away in a chariot of fire. Moses founded Israel's economy; Elijah restored it. Both men also had a symbolic presence in traditional Jewish culture: Moses represented the Law, while Elijah represented the Prophets.

Jesus, in his ministry and teaching, had already drawn several connections between himself and Moses. We've seen similarities between the two in the back-to-back miracles in John 6 of "Jesus miraculously feeding a crowd (John 6:5–14) and walking on the sea (6:16–21), incidents that narratively mirror Israel's crossing of the sea (Exod. 14:1–31) and reception of manna in the wilderness (Exod. 16:1–36)."[1]

Now, as Jesus stands with Moses and Elijah, Jesus is literally glorified in the midst of the Law and the Prophets. "While he was still speaking," the passage reads, "suddenly a bright cloud covered them, and a voice from the cloud said: 'This is my beloved Son, with whom I am well-pleased. Listen to Him!' When the disciples heard it, they fell face-down and were terrified" (Matt. 17:5–6 CSB). The cloud mentioned in the text is yet another allusion, a direct reference to Moses' experience on Mount Sinai in Exodus 24:15–16. In that encounter, Moses went up to the mountain, enveloped in clouds, to witness the manifest presence of God.

While all of these connections between Moses, Elijah, and Jesus are interesting, the high point of the transfiguration of Jesus is about more than a glowing face and a cloud. It is the moment when God speaks audibly: "This is my Son!" These words should sound familiar to students of scripture. They are the same words spoken to Jesus at his baptism: "You are my beloved Son; with you I am well-pleased" (Mark 1:11 CSB). One difference is that the words spoken at baptism were directed toward the Son as a confirmation of his divinity (*You* are my Son), but the words on the mountaintop are directed toward the disciples (*This* is my Son).

To fully grasp the significance of the words spoken on the mountain, we should note several other allusions to the Old Testament text connecting to messianic passages that align with the words God speaks on the mountain: "This is my beloved Son. I take delight in Him. Listen to Him!"[2]

"This is my beloved Son" is a quotation from the *Ketuvi'im* (the Writings) in Psalm 2:7 (CSB). "I will declare the LORD's decree," writes the psalmist. "He said to me, '*You are my Son*; today I have become Your Father.'" Psalm 2 is often labeled a "messianic Psalm," which speaks of the coming Messiah.

"With you I am well-pleased" is from the *Nevi'im* (the Prophets). It is from Isaiah 42:1 (CSB): "This is my servant; I delight in him, this is my chosen one; *I delight in him.*" This entire chapter in Isaiah, like Psalm 2, points to the Messiah—it speaks of his mission.

"Listen to Him" comes from the Torah (the Law) and is a *kesher* from Deuteronomy 18:15 (CSB): "The LORD your God will raise up for you a prophet like me from among your own brothers. You must *listen to him.*"

Until this moment in the life of Jesus, the disciples had fundamentally misunderstood Jesus's true identity. The only ones who had accurately confirmed who Jesus was by this point were the demons (Mark 5:7). So these words, spoken by God on the mountaintop, were powerful affirmations of Jesus's divine and messianic identities. Dwight Pryor sums up the full weight of these links to the Old Testament:

> God Himself answers Jesus' question by linking together three Messianic Scriptures from each of the three sections of the Hebrew Bible: the Torah (Law), the Nevi'im (Prophets), and the Ketuvi'im (Writings). God is saying, by using these three short sentences, "Jesus is my Son, the promised Messiah of Israel foretold by the prophets of Old, and He is the fulfillment of every section of Scripture. He is the embodiment of My Word; He is Word-made-flesh. Listen to Him! Obey Him!"[3]

The disciples should have understood who Jesus was when he affirmed that he had not come "to abolish the Law or the Prophets. I did not come to abolish but to fulfill" (Matt. 5:17 CSB). But they didn't. They needed his identity to be spelled out for them by God in a way that was clear and unequivocal. On the mountain, God connected the dots for Peter, James, and John—connecting Jesus to Moses and Elijah and to the promises of the Old Testament. The Mount of Transfiguration was a clear testament to who Jesus was.

Voice in the Wilderness

Another example of a "string of pearls," as the rabbis called it, is found at the outset of Mark's Gospel. When Mark begins his account of Jesus's earthly ministry, he links together three Old Testament passages that identify Jesus as the coming Messiah and John the Baptist as the forerunner. Read the opening to Mark's Gospel and pay attention to how Mark's specific word choices demonstrate who these two people—John and Jesus—are. Mark writes: "The beginning of the gospel of Jesus Christ, the Son of God. As it is written in Isaiah the prophet: See, I am sending **My messenger** ahead of you, who will prepare **your way**. A voice of one crying out in the wilderness: **Prepare the way for the Lord;** make his paths **straight**!" (Mark 1:1–3 CSB).

Now notice how this quote from Isaiah connects to various Old Testament passages. I've highlighted the connections by bolding the words to show how they align with the passages below.

> Exodus 23:20 (CSB): "I am going to **send an angel** [the Hebrew word angel is the same word for messenger used in Mal. 3:1] before you to protect you on **the way** and bring you to the place I have prepared."

> Malachi 3:1 (CSB): "See, I am going to send My messenger, and he will **clear the way before Me**."

> Isaiah 40:3 (CSB): "A voice of one crying out: **Prepare the way of the Lord** in the wilderness; make a straight highway for our God in the desert."

We have already looked at how Jesus communed with God, how he was transfigured in front of his disciples' eyes, and how he was joined by Moses and Elijah in an event filled with deep significance. Here we see that Jesus's arrival upon the scene of Jewish history was no different. In three sentences, Mark lays out exactly *who Jesus is* before he even makes an entrance into the book. He is the Messiah spoken about in every part of the Hebrew Bible. Lancaster says, commenting on Mark's technique, "By fusing the three passages, Mark identifies a messianic forerunner sent by the LORD whose testimony is validated by the Torah and the Prophets and whose job is to get everything ready for Messiah by preaching the gospel: John the Immerser."[4]

Notice the clarity with which Mark introduces both John and Jesus.

He painstakingly presents a clear message that Jesus is the one the Israelites were looking for. He does not obscure his words or present multiple options or varied interpretations. Mark is clear: John was there to make the path that the Messiah would walk clear, and Jesus perfectly walked it. Let's take a look at another example to see how Jesus spoke, using these textual allusions, with equal clarity about himself.

Which Way to God?

On his final night with his disciples, Jesus encouraged them with these words, "Don't let your heart be troubled. Believe in God; believe also in me. In my Father's house are many rooms; if not, I would have told you. I am going away to prepare a place for you. If I go away and prepare a place for you, I will come again and take you to myself, so that where I am you may be also. You know the way to where I am going" (John 14:1–4 CSB).

These words left the disciples awestruck as they silently contemplated what they meant. Thomas, an honest seeker, needed more clarification. He asked, "Lord, we do not know where you are going. How can we know the way?" Jesus said to him, "I am the way, and the truth, and the life. No one comes to the Father except through me. If you had known me, you would have known my Father also. From now on you do know him and have seen him" (John 14:5–7).

Notice that Jesus doesn't point his followers to the path to God by saying, like every other religious figure in history, "This is the way." He says, "*I am* the way." Some may criticize Christians for having a narrow-minded view of God and for being exclusive in our understanding of how we connect with God. It is *en vogue* to say, "God is infinite, so the paths to get to him are infinite, too." Our response should be, "Don't get upset with me; take it up with Jesus. He demanded we enter by the narrow gate. 'For the gate is wide and the way is easy that leads to destruction, and those who enter by it are many. For the gate is narrow and the way is hard that leads to life, and those who find it are few'" (Matt. 7:13–14). Jesus clarifies here that he is the path we walk upon to find God (John 14:6).

Jesus avoids saying, "I am the destination." In other words, he's the way because the Christian life is a walk. It's a walk we make with God, not a journey to find God.

1. God *walked* with Adam in the cool of the Garden.
2. "Enoch *walked* with God; then he was not there because God took him" (Gen. 5:24 CSB).
3. God instructed Abraham to go on a long *walk* on faith, which he obeyed.
4. God enlisted Moses to *walk* his people out of Egypt toward the Promised Land. What was supposed to be a six-month journey turned into a forty-year excursion, during which God led in a pillar of flame by night and a cloud of smoke by day.
5. God told Joshua as he entered the land of Canaan: "Moses my servant is dead. Now you and all the people prepare to cross over the Jordan to the land I am giving the Israelites. I have given you *every place where the sole of your foot treads* [wherever you walk], just as I promised Moses" (Josh. 1:2–3 CSB, emphasis mine).
6. The psalmist declared in Psalm 1:1, "Blessed is the man who does not *walk* in the counsel of the wicked, nor stands in the way of sinners, or sits in the seat of scoffers."
7. Jesus summoned his disciples with the words: "Come follow me" or "Come walk after me."

This understanding of life with God as a "walk of faith" is not a new concept. Christians were even called "the Way" after Jesus's death, burial, and resurrection in the book of Acts in two places. Acts 9 says, "But Saul, still breathing threats and murder against the disciples of the Lord, went to the high priest and asked him for letters to the synagogues at Damascus, so that if he found any belonging to *the Way*, men or women, he might bring them bound to Jerusalem" (Acts 9:1–2, emphasis mine), and Acts 19 states, "But when some became stubborn and continued in unbelief, speaking evil of *the Way* before the congregation, he withdrew from them and took the disciples with him, reasoning daily in the hall of Tyrannus" (Acts 19:9, emphasis mine). *The Way* is an accurate description of the Christian life, and it is how Jesus himself characterized himself as the path by which we come to know God.

How Much Is a Bride Worth?

If we look at Jesus through a Western lens when we read what Jesus told his followers in the upper room, we may miss the full impact of Jesus's final words at the Last Supper. In order to fully comprehend what Jesus says in John 14, we must travel back to the first century and learn more about the betrothal and engagement process when young boys and girls were married.

The parents of a young man would initiate the process of looking for a suitable wife who would typically be between the ages of thirteen and fifteen years old. They would start this process when he was around seventeen years old.[5] The task of arranging the marriage fell on the fathers. When the father had found a suitable bride, he would gather his son, the bride, and the bride's father to negotiate a bride price. The bride price was not an archaic practice of buying a human being, rather, it was a show of respect for the household that was about to lose a precious, contributing member. That bride had to be bought at a price, so the groom's father might say, "I'll give you three goats, two sheep, and an ox for your daughter."

After they had agreed upon a price, the four would share a meal together before solidifying the contract with a cup of wine. Ray Vander Laan describes what this agreement would look like:

> When it was time for a man and woman to marry, both fathers would negotiate the bride price, recognizing that the bride would be a precious loss to her family. Taking a cup of wine, the groom drank from it and offered it to the woman, symbolically saying that he wanted to make a covenant and would be willing to give his life for her. The woman sealed the engagement by drinking from the same glass. The father and son traveled home after the meal to construct a home for his future wife. The bride waited for her bridegroom to come back and get her soon.[6]

After the bridegroom and his father had left, the next step of the process began: building a place for them to live. According to the custom of that culture, the bridegroom didn't go out and look for a plot of land to begin developing, rather, he would build on to the end of his father's house. New homes were built onto existing homes occupied by the family.

The father would supervise the construction of the addition on the home. Days would turn to weeks as the bridegroom would work tirelessly on the new dwelling place for his bride. Periodically, he would approach his father with a question, "Abba, is it time?" "No son," the father would say. "Not yet." In the meantime, the bride would be at her home with her family, waiting expectantly for the arrival of her bridegroom, knowing that he was off preparing a place for her in his father's house. She may have looked on with envy as her friends or sisters were retrieved by their bridegrooms to go off and live with them, but she would remain faithful and vigilant, waiting and watching for her groom to walk down the street to take her away to be with him.

The bridegroom would continue working until the father approved the home. It was not up to the son to determine when the new addition to the house was ready—only the father knew. And when the father gave his approval, he would announce to his son, "Well done. It is time to go get your bride." Gathering his friends and family, the bridegroom would travel unannounced through the streets of the city to get his bride. As the men scurried through those narrow streets, the townspeople would follow the procession. Shouts would bellow though the highways and byways, "Behold the bridegroom comes!" and "Prepare the way for the bridegroom!" Excitement would fill the air as every young betrothed girl would wonder, "Is my groom coming for me today?" When the knock on the door came, the bride knew that her groom had kept his promise to come back to get her.

This cultural context behind the practice of betrothal and marriage sheds new light on Jesus's words on the final night of his earthly life as he speaks to his disciples. He encourages them, saying, "Let not your hearts be troubled. Believe in God; believe also in me. In my Father's house are many rooms. If it were not so, would I have told you that I go to prepare a place for you? And if I go and prepare a place for you, I will come again and will take you to myself, that where I am you may be also" (John 14:2). Because Jesus was referring to a common cultural practice, they would have immediately recognized the language as that of a marriage proposal. They would have heard him say to them:

"I love each of you so much that I'm going to give up my life as the bride price for your freedom. I'm leaving to prepare a place for you, but I will return one day to get you so you can be with me forever. I don't know the time or season. Only my father knows that. Don't be caught off guard. I will return when you least expect it, so be ready."

Keeping with the symbolism of the custom, Jesus reached for the cup of wine and said, "This cup is the new covenant in my blood, which is poured out for you" (Luke 22:20 NIV).

As each of the disciples drank from that cup, they knew what it meant: Jesus had just negotiated the price for them to belong to him. The price was his body; the covenant was sealed with his blood. It was the ultimate blood oath.

Every time the disciples celebrated communion, that same picture would have flashed through their minds: Jesus paid for me with his body and sealed his promise with his blood. This is why Paul says in 1 Corinthians 6:20, "You are not your own, for you have been bought with a price. So glorify God in your body." Everything circles back to the magnitude of Jesus's promise—he has gone, but not forever, and he has not forgotten about us. He is preparing a place in his Father's house until it is time to come back and retrieve his bride—everyone who is called by his name. It is our duty as his bride to wait expectantly, to keep the wicks of our lamps trimmed, saving ourselves for him and for him alone.

When we understand the context in which Jesus is speaking, it illuminates what he says in a fresh way. The only way a bride could get to the father of the bridegroom was to be taken there by his son. In the same way, it is only through the Son of God that we can meet the Father. By calling himself "the way" Jesus is not giving us a simple statement of exclusivity, he is giving us an encouragement that all who seek to know the Father now have a way of getting there: through marriage to the bridegroom.

Seek and Save the Lost

Luke 19 records an encounter many have sung about in a Sunday school class or children's Bible study. It's about that "wee little man" Zacchaeus, and Jesus's decision to enter his home and dine with him. What you may not realize is that Jesus's encounter with Zacchaeus is rich with truth about who Jesus is.

Zakkai—or Zacchaeus as his name is translated—was probably under five feet tall, which was short even by the standards of the first century. As if his short stature were not distinguishing enough, he was also a tax collector, which meant that he was the most hated man in town.

Whenever the Bible mentions tax collectors, it is always in the context of sinners—and for good reason. First-century Palestine was under the governmental control of the Romans, the most powerful political and military force to that point in human history. Rome frequently imposed harsh taxes on the citizens under its control, employing people from those regions to collect the taxes.

The Jews saw men like Zacchaeus as traitors to Israel—they were working directly for the rulers who oppressed them. With all the muscle of Rome behind him, Zacchaeus and other tax collectors could require upwards of twelve to thirteen different taxes a year—at any price they desired! To make matters worse, Zacchaeus was the chief of tax collectors in Jericho, one of the most prosperous cities of Israel. Because he held a top position among this despised group, he was something akin to a godfather of manipulation, habitually sinning by stealing people's hard-earned money.

Jesus stirred up a real hornet's nest when he invited himself into this hardened sinner's home. Passing by him on the street, Jesus yelled to him, "Zacchaeus, hurry and come down because today it is necessary for me to stay at your house" (Luke 19:5 CSB). To put this in context, it would be the equivalent to Billy Graham visiting Bernie Madoff, the Wall Street investor who stole millions from ordinary people investing in retirement. The religious leaders who were watching likely sniggered to themselves as Jesus sat with Zacchaeus, saying to themselves, "He's gone to stay with a sinful man!" (Luke 19:7 CSB).

After dinner, Zacchaeus stood from reclining on his side at the triclinium table (we will learn more about this way of eating in Chapter 9) and said to those gathered, "Look, I'll give half of my possessions to the poor, Lord! And if I have extorted anything from anyone, I'll pay back four times as much!" "Today salvation has come to this house," Jesus told him, "because he too is a son of Abraham. For the Son of Man has come to seek and to save the lost" (Luke 19:8–10).

What happens here? Zacchaeus's life completely changes in two verses, and we see it in the language he uses. First, notice that he refers to Jesus using the term "Lord," a term of great honor and submission that Jesus's own disciples used to refer to him. Luke inserts this term throughout his book whenever a metamorphosis happens in someone's life. When Jesus instructed Peter to cast his net in the sea for a catch in Luke 5, he initially responds, "Master, we've worked hard all night long and caught nothing. But if you say so, I'll let down the nets" (v. 5 CSB). After he hauled in the catch, he dropped to his knees and changed his perspective of Jesus, "Go away from me, because I'm a sinful man, Lord!" (v. 8 CSB). The term "Lord" is used by Luke to indicate that some type of change or transformation has occurred.

Second, notice that Jesus declares, "Today salvation has come to this house." In saying this, Jesus was playing on the connection between his own name and the word "salvation." Jesus's name in Hebrew, Yeshua, means "salvation." Perhaps with a smirk, Jesus agreed with Zacchaeus that salvation (Yeshua) had indeed come to his house. Jesus had walked in through the door!

A Shepherd Searching for His Sheep

We should also take note when Jesus calls Zacchaeus "a son of Abraham." He follows this by adding: "For the Son of Man has come to seek and to save the lost" (Luke 19:10 CSB). In saying this, Jesus refers to himself as the Son of Man, alluding to two Old Testament scriptures to reveal his true identity. Daniel 7 refers to the Messiah as the "son of man." In Daniel 7:13–14 we read:

> I saw in the night visions, and behold, with the clouds of heaven there came one like a *son of man*, and he came to the Ancient of Days and was presented before him. And to him was given dominion and glory and a kingdom, that all peoples, nations, and languages should serve him; his dominion is an everlasting dominion, which shall not pass away, and his kingdom one that shall not be destroyed.

Jesus also makes a connection to the book of Ezekiel by referencing the phrase "to seek and to save the lost." Ezekiel 34 begins, "The word of the LORD came to me: 'Son of man, prophesy against the shepherds of Israel; prophesy, and say to them, even to the shepherds, Thus says the Lord GOD: Ah, shepherds of Israel who have been feeding yourselves! Should not shepherds feed the sheep?'" The language of shepherd is a metaphor for the religious and political leadership of Israel. In Ezekiel's day, the shepherds (leaders) neglected their duty to care for the sheep (the people), and so God chastised their leadership by saying,

> You eat the fat, you clothe yourselves with the wool, you slaughter the fat ones, but you do not feed the sheep. The weak you have not strengthened, the sick you have not healed, the injured you have not bound up, the strayed you have not brought back, the lost you have not sought, and with force and harshness you have ruled them. So they were scattered, because there was no shepherd, and they became food for all the wild beasts. My sheep were scattered; they wandered over all the mountains and on every high hill. My sheep were scattered over all the face of the earth, with none *to search or seek for them* [or seek and save them] (Ezek. 34:3–6).

Ezekiel continues:

> "For thus says the Lord GOD: Behold, *I, I myself will search for my sheep and will seek them out* (seek and save them). As a shepherd seeks out his flock when he is among his sheep that have been scattered, so will *I seek out my sheep*, and *I will rescue them* from all places where they have been scattered on a day of clouds and thick darkness. And *I will bring them out* from the peoples and gather them from the countries, and will bring them into their own land. And *I will feed* them on the mountains of Israel, by the ravines, and in all the inhabited places of the country. *I will feed them* with good pasture, and on the mountain heights of Israel shall be their grazing land. There they shall lie down in good grazing land, and on rich pasture they shall feed on the mountains of Israel. *I myself will be the shepherd of my sheep*, and *I myself will make them lie down*, declares the Lord GOD. *I will seek the lost*, and *I will bring back the strayed*, and *I will bind up the injured*,

and *I will strengthen the weak*, and the fat and the strong I will destroy. *I will feed them in justice*" (vv. 11–16, italics mine).

According to Ezekiel, the leaders will not take responsibility to care for the lost people.

> Who is going to take matters in his own hand? God.
> Who is going to seek the lost sheep of Israel? God.
> Who is going to save the lost sheep of Israel? God.

Jesus connects himself to these Old Testament identities by saying that the Son of Man has come to seek and to save the lost. He is the true Messiah; he is the Lord God who will search, seek, and save his people as the shepherd of the sheep.

In addition to being a code word for the Messiah in Daniel 7, the term "Son of Man" is also an implied reference to Cain and Abel. The word *man* in Hebrew is *Adam*, and the biological son of Adam (aka the Son of Man) was Abel who was wrongly murdered by his brother Cain. The Bible states that Abel's blood is crying out for vindication. As the Son of Man, Jesus will also die an undeserved death, similar to Abel's, at the hands of his own people.

God concludes Ezekiel 34 by explaining how he is going to seek and save his lost people:

> "I will rescue my flock; they shall no longer be a prey. And I will judge between sheep and sheep. And I will set up over them one shepherd, my servant David, and he shall feed them: he shall feed them and be their shepherd. And I, the LORD, will be their God, and my servant David shall be prince among them. I am the LORD; I have spoken" (vv. 22–24).

Since this is written four hundred years after the death of King David, the passage does not make sense if taken literally. How, then, is it possible for David to be the savior of God's people? Once again, God is using an allusion to describe the Messiah and the role he will play in the future salvation of God's people. Jesus was called the "son of David" in the New Testament by a blind man named Bartimaeus in Jericho (Zacchaeus's hometown) shouting, "Jesus, son of David, have mercy on me" (Mark 10:47). When Bartimaeus assigned this title to Jesus, he was making a theological assertion about the identity of Jesus because one of the key prophetic claims about the Messiah in the Old Testament was that he would descend from the throne of David to rule a kingdom that would never end (see 1 Chron. 17:11). The Messiah was the promised "son of David," God's anointed king.

So when we read the words of Jesus in Luke and his allusion to Daniel 7 and Ezekiel 34's "seek and save" statement, we find a subtle, sophisticated, and Jewish way for Jesus to make a bold claim—that he is the promised Messiah and that he is the saving God, the shepherd of his sheep. He is claiming to be one with God, essentially saying, "I'm the one Daniel prophesied about in Daniel 7. I'm the one Ezekiel promised would come to rescue Israel. I am here to 'seek and save the lost,' and I'm starting with Zacchaeus who was a lost sheep, and now he is found."

Through the invitation of Jesus, after years of wandering from God as a turncoat tax collector, Zacchaeus finally came home. There is one final nugget we can uncover when we consider the type of tree Zacchaeus climbed to observe Jesus passing by. According to scholar Dwight Pryor, the sycamore tree was symbolically synonymous with repentance and renewal in the ancient world. Zacchaeus climbed that sycamore tree to glimpse the one who could save him, bringing "salvation" into his house.[7] He repented and turned away from his sins.

A Walk to Remember

Another example of a subtle allusion in the text of the Gospels is found in the events that follow the feeding of the multitudes. After feeding the 5,000 men (we can assume there were in upwards of 15,000 there with women and children present), Jesus "made his disciples get into the boat and go ahead of him to the other side, to Bethsaida, while he dismissed the crowd" (Mark 6:45 CSB).

The disciples, many of whom were fishermen, had made this same journey many times. But what should have been an effortless trip on a familiar body of water turned into an unforgettable experience. We read in the Gospel of Mark: "And when evening came, the boat was out on the sea, and he was alone on the land. And he saw that they were making headway painfully, for the wind was against them. And about the fourth watch of the night he came to them, walking on the sea. He *meant* to *pass by them* . . ." (6:47–48, emphasis mine).

John's Gospel tells us that they began their journey across the lake "when evening began," roughly around 6:00 p.m. (see John 6:15). Since they did not see Jesus until "the fourth watch of the night," we know that they could have been struggling in the storm for up to seven hours, paddling to the middle of the lake—a distance of no longer than four miles.

At first, the disciples saw the figure of a man walking across the waves, and they thought that he was a ghost. It would have been an easy assumption to make: Waves were crashing against the small boat, the wind was ripping across their faces, and they were probably fearful for their very lives. Every one of their senses was heightened, and their imaginations were running wild with thoughts of how they might die in the middle of this lake they'd grown up on. Exhausted and scared at three in the morning, they see a man walking toward them where they know there is nothing but water. To add to this frightening scene, the text tells us that they sensed that he *meant to pass by them*. What a strange situation!

Commentators are divided over the purpose of Jesus's actions. Some suggest Jesus attempted to surprise them on the water to see if they would notice it was him. Others believe he didn't intend to stop at all, but upon recognizing their fear, he turned toward them. One person has even suggested that Jesus wanted to remain unrecognized so he could frighten the disciples. I'm not convinced that any of these explanations make good sense of the text. In order to understand why Jesus meant to pass them by, we need to recognize a connection in this passage to the Old Testament. Again, we pay attention to key words and phrases. There are two that are significant here: the words "meant" and "pass by."

Saying that Jesus *meant* or *intended* to pass them by suggests that there was intention in what Jesus was doing. It leaves no room for chance or happenstance. Jesus willed this to happen to prove a point. This phrase is used elsewhere to describe an epiphany, something that discloses or unveils the identify of God. This rare revelation is seen a few times in scripture.

John P. Meier states, "God made striking and temporary appearances in the earthy realm to a select individual or group for the purpose of communicating a message."[8]

There are at least two notable occurrences when God intentionally *passed by* individuals. On Mount Sinai, God *passed by* Moses.

> Moses said, "Please show me your glory." And he [God] said to him, "I will make all my goodness pass before you and will proclaim before you my name 'The LORD.' And I will be gracious to whom I will be gracious, and will show mercy on whom I will show mercy. But," he said, "you cannot see my face, for man shall not see me and live." And the LORD said, "Behold, there is a place by me where you shall stand on the rock, and while my glory *passes by* I will put you in a cleft of the rock, and I will cover you with my hand until I have *passed by*. Then I will take away my hand, and you shall see my back, but my face shall not be seen" (Exod. 33:18–23, emphasis mine).

In this passage from Exodus, God reveals himself to Moses—something of his nature and character is made known—by passing him by.

In another instance of the Lord "passing by" an individual in a revealing manner, the Lord manifests himself before Elijah on Mount Horeb:

> And he [God] said [to Elijah], "Go out and stand on the mount before the LORD." And behold, the LORD *passed by,* and a great and strong wind tore the mountains and broke in pieces the rocks before the LORD, but the LORD was not in the wind. And after the wind an earthquake, but the LORD was not in the earthquake. And after the earthquake a fire, but the LORD was not in the fire. And after the fire the sound of a low whisper (1 Kings 19:11–12, emphasis mine).

What is happening in this passage in Mark 6? Instead of suggesting that Jesus was going to bypass or walk around the disciples in the boat, Mark may be intentionally linking this episode to those where God reveals himself to Moses and Elijah. New Testament scholar Richard Hays asserts, "Jesus 'passing by' the disciples should be read as an allusion to the Exodus theophany, suggests simultaneously that Jesus' walking on the water is a manifestation of divine glory."[9] By walking on the water, Jesus is showing himself to possess power and authority as the Creator. His actions preach a message to his disciples—that is what is meant by "passing them by." He was, without saying a word, proclaiming that he is the God of Moses and Elijah, and he revealed his divinity by giving evidence of his oneness with God.

But the story does not end there. In the midst of the raging storm on the Sea of Galilee, Jesus speaks a word of encouragement to his disciples: "Have courage! It is I. Don't be afraid" (Mark 6:50 CSB). The phrase "do not be afraid" is used one hundred times from Genesis to Revelation, and it is typically spoken as a word of assurance prior to a revelatory moment.

How could the disciples relax in the middle of a storm at sea? Jesus assures them, "Do not fear, I Am."[10] Much like the I Am statements we saw in John's Gospel, the reader is again reminded of Exodus 3, when God responded to Moses' question about his name, "I AM WHO I AM" (Exod. 3:14 CSB). The name speaks to God's constant presence: I always was, always am, and always will be. Isaiah repeatedly used this phrase in reference to God:

Isaiah 43:25: "I, I am he who blots out your transgressions for my own sake, and I will not remember your sins."

Isaiah 48:12: "Listen to me, O Jacob, and Israel, whom I called! I am he; I am the first, and I am the last."

Isaiah 51:12: "I, I am he who comforts you; who are you that you are afraid of man who dies, of the son of man who is made like grass."

And when Jesus was arrested by the temple police in the garden, he used God's name to identify himself to the guards. "Then Jesus, knowing all that would happen to him, came forward and said to them, 'Whom do you seek?' They answered him, 'Jesus of Nazareth.' Jesus said to them, '*I am* he.' Judas, who betrayed him, was standing with them. When Jesus said to them, '*I am* he,' they drew back and fell to the ground" (John 18:4–6, emphasis mine). Notice that when Jesus speaks these words, he is doing more than speaking a few words. At the mention of "I am," the men were hurled to the ground. Jesus associates himself with the I Am of the Old Testament, the self-chosen name of the God of Israel.

When Jesus speaks to his disciples from the storm, instead of falling away in fear, the disciples are comforted and drawn to him. And as they realize it is their teacher and rabbi, they fall down and worship Jesus as he enters the boat. Why? Because by his actions and in speaking the divine name, he has just told them who he is in a language they understand.

Again, Richard Hays points out the significance of this event: "When Jesus speaks this same phrase, 'I am,' in his sea-crossing epiphany it serves to underscore the claim of divine identity that is implicitly present in the story as a whole."[11] It is easy for Western ears to miss these subtle hints. That is why we must learn to bend our ears to an Eastern dialect to catch the full meaning behind this encounter. The message that comes across is unmistakably clear: Jesus Christ is more than just a man. He is the Creator God, the God of Israel, and the I Am of the burning bush. He is fully human, yet he is fully God simultaneously.

CHAPTER 6

A Jewish Rabbi
and the Coming Kingdom

One of the feasts that the Israelites were commanded to observe every year is described in Leviticus 23:42. It is called *Sukkot* in Hebrew, but we commonly know it as the Feast of Tabernacles. *Sukkot* has a dual significance, both historical and agricultural. Historically, *Sukkot* commemorates the forty-year period in which the children of Israel were living in temporary shelters as they wandered in the desert. But the feast is also an agricultural and seasonal celebration—a harvest festival. During the festival, participants pray for God to send rain upon the land to water the crops. The people depended upon God to provide water for the crops and to quench their thirst. There was no Dasani factory down the street or filtered water to purchase on tap.

It is difficult for those of us living in modern, Western nations to fully grasp the dependence the people had upon God to send them rain. We easily forget that the Israelites lived on the edge of the desert, and crops died regularly from the lack of rainfall. Often, by the time of the festival of *Sukkot*, not a drop of rain (yes, you read that correctly) had fallen for six months. It was the same thing every year. The residents worried that the rain would not return and the crops would fail.

This connection between the Feast of Booths and the need for rain is found in the writings of the Old Testament prophet Zechariah: "Then everyone who survives of all the nations that have come against Jerusalem shall go up year after year to worship the King, the Lord of hosts, and to keep the Feast of Booths. And if any of the families of the earth do not go up to Jerusalem to worship the King, the LORD of hosts, *there will be no rain on them*" (14:16–17, emphasis mine). For hundreds and hundreds of years, the people had participated in this feast, but some misunderstood the true significance of the festival. When Jesus came, he intended to correct their misunderstandings.

The Feast of Tabernacles spanned seven days in Old Testament times and eight days in the time of Jesus.[1] Every day, a designated priest would descend from the temple toward the pool of Siloam in the midst of a multitude of jubilant worshipers. The priest led a procession of people toward the pool singing the words of Isaiah 12:3 (NKJV), "Therefore with joy you will draw water from the wells of salvation."

After filling a golden pitcher with water, the priest would make the trek back up to the basin at the foot of the altar. Silver trumpets would be blown and palm branches would be waved in unison with chants of Psalm 118:25–27, "Save us, we pray, O LORD! O LORD, we pray, give us success! Blessed is he who comes in the name of the Lord! We bless you from the house of the LORD. The LORD is God, and he has made his light to shine upon us. Bind the festal sacrifice with cords, up to the horns of the altar!" The people would shout, "Hosanna," which means, "save us."[2] The priest then held the pitcher up before pouring out the water, symbolizing God's provision of water for the people in their desert journey.

The Mishnah described the festival this way: "He who had never seen this ceremony, which was accompanied by dancing, singing and music had never seen true joy."[3] Some simply referred to it as "the feast." And all waited patiently for the last, or "great" day. Author Roger D. Willmore describes the two newer variations to the celebration that were included on the final day at the time of Jesus:

First, when the parade of people returned from the pool of Siloam, the Priests would march around the altar seven times commemorating Joshua's victory at Jericho. Secondly, the Priests would raise the golden pitcher over the silver funnels as they had done each day previously, but this time there was no water—only an empty pitcher. This signified the disobedient generation that died in the Wilderness. Instead of a shout and the waving of palm branches as the people had done each day, they now stood in silence.[4]

On the last day of the festival, as described in John 7, this very ritual was well under way. The priests had done everything according to their custom. The people had shouted as the priest climbed the steps to the silver funnels, and then everyone falls suddenly, shockingly silent as he lifts up the golden pitcher. The city is silent. Palm branches cease to be waved. Horns are muted. Shouts are ended. All eyes are fixed upon the priest.

Then, speaking into the silence, a Galilean rabbi stands to his feet and shouts, "If anyone is thirsty, he should come to me and drink. The one who believes in me, as the Scripture has said, will have streams of living water flow from deep within him" (John 7:37–38 CSB).

You may think that Jesus *interrupts* the feast, but he does just the opposite. He actually *interprets* the festival for them.[5] He says, in essence, "You are spiritually thirsty, and I alone can satisfy you because streams of living water flow from deep within him." I have often wondered who Jesus means when he refers to "him," the one with living waters flowing within him.

For years I thought Jesus was referring to the person who drinks the living water, but it is more likely that he's actually referring to himself. Noted New Testament scholar G. K. Beale explains, "Jesus alludes to the prophecy of water flowing from the temple in Ezekiel, Joel and Zechariah. The 'heart' from which 'flow[s] rivers of living water' is Jesus himself as the new 'Holy of Holies.'"[6] Jesus is making what scholars call a "typological interpretation" of Ezekiel 47:1–12. He is saying that he is the fulfillment of the prophecies about the "eschatological Temple during the Messianic Kingdom."[7] Jesus uses allusion again when he speaks, referring to Isaiah

44:3 (CSB) and connecting the pouring of water with the giving of the Holy Spirit: "For I will pour water on the thirsty land and streams on the dry ground; I will pour out my Spirit on your descendants and my blessing on your offspring."[8]

Jesus had watched this scene unfold for the past seven days. Even more, he'd been watching this scene unfold every year since his youth. Thousands of worshipers for hundreds and hundreds of years have gone through the same motions, saying the correct words at the correct time, but they have misunderstood the significance of the ceremony. Jesus clears up the misunderstanding: It was all pointing to the Messiah, the one who now stood in their midst!

Touching the Hem

The account of the Feast of Booths in John 7 is not the only instance of Jesus making a teachable moment out of an "interruption." In Luke 8 he uses a hemorrhaging woman's disruption to teach a beautiful lesson about the kingdom of God. A woman with menstrual bleeding was prohibited from contact with others for fear of making them unclean. We find this prohibition in Leviticus 15:

> When a woman has a discharge, and it consists of blood from her body, she will be unclean because of her menstruation for seven days. Everyone who touches her will be unclean until evening. Anything she lies on during her menstruation will become unclean, and anything she sits on will become unclean. Everyone who touches her bed is to wash his clothes and bathe with water, and he will remain unclean until evening. Everyone who touches any furniture she was sitting on is to wash his clothes and bathe with water, and he will remain unclean until evening (vv. 19–21).

Later in this chapter a warning is added to keep the "Israelites from their uncleanness, so that they do not die by defiling my tabernacle that is among them" (v. 31 CSB).

For the woman we meet in Luke 8 in particular, it appears that her ailment had plagued her life for twelve long years. She had likely sought treatment from every doctor in the region, all to no avail. Mark writes about her in his Gospel account, "[she] spent all she had, yet instead of getting better she grew worse" (Mark 5:26 NIV). Her condition brought with it unwanted shame. Because of the Levitical prohibition against contact, she was despised, defiled, destitute, desperate, and discouraged. The Jewish Talmud prescribes eleven cures for this specific illness. Some of the suggestions are potions, others border on superstition:

> Take of the gum of Alexandria the weight of a small silver coin; a piece of alum the same; and a piece of crocus the same. Let them be bruised together, and given in wine to the woman that has an issue of blood. If this does not benefit, take of Persian onions three pints; boil them in wine, and give her to drink, and say "Arise from thy flux." If this does not cure her, set her in a place where two ways meet, and let her hold a cup of wine in her right hand, and let someone come behind and frighten her, and say, "Arise from thy flux."[9]

If these were some of the remedies the woman had attempted to find healing, it is safe to assume that she had tried extreme measures to rid herself of the ailment. Luke records, "While he was going, the crowds were nearly crushing him. A woman suffering from bleeding for 12 years, who had spent all she had on doctors yet could not be healed by any, approached from behind and touched the *end of his robe*. Instantly her bleeding stopped" (Luke 8:42–44 CSB).

Here is the picture Luke creates for us. We imagine her crawling, bleeding, towards Jesus with twelve years' worth of unsuccessful attempts to heal herself weighing heavily on her mind. She is desperate. But she has a glimmer of hope. Risking persecution from the thick crowd following Jesus, this woman throws all of her hope on the itinerant rabbi who had a reputation for miraculous healings. She reaches out as he passes and is able only to reach the very edge of his robe. But while this is a nice, cinematic image, filled with drama, it is hardly an accurate one. Why do I say that? Because the woman wasn't reaching out to grab a random piece of the rabbi's robe. This wasn't just an accidental touch of his garment. Instead, she was laser-focused on touching a specific part of his outer garment. The woman had a clear goal in mind, based on a very *specific* hope for healing.

Healing in His Wings

To understand why the woman was reaching for a specific portion of Jesus's outer garment, we need to understand how Jewish men at the time of Jesus dressed. One of the features of the clothing worn by Jewish men was tassels. These were located on the corner of their garments in keeping with the directions given in Numbers 15:

> The LORD said to Moses, "Speak to the Israelites and tell them that throughout their generations they are to make tassels for the corners of their garments, and put a blue cord on the tassel at each corner. These will serve as tassels for you to look at, so that you may remember all the LORD's commands and obey them and not become unfaithful by following your own heart and your own eyes. This way you will remember and obey all My commands and be holy to your God" (vv. 37–40).

God further clarified what was to go on the four corners of the cloak in Deuteronomy 22:12: "Make tassels on the four corners of the outer garment you wear" (CSB). In Hebrew, *tzitzit* is the word we translate as tassels, fringe, or hem of the garment. These tassels were a constant reminder to obey the commandments of God. Jesus, as an observant Jewish man, would have worn a one-piece, finely woven, long-sleeved tunic with an opening for his head. Some tunics of the time stretched from head to feet. His outer garment was most likely a rectangular coat called a *tallit* with four *tzitzit* hung from each of the four corners.

The *tzitzit,* or tassels, had additional significance in relation to the Messiah. Malachi 4:2 (emphasis mine) says, "But for you who fear my name, the sun of righteousness shall rise with *healing in its wings.* You shall go out leaping like calves from the stall." When Malachi writes about the "sun of righteousness," he is not referring to an inanimate celestial object, but a person. It is a reference to God himself. The "sun of righteousness" mentioned in this passage is a Hebrew idiom for the Messiah—the manifest presence of God.

The Hebrew word *kanaph* found here in Malachi is the word we translate into English as *wings.* It occurs elsewhere in the Old Testament to refer to a number of different things as well. For example, in Genesis 1:21 it speaks of the created, winged animals that soar around the earth. Isaiah 6:2 uses the word to define the wings of the seraphim. Interestingly, it is also used to refer to the corner, or fringe, of a garment. In the book of 1 Samuel, after Saul is disobedient to the Lord, the Lord sends Samuel to confront Saul and strip him of the kingdom. Saul responds by approaching Samuel and grabbing the corner or the hem (or *kanaph*) of his garment, ripping it off.

With these textual connections in mind, the Malachi passage takes on some additional meaning. In a messianic context, it suggests that the Messiah will appear, and he will have healing in his "wings"—in the corners of his garments. In other words, his arrival will be associated with the healing and restoring of his people. And this is what the crowds were seeing in the ministry of Jesus of Nazareth. But his healing was more than physical, of course. The sun of righteousness, God himself, will possess healing in his tassels—not merely physical healing, but spiritual restoration from sin and separation from the Lord.

So why did the woman reach out to touch the hem or tassel of Jesus's garment? In doing this she was saying, without saying a single word, that she believed Jesus was the Messiah. She knew the Word of God, and her actions demonstrated that she knew exactly *who* Jesus was, that he was more than just another healing rabbi. And Jesus confirms her belief by saying to her, "'Have courage, daughter,' he said. 'Your faith has saved you.' And the woman was made well from that moment on" (Matt. 9:22 CSB). She demonstrated faith by touching the hem of Jesus's robe and affirming her belief that he was the Messiah.

The Necessity of Being Born Twice

In several of his interactions with individuals, Jesus speaks in ways that seem cryptic or strange to our Western ears. One of those individuals was a religious leader named Nicodemus. John's Gospel tells us about their meeting:

> Now there was a man of the Pharisees named Nicodemus, a ruler of the Jews. This man came to Jesus by night and said to him, "Rabbi,

we know that you are a teacher come from God, for no one can do these signs that you do unless God is with him." Jesus answered him, "Truly, truly, I say to you, unless one is born again he cannot see the kingdom of God." Nicodemus said to him, "How can a man be born when he is old? Can he enter a second time into his mother's womb and be born?" (John 3:1–5).

To grasp what is happening in this conversation, we need to know more about Nicodemus. What prompted him to seek out Jesus? Most likely he was in the crowd that day and had witnessed firsthand the miracles Jesus had done. John suggests that there were some like this when he writes in John 2:23–25, just before we meet Nicodemus: "Now when he [Jesus] was in Jerusalem at the Passover Feast, many believed in his name when they saw the signs that he was doing. But Jesus on his part did not entrust himself to them, because he knew all people and needed no one to bear witness about man, for he himself knew what was in man." We also learn that Nicodemus was a Pharisee, which means he was a rabbi, a teacher of the Bible. We are also told that he was a ruler of the Jews, which means he was a member of the Sanhedrin. The Sanhedrin was the most powerful religious and political body in Judaism. This meant that he was a distinguished teacher in the community.

Perhaps hoping to avoid being seen by his fellow Pharisees, Nicodemus approaches Jesus at night. While this interaction did literally occur at night, that's not the only reason John includes this detail. "Night" is also a metaphor used in John's writing to indicate moral and spiritual darkness (see John 1:5; 3:2; 3:19; 9:4–5; 12:35; and 20:1). The context and timing of their meeting is an indication of Nicodemus's spiritual condition or a reflection upon the religious state of the people of Israel (since he is a leader and representative of the people). While discussing scripture at night was not uncommon for rabbis, Nicodemus might also have been fearful of being seen with Jesus.

Jesus disregards Nicodemus's flattery and gets right to the heart of the problem: "Truly, truly, I say to you, unless one is born again he cannot see the kingdom of God." Jesus immediately diagnoses Nicodemus's problem. Not only was Nicodemus approaching him at night (in spiritual darkness); he was approaching him without the ability to see the kingdom of God (spiritual blindness). This is significant, for Nicodemus was among the most religious of the Jewish people. It is a clear statement that without Christ to open our eyes and give us sight, we are all blind to the kingdom of God.

Reading through the Gospels, we find two phrases that look quite similar: "the kingdom of God" and "the kingdom of heaven." In reality, these phrases are synonymous. Matthew uses the term "heaven" more than other Gospel writers because he was a Jew writing to a Jewish audience. Not wanting to defame the name of God, he replaced the name of God with the word "heaven." We see this when we compare what Jesus says when he likens the kingdom of God to a mustard seed in Matthew 13:31 and Mark 4:30–31.[10] The terms are interchangeable, referring to the same reality.

Biblically understood, God's kingdom is where his presence is manifested in the world. What is interesting is that most of the time, Jesus uses the phrase "the kingdom of God" or "the kingdom of heaven" to refer to the *here and now*. In other words, he isn't referring to a distant, far-off place; he is speaking of something near, something that is close, a reality that is right here with us, if only we have eyes to see and ears to hear. Here are a few examples of the kingdom as a *present* reality in scripture:

After John was arrested, Jesus went to Galilee, proclaiming the good news of God: "The time is fulfilled, and the kingdom of God has come near. Repent and believe the good news!" (Mark 1:14–15 CSB)

Being asked by the Pharisees when the kingdom of God will come, he answered them, "The kingdom of God is not coming with something observable; no one will say, 'See here!' or 'There!' For you see, the kingdom of God is in your midst." (Luke 17:20–21 CSB)

"What do you think? A man had two sons. He went to the first and said, 'My son, go and work in the vineyard today.' He answered, 'I don't want to,' but later he changed his mind and went. Then the man went to the other and said the same thing. 'I will, sir,' he answered. But he didn't go. 'Which of the two did his father's will?' 'The first,' they said. Jesus said to them, 'Truly I tell you, tax collectors and prostitutes are *entering the kingdom of God before you*.'" (Matt. 21:28–31 CSB, emphasis added)

Jesus looked around and said to his disciples, "How hard it is for those who have wealth to enter the kingdom of God!" The disciples were astonished at his words. Again Jesus said to them, "Children, how hard it is to enter the kingdom of God! It is easier for a camel to go through the eye of a needle than for a rich person to enter the kingdom of God." (Mark 10:23–25 CSB)

In the last passage mentioned above, Jesus is not excluding rich people from entering heaven after they die; however, he is warning against missing out on the blessings and the benefits of the kingdom of heaven today because of serving money.

Jesus spoke a great deal about the kingdom of God. It was the key point of his first preaching message: "Your time has come. The kingdom of heaven is at hand." The kingdom message Jesus preached and taught was clear: The long-awaited kingdom of God had now arrived. When Jesus says that it is "at hand," he is simply saying that it is happening right now. Lancaster elaborates on the significance of this message:

Those who receive the forgiveness of their sins in this age and live by the rule of the kingdom (i.e., the Torah) in this present age can be said to have already laid hold of the kingdom of heaven, so to speak.[11]

The kingdom of heaven is both an external state when the Messiah reigns over the whole earth and an internal state of the individual who is forgiven and spiritually regenerated by the Lord.

Why is this important for us to understand? Because if we miss the teaching on the kingdom, we miss a significant aspect of the teaching of Jesus. Today, some teach that Jesus came to die for the sins of mankind. As necessary and important as that was, it was not the *only* reason Jesus came. In fact, Jesus often explained his ministry in another way. After a morning of prayer, the crowds begged him to stay with them, to which Jesus responded, "I must preach the good news of the kingdom of God to the other towns as well; for I was sent for this purpose" (Luke 4:43). Whenever Jesus healed someone, he said to them, "The kingdom has come upon you" (Matt. 12:28; Luke 11:20). In the Sermon on the Mount, Jesus began his message with, "Blessed are the poor in spirit, for theirs is the kingdom of heaven" (Matt. 5:3). Why so many references to the kingdom?

Jesus was saying to those who were willing to listen that when we humble ourselves, we experience the power and presence of the kingdom now, not just as a distant, future reality. The kingdom is not just a faraway destination we enter upon death. It's a present reality for anyone who repents and believes in Jesus. For many of us who have developed selective hearing as we read the Gospels, we may need fresh ears to hear what Jesus is teaching about the kingdom as something present among us today.

Dwight Pryor has a wonderful message series called *Unveiling the Kingdom* where he makes this very point, saying, "When Jesus announced that the Kingdom of God was 'at hand' he was not saying: 'Soon and very soon I am coming to set up a Kingdom and to rule from the New Jerusalem.' Rather, he was emphasizing the immediacy of God's power to break in and take charge of human lives—to heal, to save, to deliver and redeem—through the person of Jesus and in the power of the Holy Spirit."[12]

I believe this is a truth that we need to recover today as well. Many believers only view the kingdom of heaven as a future place we live at after death—not as a present power to live in. Unfortunately, this view of heaven paralyzes us and leads us to think that the Christian life is an escape from this world. The truth is that God is breaking into this world, bringing his justice, his power, and his presence. He comes through the preaching of the gospel and through the presence of his Holy Spirit at work among his people. God desires to be with his creation.

In fact, the teaching of Jesus about the kingdom fits the larger trajectory of the Bible. The story of redemption is a story of the high and holy God of Israel "coming down" to be with his people.[13] Recall that God first came down to walk with Adam in the "cool of the garden."[14] He descends again to make a covenant with Abraham in Genesis 15. He speaks to Moses though a flaming bush in the desert. He envelops the mountain in smoke as he distributes the commandments to Moses on Mount Sinai. Finally, he comes down as a man in the incarnation of his Son.

But the story does not end there! The Holy Spirit indwells the disciples on the mountain of Jerusalem on Pentecost in Acts 2. And we are promised that Jesus remains with his people, even to the end of this age. One day, he will appear at the end of days as Revelation 21 promises, "Behold, the dwelling place of God is with man. He will *dwell* [take up permanent residence or settle] with them, and they will be his people, and God himself will be with them as their God" (v. 3).

The kingdom of heaven comes to earth when we live holy and just lives, when we walk upright, and when we bless others around us. Do you recall how Jesus taught his followers to pray? "Your kingdom come, your will be done." The second line of that prayer parallels the first. It means that when God's will is done in our lives, the kingdom comes to our lives.

Today, we continue to pray this prayer. And as we do this, we are saying, "Jesus, take control. Take over. Lead my family. Lead my business. Lead my marriage. Lead my life."[15] Relinquishing control of one's life requires humility. The rabbis had an interesting way of illustrating this. They compared the Holy Spirit to water, which naturally seeks the lowest resting point on the ground when it is poured out.[16] In a similar manner, God's Spirit seeks out the lowest, the most humble person to rest upon. As James reminds us, God opposes the haughty but gives grace to the humble.[17]

Entrance into the Kingdom

Let's return to Jesus and his meeting with Nicodemus. Jesus gives an interesting answer, and Nicodemus's interest is piqued. So he presses Jesus further by asking what seems like an odd question: "How can a man be born when he is old? Can he enter a second time into his mother's womb and be born?" (John 3:4).

While Nicodemus is speaking of a literal birth, it may be as a way of drawing out the meaning Jesus has in mind. According to Arnold Fruchtenbaum, Jews believed that a person could be born again in six ways.[18] Nicodemus qualified for four of the six. Gentiles were "born again" when they converted to Judaism, but Nicodemus did not qualify because he was already a Jew. Another avenue for being "born again" was to be crowned a king. Again, we have no indication that Nicodemus was of the lineage of King David, so that was clearly not what Jesus had in mind.

Nicodemus did, however, qualify to be "born again" in four of the accepted ways. First, a Jewish boy was considered an adult at the age of thirteen at what is known today as a *bar mitzvah*. At this age, a boy was old enough to obey the commandments of God and was considered "born again." Nicodemus, like every other devout Jewish boy, would have already followed through with this rite of passage.

Second, a man was "born again" after his wedding ceremony took place. Although the biblical record never overtly states Nicodemus was married, we know he was a member of the Sanhedrin, and one of the requirements for entrance into the governing body of Israel was marriage.

Third, an ordained rabbi or Pharisee was considered to be "born again" after taking up his position as a teacher. Again, Nicodemus qualified as a religious teacher and leader in Israel.

Finally, a person could be considered "born again" in the first century by becoming the head of a rabbinical school in Israel. Jesus may have had this in mind when he asked Nicodemus, "Are you the teacher of Israel and yet you do not understand these things?" (John 3:10). He probably wasn't confused by the concept of being born again. He just wasn't sure how it could apply to him. After all, he represented the very best of the Jewish faith. He was an exemplar to others, a leader.

What, then, lies behind the question Nicodemus is asking Jesus? Let's take a closer look at these two questions again, particularly his follow-up question: "How can a man be born when he is old? Can he enter a second time into his mother's womb and be born?" (John 3:4). Nicodemus asked Jesus how he, as a senior citizen, could re-enter his mother's womb to be "born again." Fruchtenbaum clarifies what Nicodemus is likely asking:

> That's why he asked the question the way he did: *How is one born again when he is old?* What he is saying is, "hey, I've used up all my options." As far as he can see there is no other way to be born again except the way he suggested back in verse 4: to go back into his mother's womb, be born physically once more, and simply begin the process all over again, and be born again at the ages of 13, 20, 30, and 50.[19]

And how does Jesus respond to Nicodemus? With these words:

> "Truly, truly, I say to you, unless one is born of water and the Spirit, he cannot enter the kingdom of God. That which is born of the flesh is flesh, and that which is born of the Spirit is spirit. Do not

marvel that I said to you, 'You must be born again.' The wind blows
where it wishes, and you hear its sound, but you do not know where
it comes from or where it goes. So it is with everyone who is born of
the Spirit" (John 3:5–8).

Jesus was pointing out to Nicodemus that even if he had been "born
again" in all of the culturally acceptable ways, he was still in need of
a deeper transformation. Jesus was telling Nicodemus that he did not
qualify for the kingdom, that nothing he had done to this point would
merit his entrance. Even as the teacher of Israel, he was lacking something.
Jesus rejects the Pharisaic understanding that "all of Israel will share in
the kingdom in the coming age," teaching that a Jew by birth does not
automatically garner entrance into the kingdom. A person has to be born
again spiritually. Birth by water denotes physical birth, while spiritual birth
comes as the Holy Spirit quickens our deadened hearts to come to life.

Look to the Son to Be Saved

Nicodemus obviously has difficulty accepting this idea:

> Nicodemus said to him, "How can these things be?" Jesus answered
> him, "Are you the teacher of Israel and yet you do not understand
> these things? Truly, truly, I say to you, we speak of what we know,
> and bear witness to what we have seen, but you do not receive our
> testimony. If I have told you earthly things and you do not believe,
> how can you believe if I tell you heavenly things? No one has ascended
> into heaven except he who descended from heaven, the Son of Man.
> And as Moses lifted up the serpent in the wilderness, so must the Son
> of Man be lifted up, that whoever believes in him may have eternal
> life" (John 3:9–15).

To help Nicodemus grasp what he is talking about, Jesus references
Numbers 21. Let's take a look at the background to this passage to understand why Jesus alludes to it. In Numbers 21 the people have grown
impatient with God. Numbers 21:4–9 are the verses Jesus has in mind
when speaking to Nicodemus:

From Mount Hor they set out by the way to the Red Sea, to go around the land of Edom. And the people became impatient on the way. And the people spoke against God and against Moses, "Why have you brought us up out of Egypt to die in the wilderness? For there is no food and no water, and we loathe this worthless food." Then the LORD sent fiery serpents among the people, and they bit the people, so that many people of Israel died. And the people came to Moses and said, "We have sinned, for we have spoken against the LORD and against you. Pray to the LORD, that he take away the serpents from us." So Moses prayed for the people. And the LORD said to Moses, "Make a fiery serpent and set it on a pole, and everyone who is bitten, when he sees it, shall live." So Moses made a bronze serpent and set it on a pole. And if a serpent bit anyone, he would look at the bronze serpent and live.

Tired of the people complaining, God disperses poisonous serpents among them. Many die from the snakebites, causing the people to recognize the error of their ways and ask for forgiveness. As mediator between God and the people, Moses offers a sincere plea to the Lord asking for lives to be spared. And God offers a peculiar means for healing. He sends an antidote for the serpent's venom coursing through their bodies. He tells Moses to construct a fiery, metal serpent, to impale it upon a pole, and to hoist it into the air. Anyone who looked (a picture of faith and trust) to the serpent lived.

Why a Bronze Serpent?

At this point, many Western readers may be struggling to see the connections Jesus is making as he talks with Nicodemus about the kingdom, the Holy Spirit, being born again, and the fiery serpent of Numbers 21. But he is teaching something important to Nicodemus here in a very Jewish way. First, we should know that the Hebrew word for serpent is *nachash*, and the Hebrew word for bronze is *nechoshet*. Both of these words are derived from the same root word, a reminder of Genesis 3 where the serpent appears to Adam and Eve in the garden, most likely as a shiny, luminous snake. The word is also found in 1 Samuel 17 when Goliath steps forth to fight David dressed in bronze colored, "serpent-like" armor. Second, there are several things we should note about this passage from Numbers 21:

1. Notice that God doesn't remove the snakes or the poison. The remedy for the sin and disobedience of the people was given *after* the damage was done. It was a prescription for their sin, not a way of preventing it.
2. God takes the same word for serpent used in the garden, and he instructs Moses to create an image of it. This is hardly accidental. The serpent represents the ancient enemy of God's people.
3. Many of us might think that the construction of a golden-colored serpent is odd.[20] Didn't God prohibit the people from fashioning graven images for themselves? What about that terrible incident when Aaron constructed a golden calf? Why would God instruct Moses to make such a thing?

Jesus interprets the Numbers 21 passage for Nicodemus and he applies it to himself. He says, in essence, "What happened with Moses foreshadows the work of the Messiah. Just as the people looked to the serpent for healing, one day you will look to the 'lifted-up-one' for salvation." Who is the 'lifted-up-one'? Later in his ministry, Jesus says that he is the one to be lifted up. We read in John 12:32 (CSB): "[I]f I am lifted up from the earth I will draw all people to myself."

This phrase "lifted up" has a dual meaning of lifting up physically as well as exalting someone in majesty or glory. It connects to the work of the Messiah in Isaiah 52, where we read these words about the suffering servant, the Messiah, "See, my servant will be successful; he will be raised and lifted up and greatly exalted" (Isa. 52:13 CSB). Jesus's claim is simple and clear: "I am the Messiah, the suffering servant to be lifted up. I won't be defeated on the cross. I will be exalted. Just as the serpent gave life to those dying, I will give life to anyone who looks to me. My death will be the serum for your sin problem."

Throughout this conversation with Nicodemus at night, Jesus has been trying to open his spiritually blind eyes to the truth—that he is the Messiah and he has come to bring the kingdom. And how will this happen? God brings his kingdom into this world by reversing the curse and the effects of human sin and rebellion. The story of the serpent bringing healing in Numbers 21 is a foreshadowing of this work of reversal. Jesus will one day take the curse of hanging on a tree and turn it into a cure for sin. Galatians 3:13 says, "Christ redeemed us from the curse of the law by becoming a curse for us—for it is written, 'Cursed is everyone who is hanged on a tree.'" One commentator writes:

> Yet even in the wilderness God is responsive to the needs of these his complaining people. He provides what the context could not. The protests are answered, the cries are heard, quite undeservedly. There is a gift of healing where the pain experienced is the sharpest. Deliverance comes, not in being removed from the wilderness, but in the very presence of the enemy. The transformation from death to life occurs within the very context of godforsakenness. The death-dealing forces of chaos are nailed to the pole. God transforms death into a source of life. A sanctuary is provided in the wilderness.[21]

Through the work of the suffering Messiah, the one who is lifted up, God will bring transformation and healing to his people. The image of evil and condemnation—the serpent—becomes a sign of hope, just as the cross—a sign of death—becomes a sign of life. Entrance to the kingdom is available for those who will receive the Spirit and experience this new life.

We know from the end of Jesus's life that Nicodemus heeded his words. After Jesus's death on the cross, two men stepped forward to properly bury the body. After all of Jesus's close disciples had fled, Joseph of Arimathea, a secret disciple, and Nicodemus stepped up. While we cannot know for certain, church tradition suggests that Nicodemus ben Gurion, as he became known, was eventually martyred for his faith in Jesus.[22]

Salvation comes to those who look to the "lifted-up-one" for their healing. A glimpse of the Messiah, stepping out in faith to grab his garment—these are all it took. What matters is the object of our faith, the one in whom we place our hope. Jesus is more than a travelling healer or a good teacher. Like the shame-filled woman who was healed and the self-righteous Jewish teacher who humbly accepted his need for God, so it is with us. We have but to gaze upon the Son of God lifted high as a cure for our condition to be healed of it.

CHAPTER 7

Is Jesus Really the Messiah?

As Jesus's ministry grew in popularity, Jesus became the subject of growing scrutiny and criticism, particularly as he began working certain specific signs among the people and claiming that he was one with God. The most immediate concern of the Jewish people during the first century was their hope for the Messiah. They were waiting with anticipation for the one who would deliver Israel and make it again into the great nation it once was. This hope had become so prevalent that, according to Arnold Fruchtenbaum, there were specific protocols put into place that had to be followed to the letter if a person claimed to be the Messiah.[1]

Through careful study of the New Testament, taking into account both the Hebraic context and the Jewish culture, Fruchtenbaum asserts two Sanhedrin stages for Messianic investigation: observation and interrogation.[2] Whenever word would spread of a new messianic claim (and there were many people who claimed to be the Messiah, both before and after Jesus), a delegation was commissioned to investigate and observe them. During the observation stage, this group of investigators could not ask questions or raise objections; their sole purpose was to gather facts and determine if there was any legitimacy to the claim. This delegation would report back to the Sanhedrin after their preliminary investigation and give the Sanhedrin what they needed to move forward.

Was the movement legitimate? Was it significant? If the movement was determined to be illegitimate or insignificant, the official investigation would cease, and the so-called messianic movement would eventually fizzle out. If the delegation observed that the movement might actually be something important, then the Sanhedrin moved on to stage two: interrogation. Gamaliel's comments about the followers of Christ after his death in Acts 5:38–39 (CSB) lend credibility to this idea: "So in the present case, I tell you, stay away from these men and leave them alone. For if this plan or this work is of human origin, it will fail; but if it is of God, you will not be able to overthrow them. You may even be found fighting against God."

In the interrogation stage, according to Fruchtenbaum, the delegation would be allowed to interview bystanders, members of the movement, or the individual in question. The leaders would interact with the rabbi's teaching, raising objections where objections could be raised, even trying to trap the individual into breaking out of his "messianic" character. After this stage, the delegation would be forced to make a decision: either the individual they were investigating was the real deal, or he was a fraud.

The momentum of John the Baptist's ministry initiated a delegation from Jerusalem to cross-examine him and his teaching. John records the exchange:

> This is John's testimony *when the Jews from Jerusalem sent priests and Levites to ask him,* "Who are you?" He didn't deny it but confessed: "I am not the Messiah." "What then?" they asked him. "Are you Elijah?" "I am not," he said. "Are you the Prophet?" "No," he answered. "Who are you, then?" they asked. "We need to give an answer to *those who sent us.* What can you tell us about yourself?" He said, "I am a voice of one crying out in the wilderness: Make straight the way of the Lord—just as Isaiah the prophet said." *Now they had been sent from the Pharisees.* So they asked him, "Why then do you baptize if you aren't the Messiah, or Elijah, or the Prophet?" (John 1:19–25 CSB, emphasis mine).

The investigation begins with John the Baptist, since he was claiming to be preparing the way for the Messiah and had already amassed a significant following. The delegation came up to the place where he was baptizing people in the Jordan, and John famously addressed them, "Brood of vipers! Who warned you to flee from the coming wrath?" (Matt. 3:7 CSB). Some translations suggest that the leaders were coming for baptism, but this is not likely the case. They were coming to the place of baptism to inspect the movement for themselves.

We are told three times that this was a delegation sent from Jerusalem to ask John questions. These were not inquisitors in the crowd attempting to ascertain the identity of John. These were highly skilled Bible scholars who were probing John for answers. Eventually, their questions would cease for John, only to be redirected at Jesus. Jesus not only welcomes the questions, but sometimes initiates them.

We see the delegation appear again in Luke 5, when they are sent to analyze the ministry of Jesus after he heals a paralytic man. At first, the group is only investigating—not interrogating—Jesus. "On one of those days, as he was teaching, Pharisees and teachers of the law were sitting there, who had come from every village of Galilee and Judea and from Jerusalem" (Luke 5:17). The crowd gathered that day was not just a ragtag group of observers crowding the home in Capernaum to view a miracle. It was a well-organized coalition from "every village of Galilee and Judea and from Jerusalem." Mark described the house as packed out with people. "And when he returned to Capernaum after some days, it was reported that he was at home. And many were gathered together, so that there was no more room, not even at the door" (Mark 2:1–2).

The religious leaders are responding to the claims of the leper whom Jesus touched and healed earlier (see Luke 5:12–16; we will examine that encounter in a moment). Jesus knew why the crowd was present, which is why he asked them, "'Why do you question these things in your hearts? Which is easier, to say to the paralytic, "Your sins are forgiven," or to say, "Rise, take up your bed and walk"? But that you may know that the Son of Man has authority on earth to forgive sins'—he said to the paralytic—'I say to you, rise, pick up your bed, and go home'" (Luke 5:22–24). The motley crew of investigators travels back to Jerusalem after this encounter with enough evidence to move on to stage two of the investigation: interrogation.

An Outward Cleansing of an Inward Condition

While Jesus performed many miracles throughout his earthly ministry, he performed some specific miracles that caused the crowds to react in unique ways to him. The people who had been waiting for centuries to see the Messiah knew that they were looking for someone who would do unique things. They knew that the Messiah would fulfill Old Testament prophecy, make specific claims about himself, and he would be able to perform certain tasks that, according to Jewish sages, only God could perform. As Rome became more powerful and Hellenism spread across the continent, first-century Jews were expecting the Messiah's arrival more than ever.

The sages of Israel believed God's Messiah would perform three specific miracles to validate his identity. Fruchtenbaum lists these messianic miracles as healing a leper, casting out a dumb demon, and healing a man born blind.[3] And Roger Liebi, an expert in Jewish studies and New Testament archeology, supports this, arguing that we should classify the healing of a leper as one of the messianic miracles: "Since, in Judaism the healing of leprosy could only be expected from God, the conclusion was compelling that Jesus of Nazareth, who was healing people from leprosy, was sent from God and was acting with divine power."[4]

Leprosy was a broad term that was used in the first century to cover a host of issues: skin diseases, childbirth, menstruation, emissions from the body, unclean animals, mold, and the parasitic variant of leprosy we still have today. The word "leprosy" occurs sixty-eight times in the Bible, with fifty-five of those occurrences being in the Old Testament.

When a person had leprosy, they were considered ritually unclean. This meant that they were not allowed to touch people, and people were not allowed to touch them. It was not *sinful* to be a leper (unless they tried to enter the temple or partake in sacrificial services without engaging in proper purification rites first), but they were considered *unclean*. Leprosy was extremely contagious, so it was for the good of the community that lepers were contained and isolated until they could be made clean again. Lancaster states, "Only a human corpse is more ritually defiling than a leper"[5] A leper identified himself with ragged, torn clothes, unfixed hair, and a covered face. He would yell "unclean" if he wandered into the crowd to warn them of his proximity. A full restoration from the leprous condition was as difficult "as raising a person from the dead."[6]

Mosaic Law prohibited touching a leper to protect oneself from ceremonial defilement. From the time of the giving of the Law, there had been *no record* of any Jew who had been healed of leprosy. Miriam, Moses' sister, had been healed of leprosy before the completion of the Law. And though Naaman was healed of his leprosy, he was a Syrian Gentile, not a Jew. The power to heal a Jew of leprosy became seen as something rare, a healing that could only be done by the Messiah.[7]

So it is no accident that, after delivering the Sermon on the Mount, Jesus is confronted immediately by a leper seeking a miracle. "When he came down from the mountain, great crowds followed him. And behold, a leper came to him and knelt before him, saying, 'Lord, if you will, you can make me clean'" (Matt. 8:1–2). Luke, one of the Gospel writers and a doctor as well, described the man's appearance as "covered with leprosy" (Luke 5:12 NIV). Believing Jesus was the Anointed One (the Messiah) of God, the leper prefaced his request with "if you are willing," demonstrating his faith. He believed that Jesus, as the Messiah, could heal him when nobody else could.

It was also believed that the Messiah would absorb the diseases of Israel when he arrived.[8] The Babylonian Talmud records the name given to the coming Messiah: "The rabbis said: His name is 'the *leper scholar*,' as it is written [in Isaiah 53:4], Surely he hath borne our griefs, and carried our sorrows: yet we did esteem him a leper, smitten of God, and afflicted."[9] Interestingly, the Messiah came to be known as "the leper" because of his role in taking upon himself the diseases of the people. If you recall from our earlier look at John the Baptist and his questions to Jesus from prison, Jesus answered John the Baptist's disciples by saying, "lepers are cleansed" as validation of his messianic ministry.

When he touched the man with leprosy, Jesus absorbed the disease. Lancaster explains:

> Just as He intentionally took on Himself the leper's uncleanness in order to heal him, so too He intentionally took upon Himself human mortality in order to heal it. He intentionally took upon Himself our sin in order to cleanse us of it. He took upon Himself our guilt in

order to absorb us of it. He took upon Himself human uncleanness, allowing Himself to reach the highest level of ritual contamination by becoming a human corpse, in order to save us.[10]

Amazingly, instead of Jesus becoming unclean by his contact with the leper, the man becomes clean *and* Jesus remains clean. Jesus is not defiled by contact with disease; instead, he makes the defiled clean. This is something new.

What Kind of Healing Is This?

After Jesus touched the man, immediately, the leprosy left him. Then Jesus charged him to tell no one, but to "go and show yourself to the priest, and make an offering for your cleansing, as Moses commanded, for a proof to them" (Luke 5:13–14). Why would he instruct the man to reveal himself to the priesthood? Leviticus 13–14 outlines the protocol for someone claiming to be healed. The first step is to be quarantined for seven days. Fruchtenbaum explains what takes place next:

> If after seven days of investigation they were firmly convinced that the man had been a leper, had been healed of his leprosy, and the circumstances were proper, then, on the eighth day there would be a lengthy series of offerings. Altogether, there were four different offerings. First, there was a trespass-offering; second, a sin-offering; third, a burnt-offering; and fourth, a meal-offering. Then came the application of the blood of the trespass-offering upon the healed leper followed by the application of the blood of the sin-offering upon the healed leper. The ceremony would then end with the anointing of oil upon the healed leper.[11]

Although the protocol was laid out in Leviticus, there had been no time when it had been applied—until now. This instance would be the first time in Israel's history since the giving of the law that the priesthood would need to determine if someone had been healed of leprosy.[12] It was because of this healing that the religious leaders were forced to put together an investigative committee to determine whether Jesus was the long-awaited Messiah. Dwight Pentecost, in his book *The Words and the Works of Jesus Christ*, writes,

> The priest would make inquiry as to the means by which the man had been cleansed. This would give the cleansed man an occasion to present to the priest the evidence that the One who claimed to be Messiah had the power to cleanse lepers. This would make it necessary for the priests to investigate the claim, and the evidence would then be presented to the Sanhedrin for its investigation and final declaration.[13]

Up to this point in their investigation, the religious leaders had been open to Jesus's teaching. Nicodemus sought him by night for answers to his questions. But now, with the testimony of the leper, things were about to change. Immediately following the healing of the leper, Jesus is talking to a house filled with Pharisees and teachers of the Law, and he gives them something to talk about. While he is teaching, four men climb the roof of the building to lower their paralytic friend in front of Jesus.

At this point Jesus looks at the skeptical religious leaders and asks, "'Why do you question these things in your hearts? Which is easier, to say to the paralytic, "Your sins are forgiven," or to say, "Rise, take up your bed and walk"? But that you may know that the Son of Man has authority on earth to forgive sins'—he said to the paralytic—'I say to you, rise, pick up your bed, and go home'" (Mark 2:8–11).

The leaders know that the only one who can forgive sins is God. So Jesus is making a clear statement, asserting that he is God, one with the Father. Walking alongside the healed paralytic man with his bed in his hand are confused Pharisees and teachers of the Law. They are headed to Jerusalem with a full report for the Sanhedrin, trying to answer the question: Is this man the Messiah, or is he a blasphemer? From this point on, Jesus will be questioned repeatedly as they try to discern whether he should be accepted or rejected.

An Exorcism That Leads to a Confrontation

Though it may seem strange to us today, especially in the West, casting out a demon from a person was relatively commonplace in the first century.

History records instances of sages, rabbis, and Pharisees performing exorcisms. Jesus's disciples even report that after a short-term mission excursion "even the demons are subject to us in your name!" (Luke 10:17). However, there was one case that dumbfounded the religious leaders. Pharisaic Judaism proposed rules for casting out a demon, all of which required the person in question to respond to the commands of the exorcist. If a person was unable to speak, the typical process of exorcism was ineffective. The normal protocol for an exorcism was as follows:

1. The exorcist would establish communication with the demon, for when a demon speaks, he uses the vocal cords of the person he indwells.
2. After establishing communication with the demon, the exorcist would then have to find out the demon's name.
3. After finding out the demon's name, he could, by the use of that name, cast out the demon.[14]

Mark 5 records an example of Jesus employing this method of exorcism when he asks the demoniac, "What's your name?" It's interesting to note that up to this point in Jesus's ministry, no one has officially recognized him as the Messiah—not the Pharisees, scribes, elders, or priests. But now, he is identified—by a demon! When Jesus lands on shore after a boat trip across the lake, a demon-possessed man runs to him and shouts, "What have you to do with me, Jesus, Son of the Most High God?" (Mark 5:7). When Jesus asks the demon its name, the man responds, "My name is Legion, for we are many."

Again, as amazing as this sounds to our Western ears (and it is), for a Jewish audience of hardened skeptics, they could write this miracle off as the handiwork of a particularly skilled exorcist. It's amazing, yes, but not all that different from what other exorcists could do. But that's not the case with the miracle Jesus does in Matthew 12.

Dumb, Deaf, and Demon-Possessed

Matthew documents Jesus's encounter with a demon-possessed man, but in this case the man is unable to communicate. It's mentioned with an understated brevity, as if the Jewish audience of his book already knew the implications of what was about to happen. "Then a demon-oppressed man who was blind and mute was brought to him, and he healed him, so that the man spoke and saw" (Matt. 12:22).

Notice *how* Jesus found this man. The religious leaders brought him to Jesus to see what he would do. By going outside of the assigned rules for exorcism (since a man who could not speak was unserviceable by the standard rules of exorcism), Jesus performed the impossible—a task reserved for the Messiah—and cast out a demon without communication. The crowd was understandably "amazed, and said, 'Can this be the Son of David?'" (12:23). Their reaction makes sense, of course. They were wondering if this could be God's promised redeemer, the Messiah. Could they be witnessing the advent of the kingdom of God?

The Pharisees were obviously not happy. They were likely expecting Jesus to fail, proving that he was *not* the Messiah. So they terminated the enthusiasm of the multitudes quickly. Instead of revering Jesus as the Messiah, they reject him, accusing him of working with Satan. Mark writes, "And the scribes who came down from Jerusalem were saying, 'He is possessed by Beelzebub,' and 'by the prince of demons he casts out the demons'" (3:22). Perhaps they were afraid of losing power. In any case, the Pharisees tried to distract the crowd from Jesus's true identity. Matthew records their words as well: "When the Pharisees heard this, they said, 'The man drives out demons only by Beelzebub, the ruler of the demons'" (Matt. 12:24 CSB).

Jesus responds to their attempts to discredit him by explaining that it defies logic for the devil to oppose himself: "Knowing their thoughts, he said to them, 'Every kingdom divided against itself is laid waste, and no city or house divided against itself will stand. And if Satan casts out Satan, he is divided against himself. How then will his kingdom stand?'" (Matt. 12:25–26). "Why would Satan cast out himself?" asks Jesus. Their reasoning is sophomoric and unfeasible.

The Point of No Return: The Unpardonable Sin

At this point, Jesus mentions something that has given many believers trouble over the centuries. He pronounces what he refers to as the "unforgivable" or "unpardonable sin." In Matthew 12:31–32 (NIV) we read:

> "And so I tell you, every kind of sin and slander can be forgiven, but blasphemy against the Spirit will not be forgiven. Anyone who speaks a word against the Son of Man will be forgiven, but anyone who speaks against the Holy Spirit will not be forgiven, either in this age or in the age to come."

Many downtrodden believers have scheduled meetings with me through the years for counsel on this question, wondering if they had committed the unforgivable sin. "Pastor, I don't think God can forgive me because I did _____." And over the centuries, Christian theologians have suggested the unforgivable sin is unbelief, because without faith, one cannot be saved. Passages such as Hebrews 11 are often cited: "[W]ithout faith it is impossible to please God" (v. 6 NIV). I am persuaded, however, that this may not be what Jesus is referring to. Unbelief is merely the absence of belief. One doesn't commit the sin of unbelief; rather, he or she *remains* in it.

So what is the "unpardonable sin"? In context, I don't think Jesus is referring to the actions of an individual, but to the sin of an entire nation or people group, specifically, a sin committed by the people of Jesus's generation who rejected him as the Messiah of the Jewish people. In this sense, what Jesus is saying only applies to the Jewish people living during Jesus's earthly ministry.[15] But in a larger sense, it applies to anyone who chooses to reject Jesus as God's appointed savior.

To clarify why this is so, I want you to consider a question: Is there any sin that God cannot forgive? First John 1:9 (KJV) says that, "If we confess our sins, he is faithful and just to forgive us our sins and to cleanse us from all unrighteousness." Whether that sin be lying, cheating, divorce, addiction, greed, or sexual immorality, God forgives it if we repent and put our faith in Jesus. Jesus speaks of blasphemy against the Holy Spirit as an unforgivable sin, but again, what is this blasphemy he is referring to?

Blasphemy is simply speaking against God. The point Jesus is making is that since God the Father, God the Son, and God the Spirit are one, when we reject Jesus as the Messiah, as the majority of the Jewish people did, we cut ourselves off from any chance of salvation. So, when the Pharisees argue that "it is only by Beelzebub, the prince of demons, that this man casts out demons," they are blaspheming God by rejecting and denying the evidence that this is a work of God, done by God's anointed Messiah. When you deny God's Messiah, you sever yourself from the only means God has provided for a person to be saved.

Imagine while enjoying a cruise-ship vacation with your family, you witness a man fall overboard into the ocean. As the man treads water in the frigid waters below, the skipper runs to the bow of the boat with a ring buoy life preserver in his hand. Before he tosses it overboard, the man yells from the water, "I don't wear ring buoys. Do you have a life jacket?" Confused, the skipper screams back from the deck, "Sorry, this is the only life preserver I have!" Barely treading water from exhaustion, the man says, "I'll pass on the buoy. I only wear life jackets." By foolishly rejecting the salvation provided for him, this man has cut himself off from the only means he has to be saved. The sign-seeking first-century crowd responds to Jesus in a similar fashion.

Four times in Matthew 12 (emphasis mine) Jesus directs his comments toward the present generation, the Jewish people who are listening to him. These are the ones who have seen the signs, the evidence. They have rejected Jesus as the Messiah and have committed the unforgivable sin.

- Verse 39: "But he answered them, '*An evil and adulterous generation* seeks for a sign, but no sign will be given to it except the sign of the prophet Jonah.'"
- Verse 41: "The men of Nineveh will rise up at the judgment with *this generation* and condemn it, for they repented at the preaching of Jonah, and behold, something greater than Jonah is here."
- Verse 42: "The queen of the South will rise up at the judgment with *this generation* and condemn it, for she came from the ends of the earth to hear the wisdom of Solomon, and behold, something greater than Solomon is here."
- Verse 45: "Then it goes and brings with it seven other spirits more evil than itself, and they enter and dwell there, and the last state of that person is worse than the first. So also will it be with *this evil generation.*"

Their temporal punishment for rejecting God's Son will come at the hands of the Romans as the walls of the temple will come crumbling down in AD 70. The unpardonable sin they commit, according to Fruchtenbaum, is the "national rejection by Israel of the Messiahship of Jesus while he was present on earth, on the basis of His being demon possessed."[16]

Shift in the Ministry

As we read further in the Gospel and the ministry of Jesus continues, we note a further rejection of Jesus by the religious leaders and Jesus's own repudiation of them. This marks a noticeable shift in his ministry. Jesus's first parable comes on the heels of this encounter with the demon-possessed man, and this will now become his preferred method of teaching. Parabolic teaching was a common form of instruction for rabbis; yet Jesus provides a rationale for his shift in training method when his disciples ask him about it:

> "Why do you speak to them in parables?" And he answered them, "To you it has been given to know the secrets of the kingdom of heaven, but to them it has not been given. For to the one who has, more will be given, and he will have an abundance, but from the one who has not, even what he has will be taken away. This is why I speak to them in parables, because seeing they do not see, and hearing they do not hear, nor do they understand" (Matt. 13:10–13).

Matthew goes on to record, "All these things Jesus said to the crowds in parables; indeed, he said nothing to them without a parable. This was to fulfill what was spoken by the prophet: 'I will open my mouth in parables; I will utter what has been hidden since the foundation of the world'" (13:34–35). New Testament scholar Richard Hays argues that Jesus shifts his teaching to intentionally conceal his message at this point: "His [Jesus] teaching in parables produces a concealment of his message."[17] If we follow the chronology of Jesus's ministry, from this point on, the majority of his teaching to the crowd is with parables, but prior to this moment, his use of parables is virtually nonexistent. Jesus now shrouds the truth from the multitudes while disclosing it to the twelve, fulfilling what the psalmist predicted in Psalm 78:2 (NIV): "I will open my mouth with a parable; I will utter hidden things, things from of old."

"A parable, it seems," according to author Frank Kermode, "may proclaim a truth as a herald does, and at the same time conceal truth like an oracle."[18] Jesus, from this point forward, also "strictly charged the disciples to tell no one that he was the Christ" (Matt. 16:20). Not only did Jesus shroud his teaching; he explicitly prohibited his disciples from revealing his messianic identity.[19]

Miracles, as signs for the nation of Israel to believe, would also cease from this point forward, though Jesus promised to perform one more miracle for the people, what he calls "the sign of the prophet Jonah" (Matt. 12:39–40). In fact, this sign would be given to them twice, but the majority of the Jewish people would deny both instances. The first would come when Jesus raises Lazarus from the dead. But that miracle was only a shadow of the greater miracle to come, when God would raise Jesus from the dead. Sovereignly, both of these miracles, like the original time Jonah spent in the belly of the fish, occurred over a three-day period of time.

The Third Messianic Miracle: A Revelation That Results in Excommunication

The third messianic miracle was perhaps the most convincing of them all, and it is accompanied by the most detailed investigation by the religious leaders recorded in the Gospels. John tells us, "As he passed by, he saw a man blind from birth. And his disciples asked him, 'Rabbi, who sinned, this man or his parents, that he was born blind?' Jesus answered, 'It was not that this man sinned, or his parents, but that the works of God might be displayed in him. We must work the works of him who sent me while it is day; night is coming, when no one can work. As long as I am in the world, I am the light of the world'" (John 9:1–5).

The first of the two questions the disciples asked was whether the sin of the man's parents had led to his blindness. Over the years, the Jewish people had formulated a theology of personal sin and connected it to personal suffering. Exodus 34:6–7 explains how the generational sins of the fathers extend to the third and fourth generation. But the rabbis also cited Ezekiel 18:20 in their reasoning, which says, "The son shall not suffer for the iniquity of the father, nor the father suffer for the iniquity of the son," as a proof text for why sin would lead to death. Some also preached Psalm 89:30–32: "If his children forsake my law and do not walk according to my rules, if they violate my statutes and do not keep my commandments, then I will punish their transgression with the rod and their iniquity with stripes." They believed this was evidence that God would punish those who sinned, and that such punishment was evidence of prior sin.

But what about a man born with a condition like blindness? How could an individual commit a sin in his mother's womb and thus deserve God's judgment? The doctrine of reincarnation was denounced by the Jews, so it could not be the result of a "past life" problem. Instead, Pharisaic Judaism taught that a child could, in fact, commit a sin inside its mother's womb. During one's nine-month development, a child could demonstrate animosity or anger towards his mother, or he could kick his mother as he came into the world; therefore suffering the consequences of his own sin.[20] Jesus dismantles both of these assumptions by saying clearly, "It was not that this man sinned, or his parents, but that the works of God might be displayed in him" (John 9:3).

Mud Pies and New Eyes

"Having said these things," John continues, "he spit on the ground and made mud with the saliva. Then he anointed the man's eyes with the mud and said to him, 'Go, wash in the pool of Siloam' (which means Sent). So he went and washed and came back seeing" (John 9:6–7). In case you are wondering if this is some long-lost treatment for blindness, caking mud in a man's eyes is not the normal protocol for healing a blind person.

The context and setting of this miracle brings additional understanding to this incredible account. John 7:11 to John 10:21 records events in chronological order. Jesus travels to Jerusalem in John 7 to celebrate the Feast of Booths. As he is performing miracles in the two chapters before healing the blind man, he is joined by thousands of people who were in Jerusalem to celebrate with the rest of their Israelite brothers and sisters. Why is this significant? Because the worst possible time to send a blind man to the pool of Siloam would have been in the midst of the festival.

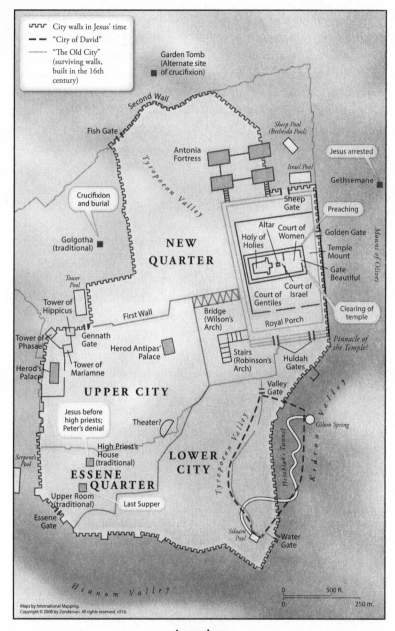

Jerusalem

For one, the city was crawling with people, packed with worshipers. Add to this the fact that the journey was roughly half a mile through the main thoroughfare. A blind man would be bumping into people along the way while simultaneously traversing a steep hill descending to the pool. The man would have fallen numerous times, all while walking with his eyes caked in mud, looking like a scene from a horror film with the damp concoction dripping down his cheeks.

But Jesus purposely directed the blind man to the pool, even in the midst of the festival. He served as a walking billboard of his grace.

The Interrogation of the Man

Because so many people would have witnessed this miracle, it immediately caught the attention of the interrogating religious leaders, who were dumbfounded by the man's healing. No one born blind had ever been healed before. The sages had reserved this miracle for the coming Messiah. Several messianic passages pointed to his coming and associated it with the healing of the blind:

> The LORD sets the prisoners free; *the LORD opens the eyes of the blind.* The LORD lifts up those who are bowed down; the LORD loves the righteous (Ps. 146:7–8, emphasis added).

> The wilderness and the dry land shall be glad; the desert shall rejoice and blossom like the crocus; it shall blossom abundantly and rejoice with joy and singing. The glory of Lebanon shall be given to it, the majesty of Carmel and Sharon. They shall see the glory of the LORD, the majesty of our God.
>
> Strengthen the weak hands, and make firm the feeble knees. Say to those who have an anxious heart, "Be strong; fear not! Behold, your God will come with vengeance, with the recompense of God. He will come and save you."
>
> *Then the eyes of the blind shall be opened*, and the ears of the deaf unstopped; then shall the lame man leap like a deer, and the tongue of the mute sing for joy (Isa. 35:1–6, emphasis added).

John didn't want us to miss the importance of this particular miracle either, so he mentions the word "blind" thirteen times in this chapter. Five of those times he notes that the man was "blind from birth" (see John 9:1, 2, 19, 20, and 32). Jesus had clearly performed something that only the Messiah was believed able to perform.

In an attempt to downplay the significance of what Jesus had done, the Pharisees responded, "This man is not from God, for he does not keep the Sabbath." But others said, "How can a man who is a sinner do such signs?" "Such signs," as the others said, refer to the three miracles we have just examined: the messianic miracles. This put the Pharisees in a precarious spot. They were intent on believing that Jesus was not the Messiah and was, instead, a blasphemer—a false prophet. Since it would have been ludicrous to argue that Jesus hadn't healed a blind man, they turned their interrogation to the one who was healed. They tried to prove that this man had not been born blind, but that he had acquired blindness sometime after birth. They turned to the man's parents with questions, as John wrote:

> The Jews did not believe that he had been blind and had received his sight until they called the parents of the man who had received his sight and asked them, "Is this your son, who you say was born blind? How then does he now see?" His parents answered, "We know that this is our son and that he was born blind. But how he now sees we do not know, nor do we know who opened his eyes. Ask him; he is of age. He will speak for himself." (His parents said these things because they feared the Jews, for the Jews had already agreed that if anyone should confess Jesus to be Christ, he was to be put out of the synagogue.) Therefore his parents said, "He is of age; ask him" (John 9:18–23).

Excommunication from the Community

The boy's parents were rightfully wary of answering the Pharisees directly, knowing that if they said something that displeased them, they could be blacklisted from the synagogue, the harshest level of excommunication anyone could experience in the community. Dissatisfied by their non-answer, they sought the man who had been healed.

So for the second time they called the man who had been blind and said to him, "Give glory to God. We know that this man is a sinner." He answered, "Whether he is a sinner I do not know. One thing I do know, that though I was blind, now I see." They said to him, "What did he do to you? How did he open your eyes?" He answered them, "I have told you already, and you would not listen. Why do you want to hear it again? Do you also want to become his disciples?" (John 9:24–27).

The frustration from this man is comical. We can hear the sarcasm ringing from his voice.

Attempting to demoralize the man, they say to him,

"You are his disciple, but we are disciples of Moses. We know that God has spoken to Moses, but as for this man, we do not know where he comes from." The man answered, "Why, this is an amazing thing! You do not know where he comes from, and yet he opened my eyes. We know that God does not listen to sinners, but if anyone is a worshiper of God and does his will, God listens to him. *Never since the world began has it been heard that anyone opened the eyes of a man born blind.* If this man were not from God, he could do nothing." They answered him, "You were born in utter sin, and would you teach us?" And they cast him out (John 9:28–34, emphasis mine).

Fruchtembaum describes the three levels of punishment practiced in the Jewish community:

In Pharisaic Judaism, there were three specific levels of excommunication. The first level is called the hezipah [or nezifah], which is simply a "rebuke" that lasted anywhere from seven to thirty days and was merely disciplinary. It could not be taken unless pronounced by three rabbis. That was the lowest level of excommunication. An example of the hezipah [or nezifah] is found in 1 Timothy 5:1. The second level is called the niddui, which means, "to cast out." It would last a minimum of thirty days and was disciplinary. A niddui had to be pronounced by ten rabbis. Examples of the second type are found in 2 Thessalonians 3:14–15 and Titus 3:10. The third and worst type of excommunication is called the cherem, which means to be "unsynagogued," to "be put out of the synagogue and to be separated from the Jewish community." The rest of the Jews considered someone under the cherem to be dead, and no communication or any kind of relationship whatsoever could be carried on with the person. This third type is found in 1 Corinthians 5:1–7 and Matthew 18:15–20.[21]

The third pronouncement, as with the case of the blind man, was equivalent to death. "A person who was put out of the synagogue could have no communication with anybody from the community from that day forward. It was similar to being dead."[22]

The healed man doesn't offer a theological discourse on the ins and outs of the means of salvation. He simply bears witness to what happened to him. Like the woman at the well in John 4, all he can do is share his testimony with the hearers. We should never underestimate the power of our own testimony.

The blind man's preaching platform was short-lived because the Pharisees took quick action to discredit him. They called him a man "born in utter sin." According to David Stern, author of the *Jewish New Testament Commentary*, the Hebrew word behind this phrase is *mamzer*, here translated as "utter sin," but a word that can also be rendered as "illegitimate son." Technically, it describes a person who is the offspring of a marriage prohibited by Leviticus 18. Jesus recruits a blind, lower-class, illegitimate beggar to school the religious elite of Israel in a lesson of messianic theology. The contrast in the text is further amplified when the two parties are placed side by side.

Having Eyes That Do Not See

The Pharisees had allowed their pride and pursuit of power to impede their understanding of the miracle and its implications. Where the man who was healed had been born physically blind, the Pharisees proved repeatedly that they were spiritually blind.

Jesus heard that they had cast him out, and having found him he said, "Do you believe in the Son of Man?" He answered, "And who is he, sir, that I may believe in him?" Jesus said to him, "You have seen him, and it is he who is speaking to you." He said, "Lord, I believe," and he worshiped him. Jesus said, "For judgment I came into this world, that those who do not see may see, and those who see may become blind." Some of the Pharisees near him heard these things, and said to him, "Are we also blind?" Jesus said to them, "If you were blind, you would have no guilt; but now that you say, 'We see,' your guilt remains" (John 9:35–41).

The blind man was physically blind, but was able to see both physically and spiritually after the miracle. On the other hand, while the Pharisees could see physically, they were spiritually blinded by their own denial of the messianic claims of Jesus.

There is one last point I have always found a bit puzzling. The blind man's answer to Jesus's question strikes me as odd. After all, how could he *not* know who had healed him? But if we look back at his day, it makes sense. His day had begun like any other—he probably stood at the same spot to beg for money at the same time every single day. Because of its proximity to the temple and the influx of visitors for the Feast of Booths, his begging cup may have been fuller than usual, but other than that, it was a normal day.

Then, over the sound of the crowd outside, he may have heard Jesus preaching in the temple, "As long as I am in the world, I am the light of the world." Shortly after hearing these words, a man kneels beside him and spits in the dirt. Sounds of mud caked together in a ball penetrated his ears before feeling the moist mud pressed into his eye sockets. The silence is broken with the words, "Go wash in the pool of Siloam."

His heart is pounding as his blood pressure rises. Although he is unable to visualize the face, he recognizes that voice—the man from the temple. This is the Nazarene's voice. The blind man is presented with a choice. Will he trust and obey him? Obeying this strange command would be laborious because of the thousands who had crowded the narrow streets of Jerusalem. But he takes a risk and embarks on the long journey down to the pool of Siloam without an escort. He repeatedly apologizes as the pilgrims he bumps into form a path for him to follow.

Upon arriving at the waters, he plunges his mud-covered face underneath. As the clay washes from his sockets, his darkness is pierced by a ray of hope. Penetrating eyes that had never until this point seen the light of day are now opened. When he emerges from the water, reality sets in. "I can see," he says to himself. Then louder, "I can see." Before long, the once blind man is yelling, "I CAN SEE! I was born blind, but now I CAN SEE!"

The account of the man born blind serves several purposes. It provides historical evidence that Jesus truly is the Messiah—but it does even more. Jesus was a Jewish rabbi who taught in pictures, not just in proofs. The healing of the man born blind is proof of who Jesus is, but it is also a picture of our salvation. This man was born into darkness, like the rest of mankind, but Jesus shined his light upon his darkened heart. Although he benefited from the miracle, it wasn't intended only for him. The man was healed and became a walking billboard, a trophy of God's grace. His pain would be the platform upon which he would preach the gospel. His suffering was the means by which God would draw others to himself.

Aren't you glad God does the same with us?

CHAPTER 8

A Colt-Riding, Table-Turning, Tree-Cursing Messiah

Jesus's entry into Jerusalem just before his trial, crucifixion, and death demonstrates God's sovereign control over these events.

> Now when they drew near to Jerusalem, to Bethpage and Bethany, at the Mount of Olives, Jesus sent two of his disciples and said to them, "Go into the village in front of you, and immediately as you enter it you will find a colt tied, on which no one has ever sat. Untie it and bring it. If anyone says to you, 'Why are you doing this?' say, 'The Lord has need of it and will send it back here immediately'" (Mark 11:1–3).

As we will see, Jesus reveals some of his deeper awareness of the divine plan when he gives the disciples detailed instructions to put into motion the events of his last earthly days. Over the events of the next few days, Jesus displays his complete control in showing us that nothing happens by accident in the economy of God. We are reminded of his words to his disciples in John 10:18: "No one takes [my life] from me, but I lay it down of my own accord. I have authority to lay it down, and I have authority to take it up again."

Humbly Fulfilling Prophecy

Let's take a closer look at the request Jesus makes for a young colt. First, we can assume that the animal Jesus speaks about in this passage was not there—it was clearly out of sight. If not, Jesus would have simply pointed to the colt and asked for it: "You see that donkey over there. Bring the animal to me." Matthew adds that there was a mother donkey with her colt, which heightens the drama. Here we have a young animal that likely does not want to leave its mother. Further, Mark records that the colt had never been ridden before.

Why does Jesus ask for a colt? Matthew points out that this is to fulfill a prophecy. He writes: "This took place to fulfill what was spoken by the prophet, saying, 'Say to the daughter of Zion, "Behold, your king is coming to you, humble, and mounted on a donkey, and on a colt, the foal of a beast of burden"'" (21:4–5). The phrase "daughter of Zion" refers to Mount Zion, the city's highest and most prominent hill. The "daughter" of Zion is a reference to the city of Jerusalem, a picture of the city as a lovely maiden whose children are her inhabitants. Five hundred years earlier, the prophet Zechariah predicted that the people of Jerusalem would worship the Messiah as their king. However, he would not come as expected, but would arrive in humble circumstances mounted on a donkey (Zech. 9:9).

All four Gospels make note of the town where Jesus stopped before entering Jerusalem: When they reached *Bethpage*, Jesus sent two disciples into Jerusalem (emphasis mine, see Matt. 21:1; Mark 11:1; Luke 19:29; and John 12:1). This town is at the city limits of Jerusalem, just two miles over the hill. Fleming narrates in layman's terms what happens here, "When Jesus got to a black and white sign that said 'Jerusalem City Limits, Elevation 2,700 feet, Population 80,000,' he leaned on that sign and waited while two disciples went to get the donkey."[1] Clearly, Jesus is entering the city with a purpose. He has come to fulfill prophecy.

Yes, it is an unlikely entrance for a king. We might envision chariots pulled by white pedigree horses entering the holy city with trumpets blasting, and a procession of people following him. Instead of riding into town seated on a horse, ready for battle, Jesus entered on a colt, signifying peace. His choice of a ride also reenacts Solomon's entry into Jerusalem. In 1 Kings 1:38–40, David orders that his son Solomon ride a donkey before he is anointed king of Israel. Just as Solomon, the "son of David," came to Jerusalem before his anointing as king, Jesus enters the town as the final "son of David."

The entire life of Jesus is a witness to his humility. We've already seen that the creator of the universe was not born in a castle but in a cave. His announcement went out to shepherds, the lowest society class in Israel, slightly above the tax collectors in the minds of the people. But we must never mistake his meekness for weakness. Every choice to be humble was intentional.

The Jewish sage Rabbi Jochanan suggested, "Wherever you find the greatness of the Holy One, blessed be He, there you find His humility. This is written in the Torah, repeated in the Prophets, and stated a third time in the Writings."[2] Joachanan identified seven scriptures where God's affection for and favor towards the humble is connected directly to his power.

1. Psalm 138:6: "For though the LORD is high, he regards the lowly, but the haughty he knows from afar."
2. Isaiah 57:15: "For thus says the One who is high and lifted up, who inhabits eternity, whose name is Holy: 'I dwell in the high and holy place, and also with him who is of a contrite and lowly spirit, to revive the spirit of the lowly, and to revive the heart of the contrite.'"
3. Isaiah 66:1–2: "Thus says the LORD: 'Heaven is my throne, and the earth is my footstool; what is the house that you would build for me, and what is the place of my rest? All these things my hand has made, and so all these things came to be, declares the LORD. But this is the one to whom I will look: he who is humble and contrite in spirit and trembles at my word.'"
4. Psalm 10:18: "O LORD, . . . You will incline your ear to do justice to the fatherless and the oppressed."
5. Psalm 68:4–5: "Sing to God, sing praises to his name; lift up a song to him who rides through the deserts; his name is the

LORD; exult before him! Father of the fatherless and protector of widows is God in his holy habitation."

6. Psalm 146:5: "Blessed is he whose help is the God of Jacob, whose hope is in the LORD his God."

7. Deuteronomy 10:17–18: "For the LORD your God is the God of gods and Lord of lords, the great, the mighty, and the awesome God, who is not partial and takes no bribe. He executes justice for the fatherless and the widow, and loves the sojourner, giving him food and clothing."

In light of this consistent Old Testament witness, passages like the one we find in the New Testament letter of James make good sense: "God resists the proud but gives grace to the humble." Pride is not fitting to those who approach God because it is not fitting attire for being in the presence of a king. The greatest form of humility is our repentance, and when we turn away from our sin and admit our need for God's forgiveness, he clothes us in robes of righteousness—his own clothing to cover our sinful shame.

Complete Authority

Although Jesus was meek and mild, he wasn't weak. He could call down at any moment "twelve legions of angels from heaven" (Matt. 26:53). Just as we earlier looked at Matthew as the most Hebraic of the Gospel writers, the Gospel writer Mark was the one who focused on communicating Jesus's authority over all things.

In Mark 1:13, we see Mark highlighting Jesus's authority over the animals. Mark is careful to tell us, "And he was in the wilderness forty days, being tempted by Satan. And he was with the wild animals." The word "with" in the language of the New Testament implies being in harmony or communion with. Jesus had no need to fear wild animals because he was in harmony with them as a direct result of his authority over them. Not only does he have authority over the animals, but Jesus also has authority over the angels. Mark continues by telling us, "and the angels were ministering to him." Normally, man was made lower than the angels, but in this case the angels are the ones ministering to Jesus (c.f. Ps. 8:5). Both the animals and the angels serve this man. Will we?

In Mark 1:22 we read about Jesus's authority as a teacher: "And they were astonished at his teaching, for he taught them as one who had authority, and not as the scribes." Jesus also demonstrates his authority over sickness, as we see in Mark 1:30–31 (CSB): "Simon's mother-in-law was lying in bed with a fever, and they told him about her at once. So he went to her, took her by the hand, and raised her up. The fever left her, and she began to serve them." He even had authority over nature and the demonic, as we read in Mark 1:34: "And he healed many who were sick with various diseases, and cast out many demons. And he would not permit the demons to speak, because they knew him."

Jesus displayed his authority over defilement when he healed a skin disease, in Mark 1:41–42 (CSB): "Moved with compassion, Jesus reached out his hand and touched him. 'I am willing,' he told him. 'Be made clean.' Immediately the leprosy left him, and he was made clean." Jesus displayed authority to forgive sins, something only God could do, in Mark 2:10–11 (CSB): "'But so that you may know that the Son of Man has authority on earth to forgive sins'—he told the paralytic—'I tell you: get up, take your mat, and go home.'" He proved he was Lord over the Sabbath in Mark 2:27–28 (CSB): "Then he told them, 'The Sabbath was made for man and not man for the Sabbath. Therefore, the Son of Man is Lord even of the Sabbath.'"

Finally, Jesus could extend his authority to others. We see this when he gives his disciples delegated authority to cast out demons and preach in Mark 3:14–15 (CSB): "He also appointed twelve—whom he also named apostles—to be with him, to send them out to preach, and to have authority to drive out demons."

Mark's cumulative case for the authority of Jesus points us to one truth: Jesus does things with the authority of God. We are left to conclude that this man *is* God, because only God possessed sole authority to heal, forgive sins, set people free from Satan, and to disseminate that authority to others. In the Old Testament, Job learned this lesson when he confronted God face to face after enduring great personal hardship. God relentlessly drove his point home in the final chapters of Job, reminding Job that there is a distinct difference between the Creator and his creation. When God is finished with his speech, Job can only respond with these words, "I know that You can do anything and no plan of yours can be thwarted" (Job 42:2 CSB).

Could This Be the Son of David?

Jesus's entrance into Jerusalem is not a quiet affair. He is met by crowds of people who begin spreading garments on the road. According to 2 Kings 9:13, it was not uncommon for people to lay their garments in the road for a leader to ride over. They did this as a sign of their respect and to indicate their submission to his authority.[3] Additionally, branches were cut and spread onto the garments that lined the streets. John 12:13 names the branches as "palm branches," which were symbols of salvation for the Jews. And salvation was the word on their minds and on their lips. Collectively, the multitude cried out, "Hosanna to the Son of David; blessed is He who comes in the name of the Lord, Hosanna in the highest!"

The Hebrew word *hosanna* is a plea for salvation: "Save us now!" The people were at the right place, but for the wrong reasons, participating in the wrong feast day. Palm branches, cries of *hosanna*, and shouts of "blessed is he who comes in the name of the Lord" are all elements associated with the Feast of Tabernacles.[4] But this was the Passover, a celebration of a different kind.

The title the people spoke, "Son of David," was a common messianic title. It indicates that the people believed Jesus to be the Messiah they had been waiting for.[5] The shouts of *hosanna* allude to Psalm 118:25–26: "Save us, we pray, O LORD! O LORD, we pray, give us success! Blessed is he who comes in the name of the Lord! We bless you from the house of the Lord."

Simply by saying *hosanna*, the people were declaring to God that they were tired of their oppression, through with their corrupt leaders. They were asking for liberty, for victory. Unfortunately, the bystanders were not interested in salvation from their own sins, but in salvation from the Romans. What the crowds missed was an understanding of why Jesus had come. He had not come to offer them a military victory over Rome. He came to establish a heavenly kingdom on earth and to conquer the age-old enemies of Adam's children—sin, death, hell, and the grave. Jesus was fighting a cosmic battle, bringing rebellious children back into the family of God by making peace with God, not war on Israel's current national enemies.

In case we are tempted to judge them for their short-sighted focus on freedom from Rome, we should consider how common it is to look for human leaders to deliver us from our own problems. A quick look at American politics will show that we are no different from the Jews in this regard. We would be wise to refrain from throwing proverbial stones at the Jewish people for their misunderstanding of Jesus's ministry! In fact, they had good reason to think the way they did. Many prophecies of the Old Testament point to a messianic time of vengeance aimed at Israel's enemies. The people were understanding the scriptures correctly; the Messiah will come at some point to bring judgment. But he had another mission to accomplish first. God's *own people* needed to be saved from the consequences of their sin.

Cleansing the Temple

The first act of Jesus as he enters Jerusalem during Passover week drives home the reality that Jesus will upset the expectations of the people. Rather than confront the Roman occupiers, Jesus immediately heads to the temple to clean house. In Mark's account of Jesus cleansing the temple, the event is sandwiched between two prophetic events involving a fig tree. As Western Christians, we often miss the significance of these events when we read this account.

Figs are harvested from mid-August to mid-October in Israel. After this, the tree's branches remain undeveloped for the remainder of the winter until springtime, when green buds start to swell again on the branches. The buds sprout around March or April. Interestingly, the little figs grow on the branches before the leaves do. So if you spot a fig tree loaded with leaves, you can expect it to be packed with little fig buds. When Jesus spotted the fig tree in Mark 11, he noticed that it was filled with leaves, and he expected to find fruit accompanying its apparent health.

Instead, he found a tree covered in leaves with no fruit! Jesus cursed the tree because he was hungry and the tree didn't provide what it promised, but his words and actions are prophetic, illustrating a deeper, spiritual reality. The account serves as a visual parable to portray what was happening to the nation of Israel.

Picture the sprawling temple in Jerusalem as a fig tree—full of signs of what should have been fruit, but instead, there is nothing. It is all empty appearance with nothing that can satisfy spiritual hunger. Despite its religious commerce and constant activity, the temple was filled with hypocrisy. Jesus was likely referencing his earlier teaching from the Sermon on the Mount: "You will recognize them [false prophets] by their fruits. . . . A healthy tree cannot bear bad fruit, nor can a diseased tree bear good fruit. Every tree that does not bear good fruit is cut down and thrown into the fire. Thus you will recognize them by their fruits" (Matt. 7:16–20).

We should also keep in mind that this was not Jesus's first time in the temple. Three years earlier, at the beginning of his ministry, he had also entered the temple, made a whip of cords, and drove out the corruption that had taken root there (see John 2:13–22). Now, at the end of his earthly ministry, he returns to do the same thing. Nothing has changed.

The first-century temple was divided into four areas. The largest of the four sections, the court of the Gentiles, was designated for merchants to sell sheep and doves for sacrificial offerings, as well as to exchange foreign currency to the Hebrew shekel. Offering sheep and doves for purchase was common. Not everybody in first-century Jerusalem raised sheep or doves at their homes, but all were expected to offer a sacrifice to God. So the idea was simple: allow these people to pay money—a sacrifice, no doubt—in exchange for an animal to fulfill the requirements of the law.

Trouble in the Temple

The Sadducees monitored this area of the temple, which turned out to be a crucial inlet of financial gain for them and for the high priest. The corruption of the priesthood was a stain upon the people of Israel. Traditionally, the high priest was selected by drawing lots among the Levites. When Herod came to power, he ignored the biblical protocol and appointed the new high priest himself. However, corruption began years earlier, in 172 B.C., when Antiochus Epiphanes illegally appointed Jason to the role of high priest.[6] From that time forward, the position was bought with bribes from wealthy Sadducean families who agreed to keep peace with Rome in exchange for wealth from the temple tithes and animal sales, which they had increased exponentially.

The priestly family in control during the time of Jesus was the house of Annas. He served for nine years and then appointed his son-in-law Caiaphas. Much like a Mafia crime family, the family of Annas was crooked and corrupt. Annas himself was the Godfather who oversaw the buying and selling of animals for sacrifice that, unsurprisingly, all came from his herd. Also, his family controlled the money changing in the temple with "Booths of Annas," as they were known. Annas turned the temple into a very lucrative enterprise. His sons were the treasurers, and they assisted in hoarding riches from visitors coming to Jerusalem for the three pilgrimage feasts. Fruchtenbaum describes the perversion in the temple during the first century:

> According to the Mosaic Law you had the perfect right to bring your own sacrifice into the temple compound. However, it had to be without spot or blemish, and therefore it had to be inspected by the priesthood before it could be sacrificed. If you chose to bring your own sacrifice the priests, who were working on behalf of Annas, would simply find something wrong with your sacrifice. You had two options. You could go back home and get another one, and if you lived near Jerusalem that would be possible. If you lived up in Galilee, which was a three-day journey, six days round trip, that would not be practical. So in one part of the temple compound they had these stalls erected with sacrificial animals already stamped with the Sadducees stamp of approval. You could purchase your sacrifice from them and they were sold at highly inflated prices. And the money went into the pockets of Annas and his family.[7]

On top of this corruption, the overseers demanded a temple tax of half of a shekel from every traveler, not to mention the markup of the exchange rate for those from different nations. The poor were not excluded from the effects of the corruption, either. Leviticus 12 required the poor to offer a dove. In the village, one could purchase a dove for, say five cents, but if you bought one in the temple it would have been the equivalent of a four-dollar markup. John MacArthur writes,

> It was a system of perversion, prostitution, travesty, extortion, monopoly, just a horrendous operation of noise and traffic. It was anything but a house of prayer. Jesus went in and just ripped into all of this. He started driving out the people buying and selling, the people bringing in their

animals and taking them out. He overturned the tables. He started
kicking over stools on which the money changers sat, thrown over
their tables, scattering their money everywhere, debris flying all over
this massive courtyard with hundreds of thousands of people in it and
throwing over the stools that the dove sellers were sitting on. Every crook,
every exploiter of the poor, and all the rotten Sadducees and priests
that oversaw the operation fell under His attention and His authority.[8]

If disrupting commerce wasn't enough, Jesus attacked the crooked
infrastructure directly by saying, "Is it not written: 'My house will be
called a house of prayer for all nations'? But you have made it 'a den of
robbers'" (Mark 11:17 NIV). With these words, Jesus was engaging in the
rabbinical technique we looked at in an earlier chapter known as "stringing
pearls." His reference to a "house of prayer for all nations" comes from
Isaiah 56:7, where God extends salvation to those formerly excluded from
it, including the Gentiles, the exiles, and the foreigners. Jesus was saying
that the temple did not belong to Israel to do as it pleased; it existed as
a witness for all the nations. Moreover, the temple had been denigrated
into a "den of robbers," a reference to Jeremiah 7:11.

With this reference, Jesus was saying that the sanctuary, supposedly
a place sanctified by God, had instead become a hideout for bandits and
thieves. The prophet Jeremiah had pointed out that people were stealing,
murdering, committing adultery, swearing falsely, and offering up worship
to false gods in the house of the Lord. Jesus effectively sealed his fate with
this pronouncement, for the "chief priests and the scribes heard it and
were seeking a way to destroy him, for they feared him, because all the
crowd was astonished at his teaching" (Mark 11:18).

Dead Trees

The day after his confrontation with the leaders in the temple, Jesus led
his disciples by the same path and stopped at the same fig tree he had
previously cursed. "As they passed by in the morning, they saw the fig tree
withered away to its roots. And Peter remembered and said to him, 'Rabbi,
look! The fig tree that you cursed has withered'" (Mark 11:20–21). In case
we miss the significance of this incident, Mark is careful to tell us that

the tree has *withered from the roots*, a sign of the totality of its destruction. A tree full of leaves just a day earlier is now withered and sagging.

The disciples would not have forgotten that visual lesson, and it effectively serves as a prophetic foreshadowing of the coming destruction of the temple. Jesus promised his disciples, speaking of the destruction of the temple, that "there will not be left here one stone upon another that will not be thrown down" (Mark 13:2). His point was clear: Mere activity does not equate to acceptable worship. God had rejected the worship of the temple system, because something more was needed.

Today, as Western Christians, we can still glean wisdom from this encounter. Though we are not Jews worshiping in the Jerusalem temple, we often are guilty of going through the motions in our worship. But Jesus reminds us that no matter how spiritual we may appear, our outward activity does not always reveal the heart of an individual. The leadership of Israel could speak the right words, but their hearts were miles away from God. May the same not be said of us!

God despises actions without integrity and activity without worship, both of which were taking place in his house.

Spotless Lamb of God

For us today, it is difficult to fully grasp the hornet's nest Jesus stirred up that day when he came to the temple. Imagine walking into the Vatican in Rome in broad daylight, flipping pews, throwing tables, and speaking judgment against the papacy. What kind of response would you get? Probably a one-way trip to a Roman penitentiary. So if we wish to understand the hatred and the intense barrage of questioning Jesus was about to endure, we need to grasp the context of this week and the events happening in Jerusalem.

First, we need to realize that it was the week of Passover, one of the busiest times of the year.

The city was busy preparing for this feast. From the tenth day of Nisan until the fourteenth day, each family would set aside a lamb for careful observation by the priesthood to determine if it was without spot or blemish for sacrifice. (Nisan was the first month of the Jewish calendar, normally April, when Israel left the bondage of the Egyptians.) If the animal turned out to be an acceptable offering, it was slain on the afternoon of the fourteenth of Nisan before the celebration officially began on the night of the fifteenth (see Exod. 12:3–6).

At the end of chapter 11, John records Jesus's arrival to Bethany, a suburb of Jerusalem, on the eighth of Nisan, two days before the selection of the Passover lamb: "Now the Passover of the Jews was at hand, and many went up from the country to Jerusalem before the Passover to purify themselves. They were looking for Jesus and saying to one another as they stood in the temple, 'What do you think? That he will not come to the feast at all?' Now the chief priests and the Pharisees had given orders that if anyone knew where he was, he should let them know, so that they might arrest him. Six days before the Passover, Jesus therefore came to Bethany, where Lazarus was, whom Jesus had raised from the dead" (John 11:55—12:1).

Jesus spends a night in Bethany with his closest friends, Lazarus, Mary, and Martha. The following day he embarks on his final ascent to Jerusalem. On the way from Bethany, he passes through Bethpage, where he instructed his disciples to find him the unridden colt for his ride into Jerusalem (Mark 11:2). This is on the ninth of Nisan. Finally, on the day of his entry, he is received by the people. As the true Passover lamb, "Jesus was set aside on the tenth day of the month with the Triumphal Entry. The purpose of the Triumphal Entry was not so much to present Himself as King of the Jews, for He had already done that. The purpose was to set Himself aside as the Lamb of God. From the tenth day of the month until the fourteenth day of the month, He was tested by four groups: the Pharisees, Sadducees, Scribes, and Herodians."[9]

Over the course of the next few days, God's Passover lamb will be inspected and tested. But notice who questions Jesus:

1. Priest and Elders: Mark 11:28, "By what authority do you do these things?"
2. Pharisees and Herodians: Mark 12:13–17, "Is it lawful to give tribute to Caesar?"
3. Sadducees: Mark 12:18–27, "What will marriage be like in heaven?"
4. Pharisees: Mark 12:28–34, "Of all the commandments what is the greatest?"

David Daube describes the type of questions that are asked here, all of which were common arrangements of rabbinic discourse: "a legal question (*health*); a vulgar question (*bout*) designed to ridicule a belief; a question of principles of conduct (*derech eretz*); and a question based on a narrative interpretation (*aggadah*)."[10] After every scrupulous question, Jesus passed their exams to prove he was the acceptable Passover sacrifice. The interrogators even affirm his identity: "And after that no one dared to ask him any more questions" (Mark 12:34). Jesus proved to be without spot or blemish. As Paul would later concur in his letter to the Corinthians, "For Christ, our Passover lamb, has been sacrificed" (1 Cor. 5:7).

Jesus's death had to take place on Passover, according to the Jewish calendar, for him to be our Passover lamb. Otherwise, there would be no acceptable atonement. Attempts to kill him prior to his time were premature, as he reminded his mother at a wedding early in his ministry, "My hour has not yet come" (John 2:4). In John 7, he also explained to his brothers, "My time has not yet come" (John 7:6). Again, he explains to his disciples as they prepare for Passover, "My appointed time is near" (Matthew 26:18 NIV). A day sooner would be too early. A day later would be too late. Jesus died at the exact moment in time the Father predestined for him to be killed as an acceptable sacrifice for our sin.

Did an Italian Painter Hijack the Jewish Passover Meal?

Most Christians have some familiarity with the connection between Jesus's death and the Passover celebration. But some of our understanding of this feast has been influenced by non-Jewish traditions and interpretations.

One of the most well-known and widely recognized religious paintings in the Western world is Leonardo da Vinci's *The Last Supper*. His work of art has captivated the minds and hearts of Christians for centuries. Da Vinci devoted three years of his life (from 1495 to 1498) to this masterpiece during the Italian Renaissance period. It is intended to depict the Last Supper, particularly the moment after Jesus announced that one of the Twelve would betray him (John 13:21). It displays Jesus in the middle of the table, flanked on both sides by his twelve apostles. James is immediately on his right; John is immediately on his left. Judas is seated next to John.

The work has been scrutinized by everyone from pastors to artists and mathematicians for its symbolism, theological insights, and psychological complexity. In May of 1999, an effort was made to restore the painting to its original glory after being damaged by exposure over the years of being displayed, and it was completed beautifully. *The Last Supper* remains one of the most important paintings of the Renaissance and, perhaps, of human history.

As a child, I can still remember gazing at this picture as it hung in the living room of my grandparents' home. Sadly, however, the painting is not based on cultural realities about Jesus or the Last Supper. Da Vinci was an Italian artist and mathematician, but not a biblical theologian. We certainly cannot fault him for painting certain elements of the final meal inaccurately. My point is not to criticize the choices he made in his painting—after all, every artist takes liberty to interpret what he chooses to paint. What we need to be careful of is allowing a popular depiction of a biblical event to color our perception of the truth. We face a similar challenge with movies about Jesus or other biblical characters today. They reflect an interpretation of events, and not all of them are informed by insights into the Jewish culture of Jesus.

So let's revisit the events leading up to the Last Supper and see how the details of the meal compare to the traditions captured in the famous painting by Leonardo da Vinci. The disciples knew that they would need to find a place to eat the traditional Passover meal, but they didn't know what kind of plan Jesus had in mind. So they asked him:

> "Where will you have us go and prepare for you to eat the Passover?" And he [Jesus] sent two of his disciples and said to them, "Go into the city, and a man carrying a jar of water will meet you. Follow him, and wherever he enters, say to the master of the house, 'The Teacher says, Where is my guest room, where I may eat the Passover with my disciples?' And he will show you a large upper room furnished and ready; there prepare for us" (Mark 14:12–15).

Here is where we need to stop for a moment. Does this detail strike you as unusual? If it doesn't, it should. In a crowded city with hundreds of thousands of pilgrims arriving for Passover, the disciples need to find a man with a water jug and follow him. We might think this an impossible task, but we miss something that would have stood out to the disciples. You see, men didn't carry water jugs; women did. Think of Rebekah in the Old Testament or the Samaritan woman in the New Testament who were at the well to draw water. You don't typically find men drawing water with them. In fact, it was considered embarrassing for a man to carry a water jug in public, as Robert Boyd explains in his book *World's Bible Handbook*:

> The custom of carrying water in the Holy Land is ancient. However, it was and is the woman's job to go to the well or spring with a pitcher and carry water to [her] home. When the Gibeonites deceived Joshua (9:3–27), he judged them and made them servants to chop wood and carry water. This punishment may seem mild to us, but how humiliating it was to a man—carrying water in public—a woman's job! This helps us to better understand how easy it was for the disciples to identify the man carrying the water pot when Jesus sought an upper room [in which] to eat the Passover. It was not a question of seeking one man out of many carrying a water pot—this man would stick out above all others, in that he alone would be carrying one. A man may carry a water skin, but seldom does one carry a water pot.[11]

Another explanation for this unusual situation is that the man was an Essene. James Fleming suggests that "a man carrying a water pot would have been an Essene taking water to the Essene quarter just inside the Gate of the Essenes. . . . The Essenes would most likely have gladly allowed one of their guest chambers to be used by this popular Galilean rabbi who was a relative of John the Baptist."[12] Regardless, it should stand out as somewhat countercultural. In the end, while it's unusual, we don't know the reason why the man was carrying a jug of water or who he was.

Little did this man know, of course, that he would be hosting the God of the universe and his disciples for Passover. I sometimes wonder what that jug of water was used for. Maybe the man served his guests water to drink after a long day walking in the Judean heat. Or maybe it was the water Jesus poured into the basin to clean the disciple's feet on the eve of Passover. While it is only speculation, when I think about these unknown, secondary characters in the story of Jesus, it teaches me that Jesus can use anyone at any time to accomplish his plans. Even if all he asks us to do is carry a water jug.

Leonard da Vinci's *The Last Supper*

After walking around the city and finding the man with the jug, the disciples set up for the supper in the upper room. They would likely be coming in right at dusk to celebrate the Passover meal at its traditional time. The celebration began when the sun went down because the Jewish people counted their days from sundown to sundown. Mark tells us the time: "And when it was *evening*, he came with the twelve" (Mark 14:17, emphasis mine). Later, when Judas leaves the gathering to betray Jesus, we learn that this happens at night (John 13:30).

This is where we find the first major discrepancy with the painting of the Last Supper.[13] If you notice the windows at the back of the painting, you see a blue sky on a sunny day with beautiful rolling hills in the distance. The light from this scene washes in and floods the room with brilliant afternoon sun. This is wonderful for lighting a canvas, but it does not match with the events the painting is supposed to depict. Not only do the windows reveal striking afternoon light, but they are framed by peaked mountains surrounded by green grass. It's a scene reminiscent of an Italian mountain range, not a scene from downtown Jerusalem.

Another discrepancy in the painting is the menu for the dinner. In the painting, the table is lined with puffy French bread and grilled fish. Da Vinci probably incorporated fish into the meal because the Christians used it as a symbol for Christ. Unfortunately, this was not the meal for the Passover. The Jews ate roasted lamb with unleavened bread and bitter herbs. In addition, the arrangement of the table in the painting is culturally inaccurate. It depicts the men seated behind a banquet table on benches, something you would find in a formal Roman dining hall. But first-century Jews would not have sat erect behind a linear table to eat. They would have reclined on cushions, lying on their sides next to a low table called a *triclinium*, a word that translates as *three couches*. This U-shaped table would sit roughly a foot off the ground, and those eating would lie beside it to eat their meal (see image on page 180).

Large cushions surrounded the table, and the middle section was left open for serving the food and entertainment. Each guest would recline on his left side with his legs protruding away from him so that his right hand was free to pick up pieces of food from the table. Because their legs extended away from the table, servants could wash their feet as they enjoyed the meal. In John 13, the text states that "[Jesus] rose from supper. He laid aside his outer garments, and taking a towel, tied it around his waist. Then he poured water into a basin and began to wash the disciples' feet and to wipe them with the towel that was wrapped around him" (John 13:4–5). The disciples were already seated at the table and were partaking of the meal when Jesus began washing their feet.

This style of eating is also found in Luke 7:36–38, when Jesus eats at the home of a Pharisee:

> One of the Pharisees asked him to eat with him, and he went into the Pharisee's house and reclined at table. And behold, a woman of the city, who was a sinner, when she learned that he was reclining at table in the Pharisee's house, brought an alabaster flask of ointment, and standing behind him at his feet, weeping, she began to wet his feet with her tears and wiped them with the hair of her head and kissed his feet and anointed them with the ointment.

Again, if we wish to picture the scene as it happened, we should understand that the penitent woman would have approached Jesus from behind to anoint his feet. His legs were extending behind him as he reclined at the table.

Another cultural detail that we might miss is the position held by the host of a traditional Jewish dinner. The host of the banquet did not sit in the middle of the table as Leonardo da Vinci has portrayed Jesus in his painting. He would sit in the spot second from the right.[14] The person immediately to the host's left was the honored guest, and the person to his right would have been a confidant or close friend. The image below depicts a more likely seating order for the supper.

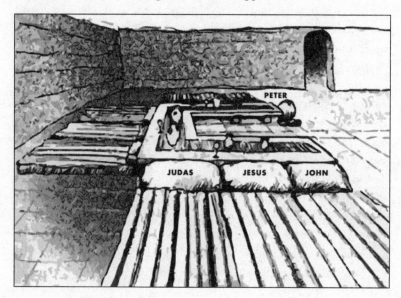

Possible Table Seating Arrangement at the Last Supper

The servant who had easy access to replenish drinks or food throughout the evening would occupy the final seat closest to the door. Peter may have sat in this position across from Jesus, and this could explain why Peter had to communicate to John with hand signals during the dinner.

> After saying these things, Jesus was troubled in his spirit, and testified, "Truly, truly, I say to you, one of you will betray me." The disciples looked at one another, uncertain of whom he spoke. One of his disciples, whom Jesus loved, was reclining at table at Jesus' side, so Simon Peter *motioned to him* to ask Jesus of whom he was speaking (John 13:21–24, emphasis mine).

If Peter was in the servant's seat, Jesus was likely teaching Peter, the rock on whom he would build his church, humility by placing him there. Jesus stated in Luke 22:26–27, "[L]et the greatest among you become as the youngest, and the leader as one who serves. For who is the greater, one who reclines at table or one who serves? Is it not the one who reclines at table? But I am among you as the one who serves." Jesus had also taught his disciples that the last will be the first in Matthew 19:30. Everyone, including Peter, would have received and understood the servant-leader lesson that Jesus was communicating.

The Betrayal of Judas

As the supper progresses, we should take note of what John does when he inquires about Jesus's betrayer. "Then, leaning back on Jesus' breast, he said to Him, 'Lord, who is it?'" (John 13:25 NKJV). This may sound like a strange position to a Western audience. If a man today were seated upright in a chair at a banquet table, leaning over to his left and putting his head on another man's chest would not only be uncomfortable; it would be quite awkward! But if we understand the cultural form of eating a meal at that time, this makes sense. When John leaned over to Jesus and rested his head on his chest to ask a question, it may have been an attempt to avoid attracting attention to the inquiry. It was a touchy subject, after all (and Peter was clearly curious about it).

We can be relatively sure that we know where Judas was sitting. We can assume he occupied the spot reserved for the honored guest because he was able to dip his hand into the same dish as Jesus. Matthew 26:23–24 records this for us when Jesus says to his disciples: "He who has dipped his hand in the dish with me will betray me. The Son of Man goes as it is written of him, but woe to that man by whom the Son of Man is betrayed!" Notice that Jesus is using strong and persuasive language here, almost as if he was trying to persuade Judas to rethink what he was about to do by giving him the choice seat of honor.

Some have suggested that Judas was actually a good man who became disillusioned along the way. I've heard some teach that Judas was a misguided, card-carrying political zealot who grew impatient with Jesus because he hadn't started an insurrection against the Roman oppression.

And he would not be the only one to misunderstand the ministry of Jesus. Most of the disciples Jesus chose were zealous for the return of the Messiah, and they expected the Messiah to come with vengeance and destruction before restoring peace to Israel. Anything less than a full upheaval of the Roman occupation would not be sufficient. They knew that blood would need to be shed to usher in the kingdom of God. They just assumed it would be Roman blood, not the blood of their beloved rabbi.

Others, trying to discern the motive for Judas's betrayal, have suggested that he was misguided in his perception of the ministry. He sold Jesus out for a very small sum, a measly thirty pieces of silver, the price for purchasing a slave. It certainly was not a large enough sum to begin a military revolution. Consider that Judas had seen Jesus heal the sick, walk on water, give sight to the blind, and raise the dead. He must have known the power Jesus had, and that taking out a legion of Roman soldiers was something he could have done in the blink of an eye. So perhaps Judas was hoping to force Jesus's hand, to put him in a position where he would have to confront the Romans.

While we cannot know the motives of Judas, there are two scriptures that offer some insight. After Jesus finished proclaiming that one of his followers would betray him, John 13 records what happened to Judas: "Then after he had taken the morsel, Satan entered into him. Jesus said to him, 'What you are going to do, do quickly'" (John 13:27). And even before this happens, we know that Jesus is aware of Judas and the true identity of the one who is going to betray him: "Did I not choose you, the twelve? And yet one of you is a devil" (John 6:70). What we do know is that Judas was used by God to bring about the culmination of the kingdom of heaven.

This happened in fulfillment of Old Testament prophecy. Psalm 41 predicted that one of Jesus's closest friends would turn on him: "Even my close friend in whom I trusted, who ate my bread, has lifted his heel against me" (Ps. 41:9; Matt. 26:14–16, 48–49 is the fulfillment of this prophecy). Zechariah predicts the exact amount of silver and the manner in which the money would be eventually used:

> Then I said to them, "If it seems good to you, give me my wages; but if not, keep them." And they weighed out as my wages thirty pieces of

silver. Then the Lord said to me, "Throw it to the potter"—the lordly price at which I was priced by them. So I took the thirty pieces of silver and threw them into the house of the Lord, to the potter. Then I broke my second staff Union, annulling the brotherhood between Judah and Israel (Zech. 11:12–14; Matt. 27:2–5 is the fulfillment of this prophecy).

Not only was Judas paid thirty pieces of silver; he would later regret his actions, return the money to the Jewish leaders, and they would use the silver to buy a field known as the Potter's Field. In all of this, we see the hand of God at work, using Judas to bring about the death of Jesus.

There are also clues about Judas's fate in the Gospels, if we look closely. Judas Iscariot never seems to have had a life-changing encounter with Jesus. There are no recorded instances of Judas revealing the person and work of Christ, which is surprising given his dramatic role in events near the end of Jesus's life. Other characters like Nathaniel, Peter, John, Andrew, James, Nicodemus, and even the Samaritan woman all recognized that Jesus is the Christ, but that is never said of Judas. In addition, when the disciples are listed, there are always slight variations in their order. Some scholars believe the order hints at the intimacy of their relationship with Jesus (see in particular Matt. 10:2–4; Mark 3:16–19; Luke 6:14–16). In every account, Peter, James, John, and Andrew are always listed first—but Judas is always last, which may explain his disassociation from Jesus and the others.

Finally, and most revealing of Judas's character, are the three times he speaks in the Gospels. We see his greed when he confronts Mary for wasting her expensive ointment by anointing Jesus's feet. John 12:3–6 records this account:

Mary therefore took a pound of expensive ointment made from pure nard, and anointed the feet of Jesus and wiped his feet with her hair. The house was filled with the fragrance of the perfume. But Judas Iscariot, one of his disciples (he who was about to betray him), said, "Why was this ointment not sold for three hundred denarii and given to the poor?" He said this, not because he cared about the poor, but because he was a thief, and having charge of the moneybag he used to help himself to what was put into it.

What looks outwardly to be heartfelt desire to care for the poor turns out to be a ploy to hinder a woman from showing extravagant adoration toward Jesus. Judas was disgusted by the woman's act of worship. The other documented dialogues with Judas (Matt. 26:25; Luke 22:48) reveal his interactions with the religious leaders as he prepares to betray his rabbi and teacher.

Judas concealed his true identity from the disciples until the end of his life. At the Last Supper, none of the eleven had any idea that Judas was an instrument being used by Satan. Matthew records another perspective on the final meal with Jesus in Matthew 26. Jesus shocks the group by stating,

> "Truly, I say to you, one of you will betray me." And they were very sorrowful and began to say to him one after another, "Is it I, Lord?" He answered, "He who has dipped his hand in the dish with me will betray me. The Son of Man goes as it is written of him, but woe to that man by whom the Son of Man is betrayed! It would have been better for that man if he had not been born" (Matt. 26:20–24).

Jesus's statement sent a shockwave through the hearts of his followers. But what is interesting is that each of the men immediately doubted himself, rather than accusing someone else. Each one asks, "Is it I, Lord?"

"Lord" is not a typical phrase for disciples to use when referring to their teacher. The address is honorific and hints that each of the men may have viewed Jesus as the Messiah. But notice when it is Judas's turn to speak. Verse 25 records his response, "Judas, who would betray him, answered, 'Is it I, Rabbi?' He said to him, 'You have said so'" (Matt. 26:25).

Notice that Judas uses the word "rabbi" to refer to Jesus, the common address to a teacher. At the end of the discipleship experience, Judas still looked at Jesus as a teacher, not as someone worthy of special honor. Even though he had heard the sermons Jesus preached, witnessed many of the miracles Jesus performed, and watched people healed before his eyes, he did not believe. He was one of the twelve sent out to cast out demons and prophesy about the kingdom. He was one of the seventy-two who were commissioned and empowered to preach the good news to anyone who would listen and heal anyone willing to receive it. But it was not enough to convince him.

Judas may have enjoyed Jesus's teaching and may have admired Jesus's ministry, but when push came to shove, he was still in control of his own heart. He had not surrendered his life to Christ. He was still the captain of his own ship, seated on the throne of his heart. He was as close to Christ as you could be, humanly speaking, and yet he completely missed out on a committed relationship with him.

Don't Be a Judas

In this, Judas is a welcome reminder for us today. We can be around godly people. Your dad may be a deacon, and your mom may sing in the choir. You may have attended Sunday school or church groups for years. Maybe you were baptized as a child and raised in a Christian home, but when it comes to Jesus, he is nothing more than a good teacher. You call him rabbi but continue to live your life on your own terms.

Jesus warned that those who do not accept him as Lord, as the Savior to whom their lives now belong, can disguise themselves as Christians but they remain lost in their sins. In Matthew 7, Jesus laid it out plainly stating,

> "Not everyone who says to me, 'Lord, Lord,' will enter the kingdom of heaven, but the one who does the will of my Father who is in heaven. On that day many will say to me, 'Lord, Lord, did we not prophesy in your name, and cast out demons in your name, and do many mighty works in your name?' And then will I declare to them, 'I never knew you; depart from me, you workers of lawlessness'" (Matt. 7:21–23).

No one wants to stand before the judge of the world and hear that he doesn't know you.

> "Hey Jesus, do you remember me? It's Jeff!"
> "Have we met before?" Jesus asks.
> "Jesus, it's me, Stacy. I went to church on Easter and Christmas!"
> The haunting reply we never want to hear: "Do I know you?"[15]

The real question is not: "Do you know Jesus?" The question that matters in the end is: "Does Jesus know you?" If you know him from a distance but have not surrendered your life to him, the only way you can be known by him is to turn in repentance from your reliance upon yourself and place your faith entirely in him, trusting that only he can save you from the consequences of your sin and bring you to God. Knowing Jesus as a disciple is more than just reciting words at the right place in a prayer (a very non-Jewish way of thinking about salvation). True discipleship requires obedience to Jesus. We understand that our lives now belong entirely to him, and he rules and reigns over our life. "Disciple" is just another word for "student," and with Jesus, school is always in session.

Know the Real Jesus

Throughout this chapter I've tried to show that even if we know the story of Jesus's final days, a story many of us have heard hundreds of times, there are still details that have been lost in translation. Whether we've simply wrongly assumed that first-century Jewish culture is similar to our own or taken our cues from a popular Renaissance painting, we've incorporated understandings of Jesus that don't match reality. Don't get the wrong idea. Da Vinci's painting is wonderful in many ways, and there are still many things we can learn from it as a work of art. But it also illustrates the danger we face in detaching Jesus from the context in which he lived.

Over the past 2,000 years, much has been said about the person and the teachings of Jesus, and the majority of what we know is good and reliable. But we still need to study the Bible, to dig out the truth for ourselves, and to be willing to move beyond our cultural assumptions of who we think Jesus is to uncover the Jesus who has sometimes been forgotten.

Is the Jesus we know the man who was born to a virgin, reared in a Jewish land, and raised in a Hebraic culture, or is he a Jesus of our own imagination who resembles an American pastor or a life coach?

More than ever, as followers of Jesus we need to learn to know our rabbi. We want to understand the man and learn to follow the way of life he taught us to live.

CHAPTER 9

Which Jesus Will You Choose?

If you've read the Gospels and encountered the apostle Peter, you may have noticed that he was born with a foot-shaped mouth. Though his birth name was Simon, he would later receive the nickname Petros, which means "rock," from Jesus. The Aramaic form of his name is Cephas, which is translated as "stone." Today he might have the nickname Rocky. But what's in a name, anyway? Well, when Jesus gives you a name, it reveals something, and in this case it revealed the type of person Jesus expected Peter to become. Jesus called Peter when he was a spontaneous, rash, and reckless fisherman, and chiseled him into a strong, steadfast, and stable follower. In virtually every Gospel account, Peter's name is the first to be listed:

Matthew 10:2: "Peter, Andrew, James and John . . ."
Mark 3:16: "Peter, James, John, and Andrew . . ."
Luke 6:14: "Peter, Andrew . . ."
Acts 1:13: "Peter, John . . ."

Clearly, he was central among Jesus's disciples and a key figure in the early church. But who was Peter?

Peter and his brother Andrew oversaw a local fishing business in Capernaum when Jesus summoned them to drop their nets and follow him. The rest of the Gospels give us wonderful details about Peter, and we witness a complete metamorphosis as he moves from a position of unbelief to belief and eventually to sold-out commitment and servant leadership. In Luke 5, Jesus asked Peter to drop his nets for a catch. Peter responds with some doubt at first, though he reluctantly agrees to do it: "Master, we toiled all night and took nothing! But at your word I will let down the nets" (v. 5). In this first scene we get a sense of the man. When the catch looks to overwhelm the fishermen, Peter swings to the other extreme. He drops to his knees and says, "Depart from me, for I am a sinful man, O Lord" (v. 8). Peter probably did not know who Jesus was at this point, but he immediately expressed a willingness to submit to Jesus.

Peter would later exercise courageous faith in Christ by walking out upon the waves of the Sea of Galilee toward the ghost-like figure of Jesus, in obedience to Jesus's command. While the others cowered in fear, Peter stepped over the rail of the boat and experienced the impossible. Then, at Caesarea Philippi, Peter answers Jesus's question, "Who do you say that I am?" by saying, "You are the Christ, the son of the living God." He was one of the first to believe that Jesus was more than an ordinary man and to put his faith in him.

As we explore the Gospels further, we notice that Peter held a position in Jesus's inner discipleship group of four (John, James, Peter, and Jesus himself), and he was also privy to five encounters to which not all the other disciples were privy:

1. The healing of his mother-in-law (Mark 1:29–31)
2. The raising of Jairus's daughter from the dead (Mark 5:35–43)
3. The transfiguration of Jesus (Mark 9:2–8)
4. The Olivet Discourse, when Jesus explained end-time events (Mark 13)
5. With Jesus in the Garden of Gethsemane, just prior to his trial and crucifixion (Matt. 26:36–46)

Peter's name is mentioned more in the Gospels than any other person except Jesus. What is interesting is that no one stands up more for Jesus than Peter, yet no one is rebuked more frequently than Peter! He was wholehearted and a bit hot-headed. Consider what he says to Jesus at the Last Supper as he declares his commitment: "Even if everyone falls away, I will not" (Mark 14:29 CSB). And yet shortly afterward, he would do just that. Peter had good intentions, but in the end he had to learn the truth about a sinful heart: that even good intentions are not enough. We all need a savior from our selfishness and sin.

No Cock Crows at Night

Peter was a man filled with faith, so why does he crumble under the pressure in a courtyard on the night of Jesus's arrest? How does someone who had experienced everything that Peter experienced come to the place where he denies the one he loves? One of the reasons is that even though Peter had spent three years with Jesus, he still misunderstood the Messiah in at least three important ways.

1. He misunderstood Jesus's role. Jesus had to correct the disciples' faulty perceptions about his ministry purpose on three occasions (Mark 8, 9, and 10). He is forced to rebuke Peter on one occasion for thinking like the devil: "Get behind me, Satan!" (Mark 8:33). Even though Jesus repeatedly said that he would be betrayed and killed, Peter failed to grasp the true nature of Jesus's mission.

2. He miscalculated his own role. In the garden of Gethsemane at the arrest of Jesus, Peter drew his sword and sliced the ear off of Malchus, one of the priests. For Peter, it was "game on." He was ready for the kingdom of heaven to come at that moment, even if it came through his own violent efforts. But that wasn't God's plan. Jesus intervened, healed the man's ear, and ended the violence. Peter was perplexed.

3. He misjudged his surroundings. Peter was surrounded by rejecters and worldly influences the night he denounced his connection with Jesus in the courtyard. Pressure from the crowd likely caused him to cave in.

Let's take a close look at the account of Peter's betrayal of Jesus and try to place ourselves in the first-century context as we attempt to understand what was going on in Peter's head.

While Peter was in the courtyard below, one of the high priest's maidservants came. When she saw Peter warming himself, she looked at him and said, "You also were with Jesus, the man from Nazareth."

But he denied it: "I don't know or understand what you're talking about!" Then he went out to the entryway, and a rooster crowed.

When the maidservant saw him again, she began to tell those standing nearby, "This man is one of them."

But again he denied it. After a little while those standing there said to Peter again, "You certainly are one of them, since you're also a Galilean!"

Then he started to curse and swear, "I don't know this man you're talking about!"

Immediately a rooster crowed a second time, and Peter remembered when Jesus had spoken the word to him, "Before the rooster crows twice, you will deny me three times." And he broke down and wept (Mark 14:66–72 CSB).

Some have viewed the word translated as "swear" here as an example of Peter uttering a profane word, but "to swear" simply means that he was adamant about the truthfulness of what he was saying. This may mean that Peter took oaths in the course of his denial, something Jesus forbade his followers from doing.[1] In Matthew 5, Jesus warned, "Don't take an oath at all: either by heaven, for it is the city of the great King. . . . But let your 'yes' mean 'yes,' and your 'no' mean 'no.' Anything more than this is from the evil one" (Matt. 5:34, 37 CSB).

Regardless, as the accusations came in, Peter's allegiance to Jesus went out the door. Time stood still as the cry of the rooster reverberated through the midnight air. Not only did Peter hear the sound, but we learn that Jesus heard it as well. Luke, the doctor, recorded a key detail for us: "And immediately, while he was still speaking, the rooster crowed. *And the Lord turned and looked at Peter*. And Peter remembered the saying of the Lord, how he had said to him, 'Before the rooster crows today, you will deny me three times'" (Luke 22:60–61, emphasis mine).

Picture the scene as Jesus lifts his bloodstained, bruised head and gazes over into Peter's eyes. Peter realized that he had done what he said he wouldn't do. He had abandoned Jesus. "And he went out and wept bitterly" (Luke 22:62). The weight of his sin melted his heart. It was too much for him to bear. Peter the rock had crumpled into a pile of rubble.

Rooster or Man?

There is an interesting detail in this account that may shed some new light on what is happening. Over the years, I've wondered about the presence of roosters in Jerusalem. In my study of the cultural background of the Bible, I've found that crows and members of the crow family are considered dirty animals that rummage through anything and everything. According to the Mishnah, a collection of Jewish oral laws, roosters and chickens were banned from the city of Jerusalem while the temple stood.[2] This ban was enacted out of concern that the animals would wander into the Holy Place or the Holy of Holies and defile the altar. So it would seem strange to find a rooster crowing, especially this close to the temple. But if it was not a rooster that crowed, what or who made the noise in the courtyard that night?

One position in the temple is known as the "temple crier." This individual would announce certain events throughout the year, as well as the morning services in the temple, which would begin with the sound of a trumpet blast that signaled for the Levites to find their posts. At the blast, the priests would prepare themselves for the service, and the people would gather for worship. It is interesting to note that another name for the "crier" was the "rooster," a fact that has been confirmed by several scholars and historians over the years.[3] The Mishnah documents three places where a "rooster" blows a blast on the trumpet:

> Mishnah Sukkah 5.4 reads: "They had trumpets in their hands when the crier cried [rooster crowed]. They sounded a *tech*, *teruah*, and *tekiah* (these are sounds of the shofar horn) [which signaled that they should proceed to the Shiloah spring to draw water].

> Mishnah Tamid 1.2 refers to a time when the supervising priest would arrive at the temple. "There is no set time; sometimes he comes when the cock crows, or close to it, sometimes before, sometimes after."

Mishnah Yoma 1.8 records that "every day they used to remove the ashes from off the Altar at cock-crow, or near to it, either before it or after it; but on the Day of Atonement [they did so] at midnight, and on the Feast at the first watch. And before the [time of] cock-crow drew near the Temple Court was filled with Israelites"[4]

We all know that cultural idioms can morph and change over time as the culture changes. For example, if you were to say, "the eagle has landed" a century ago, most people would assume you were referring to a bird resting from a long flight. That same phrase is now a cultural idiom used today in reference to the original moon landing by Apollo 11. We might use it today to speak about a plane touching down or the completion of a difficult project. Or to give another example, a century ago, a ship would most likely refer to a boat on the ocean. Today, it could just as likely apply to a spacecraft. Idioms change over time and can even develop different meanings depending upon the time period.

If the Gospel writer was referring idiomatically to a man and not an animal, it slightly changes the way we understand the passage as well as some other passages we read in scripture.

When Did the Horn Blow?

The Romans divided the night into three-hour blocks called "watches." The first watch began at sundown and ended at 9:00 p.m., the second watch went to midnight, the third watch ended at 3:00 a.m., and the fourth watch stopped at sunrise or 6:00 a.m. The rooster ("cock-crier") traditionally crowed at the third watch between midnight and 3:00 a.m. His trumpet blast signaled the changing of the temple guard, and as the ESV footnote points out, the rooster was crowing at this time (between the hours of midnight and 3:00 a.m.). Furthermore, the text also states that some time had elapsed between Peter's first denial and his third. It indicates about an hour of time had passed: "And after *an interval of about an hour* still another insisted, saying, 'Certainly this man also was with him, for he too is a Galilean'" (Luke 22:59, emphasis mine).

Here is why I'm convinced that the "rooster" is really referring to a temple crier, not an animal. My grandfather and uncle raised roosters most of their lives. And despite what you might think, I've rarely heard roosters crow before dawn. I've certainly never heard one wait a long time between intervals of crowing. When roosters get to crowing, it's nonstop. If this rooster began at 3:00 a.m., that fateful final rooster cry would have come at daybreak, around 6:00 a.m., an interval of several hours. Ancient translators rendered the Greek word as "cock-crowing," yet all modern translations now read "rooster crowed." In this case, the historical and traditional evidence suggests to me that we are closer to the truth when we realize that the "cock-crower" is not referring to an actual rooster but is a Hebrew idiom for "temple crier."

Regardless of which view is correct (if it is an animal or a man), the truth of the text remains the same. Peter, in a moment of sinful weakness, caved under the pressure of the bystanders. He denied his master and rabbi on the very eve of Jesus's death.

But thankfully, the story doesn't end there. Peter would eventually be given another chance to speak with Jesus after the resurrection when Jesus served him breakfast on the Sea of Galilee. We read about this in John 21. After a long night of unsuccessful fishing, Jesus reunites with his disciples back where it all began—out on the water fishing. Like the first time they met, he again instructs them to throw their nets on the other side. And miraculously, they pull in a monstrous haul.

The familiarity of the event is all too clear to Peter and John. Recognizing Jesus, Peter plunges into the water and swims for land. "When they got out on land, they saw a charcoal fire there, with fish lying on it, and bread" (John 21:9). Jesus is cooking bread and fish, reminiscent of the miracles he performed with them, and there is also a charcoal fire, a reminder of another charcoal fire recorded in John 18:18 in the courtyard where Peter denied Jesus.

Jesus sets the stage for restoration by restoring Peter in the same way that Peter had fallen. In response to Peter's threefold denial of him, Jesus asks Peter a question three times—not for his own understanding, but for Peter to experience the depth of his restoration. Jesus knew Peter would be committed to him, and he wanted to make sure Peter knows it. In that culture, something done three times was considered permanent. Here we witness three denials, three confessions, and three commissions from Christ. There was no trial period of examination. There were no strings attached, nor any stipulations. Jesus freely offered full restoration. By his actions, Jesus is saying to Peter: You don't serve God *for* redemption, you serve him *from* redemption.

Jesus the Christ or Jesus Barabbas?

If we return to the eve before Jesus's death, we come to the scene of Jesus's trial. The trial begins under the cloak of darkness, as Jesus is tried for crimes he didn't commit. The high priest and his family bring trumped-up charges: "And as soon as it was morning, the chief priests held a consultation with the elders and scribes and the whole council. And they bound Jesus and led him away and delivered him over to Pilate" (Mark 15:1). The corrupt leaders want him dead because he has dared to judge and expose their corruption.

Though the Sanhedrin had already formalized a sentence against Jesus the night before, they had no legal power to carry it out. According to the laws of the land, for Jesus to be condemned to death, it had to be done by a Roman court. The governing body of Israel met together to formulate charges they believed would hold up in this court and then led Jesus to Pilate. At this point, Jesus had been held captive from 3:00 a.m. to daybreak.

Pilate was the legal representative of the Roman government in Judea. He held the office for a total of ten years, which shows that Rome trusted him. The Jews, however, despised him, particularly for two specific incidents. Josephus tells us of a time when Pilate and his troops rode into Jerusalem with an image of an eagle on each of their poles.[5] Since the Jews opposed idolatry, previous governors had avoided this tradition. Pilate, whether out of ignorance or cockiness, disregarded that practice. A riot broke out, forcing him to remove the birds. At another time, Pilate began construction on a new aqueduct system for Jerusalem, and he resourced the project with funds from the temple treasury. As you can imagine, the Jews were enraged by his actions.

So the Jewish leaders did not like Pilate, but appealing to Pilate was their only hope if they wished to kill Jesus. As Pilate questions him, Jesus is standing with his outer garment saturated with blood and sweat. His face is bruised from physical blows by the priests. He hasn't washed off the spit in his beard.

Pilate would have taken one look at this man and immediately understood that he had been placed in a dilemma he couldn't win. Pilate may have believed that Jesus was innocent before he even began the interrogation—he may have realized that Jesus was being set up. But he had to present him to the crowd for a final ruling in order to do two things: avoid an uprising against him (because the Jews disliked him) and, unknown to him at the time, to fulfill the prophecy of Isaiah 53:7. This prophecy reads: "He was oppressed, and he was afflicted, yet he opened not his mouth; like a lamb that is led to the slaughter, and like a sheep that before its shearers is silent, so he opened not his mouth."

Ancient sources confirm that a Roman governor could set a prisoner free each Passover at the request of the people as a demonstration of mercy. So Pilate, perhaps in an effort to keep with tradition and appease his sense of justice, offered the people a choice between Jesus and a man named Barabbas. Mark describes Barabbas as a "rebel and a murderer." John labels him a "robber," and Matthew calls him a "notorious prisoner." Pilate probably assumed that when faced with a choice between Jesus and Barabbas, the people would almost certainly choose to free Jesus. Why would they ask him to pardon a known criminal?

Initially, it appears that the crowd may have wanted to release Jesus. Notice how Pilate presents him: "Do you want me to release for you the King of the Jews?" (Mark 15:9) as if he were reiterating the belief of the crowd. Also, Pilate "perceived," and we have no reason to believe the crowd didn't as well, "that it was out of envy that the chief priests had delivered him up" (Mark 15:10).

In the middle of his proposal, Pilate is interrupted by a message from his wife telling him that he should have nothing to do with this righteous man, Jesus. The chief priests seize this opportunity to stir up the crowd in support of releasing Barabbas, and their efforts were effective. Three times Pilate attempts to dissuade the crowd from crucifying Jesus, but the die had been cast. Nothing less than Jesus's death would silence their bloodthirsty cries.

Which Jesus Do You Want?

I highlight this choice the people faced between Jesus and Barabbas because, through it, Mark paints for us a clear portrait of the substitutional sacrifice of Christ. We should first note that Barabbas was not this man's first name. Matthew 27 records his full name for us: "At that time they had a well-known prisoner whose name was Jesus Barabbas. So when the crowd had gathered, Pilate asked them, "Which one do you want me to release to you: Jesus Barabbas, or Jesus who is called the Messiah?" (Matt. 27:16–17 NIV). Although some translations don't include Jesus Barabbas in the text, they do provide a footnote that indicates the full name: "Other manuscripts read Jesus Barabbas."

Jesus Barabbas was the polar opposite of Jesus the Messiah. He had been judged and legally condemned for the crimes he committed. He deserved death and could do nothing to free himself from the sentence he received. On the other hand, Jesus the Messiah was an innocent man. He did nothing wrong, yet he was charged for crimes he did not commit. Barabbas was supposed to die but he was released. Instead, Jesus took his place.

The truth of this passage hits close to home when we understand that you and I are Barabbas. What do I mean? Well, Barabbas's Hebrew name consists of two parts. That word *bar* means "son of," and the term *abbas* means "father." So Barabbas, when translated into English, means "son of the father." As I suggested earlier, Barabbas serves as a representative type of all of us—the sons (and daughters) of our fathers. We are all descendants of our first father, Adam, separated from God because of our sin. We have robbed God of his glory, we are imprinted by sin, and we are bound for hell until Christ enters our lives, calls our names, and sets us free by substituting himself in our place of condemnation and punishment.

Barabbas knew that he had zero chance of being set free that day. He was likely pondering his imminent death moments before a Roman soldier entered his cell. Previous crucifixions might still be ringing in his ears as he listens to the soldiers hammering the nails through skin and wood. He may have envisioned the agony of struggling for breath as he would hang suspended from the tree.

Into this silence his name is called. Keys jingle as his prison door is flung open. "Get up, come with me," yells the jailor. Hesitantly, Barabbas stumbles to his feet as the chains that bound him are removed. A cacophony of cheers echo through the prison hallway from the riotous crowd as he walks into the courtyard. He is prepared for the worst, yet unexpectedly, he hears his name being chanted repeatedly by the crowd, "Barrabas, Barrabas, Barrabas." Within seconds, he is wobbling into the crowd as a freed man. He looks back, and what does he see? A bloody man standing silently, looking at him with pity.

Barabbas is the only man who can say that Jesus physically and historically took his place of punishment. But every believer who trusts in Jesus by faith knows that Jesus has made that same offer to us. Though we each deserve judgment, condemnation, and an eternal place in hell, the gospel tells us that Jesus bore our sins and absorbed the wrath of God. He became our substitute that day, just as he did for Barabbas.

My God, My God or My Father?

In less than six hours, Jesus has been stabbed in the back by one of his disciples. He has been denied by a close friend, rejected by the Sanhedrin, sold out by Pilate, and now traded for a criminal by the crowds. But the extent of his suffering was far from over. As he hung from the cross, Jesus uttered seven different things. Nestled in the middle of these seven phrases, there is one that has troubled theologians for years: "My God, My God, why have you forsaken me?" (Matt. 27:46 NIV). Matthew 27:46 is the only portion of Jesus's words from the cross that we have recorded in Hebrew, an indication that Jesus spoke in Hebrew and not just the local tongue of Aramaic. Many of the people surrounding the cross wouldn't have had any idea what he was saying. The Roman soldiers surmised that he was calling for Elijah because they heard him saying, "Eli, Eli." But Jesus wasn't calling for Elijah, he was crying out to God.

As we've seen many times throughout this book, when a rabbi wanted to teach a lesson from a particular passage, he didn't direct his audience to a chapter and verse. Instead, he quoted the beginning of the passage. That first line would make sure that everybody listening was on the same page—the rest of the passage and all of the lessons they had learned about it would spring instantly to mind. So when we look at this particular saying from the cross, "My God, my God, why have you forsaken me," we should read this not just as a random quote from Jesus as he is taking his last breath. He is *still* teaching his disciples, even in his death. "Eli, Eli," is from the beginning of Psalm 22.

Rich Words from the Cross

Psalm 22 is a prophetic passage that points to the coming Messiah. It is written in the first person, and it describes in great detail the agony of death. Verse 7 reads: "All who see me mock me; they make mouths at me; they wag their heads." Verse 12 continues: "Many bulls encompass me; strong bulls of Bashan surround me; they open wide their mouths at me, like a ravening and roaring lion. I am poured out like water, and all my bones are out of joint; my heart is like wax; it is melted within my breast." The psalmist describes a disheartening situation. Verse 6, however, contains a particularly important detail: "But I am a *worm* and not a man, scorned by mankind and despised by the people" (Ps. 22:6, emphasis mine).

I point this verse out because the word "worm," or *tola'at* in Hebrew, is used to describe an insect that devours plants. If you look this word up in a Hebrew dictionary, you will find the same word can be translated as "crimson, scarlet, or purple."[6] This is because in ancient times, the little *toleah* worm was crushed to extract a reddish purple dye.

The color crimson (a purplish red) is found throughout the pages of the Bible. Crimson was used in the construction of the traveling tabernacle in the desert: "[Y]ou shall make the tabernacle with ten curtains of fine twined linen and blue and *purple* and scarlet yarns" (Exod. 26:1, emphasis mine). In the permanent temple in Jerusalem, God instructed that they make "the veil [of the temple] of blue and purple and *crimson* fabrics and fine linen" (2 Chron. 3:14, emphasis mine). Rahab hung a *scarlet* colored cord from her window in Jericho so the Israelite army would spare her and her family from destruction (Josh. 2:17–21). When Pilate condemned Jesus to crucifixion, the soldiers escorted Jesus into the Praetorium and clothed his battered body in a *scarlet* robe before twisting a crown of thorns upon his head (Matt. 27:27–30).

Hundreds of miles from Jerusalem, Paul would share the gospel with the first European convert, Lydia, who was a dealer of purple cloth in Philippi. The Zondervan Encyclopedia of the Bible provides additional insight as to the color of cloth Lydia was selling: "The *purple* or *crimson*, which dyed the cloth that Lydia sold, was a local manufacture from the madder root, a cheap rival of Phoenician murex dye."[7] Given the prominence of this color through the Bible, I don't believe it's an accident that this woman sold crimson-dyed clothes.

Every color in the temple had meaning, and both crimson and scarlet were commonly associated with sin. God spoke through his prophet Isaiah, "Come now, and let us reason together," says the LORD, "Though your sins are like *scarlet*, They shall be as white as snow; Though they are red like *crimson*, They shall be as wool" (Isaiah 1:18 NKJV). Why is this significant? Because part of what Jesus was identifying with in Psalm 22 was the notion that he was being "crushed like crimson."

When we understand some of the possible ways crimson was used and what it represents, we see that at one level Jesus is identifying himself with sin. It brings to mind Paul's words to the church at Corinth, "He made the one who did not know sin to be sin for us, so that in him we might become the righteousness of God" (2 Cor. 5:21 CSB). Jesus was being crushed like a worm for us, and turned into crimson—sin—in our place.

By reciting the first lines of Psalm 22, Jesus encourages his listeners to develop a deeper understanding of what is happening to him as he hangs dying on the cross. Although the passage begins with agony and despair, it ultimately ends with triumph and victory. Listen to final verses:

All the ends of the earth will remember and turn to the Lord. All the families of the nations will bow down before you, for kingship belongs to the Lord; he rules over the nations. All who prosper on earth will eat and bow down; all those who go down to the dust will kneel before him—even the one who cannot preserve his life. Their descendants will serve him; the next generation will be told about the Lord. They will come and declare his righteousness to a people yet to be born—they will declare what he has done (Ps. 22:27–31 CSB).

Richard Hays says that "to read Jesus' cry from the cross in Mark 15:34 as an intertextual evocation of Psalm 22's promise of hope is not simply an exegetical cop-out, a failure of nerve that refuses to accept Mark's bleak portrait of Jesus' death at face value. Rather, it is a reading strategy that Mark himself taught us through his repeated allusive references to snatches of Scripture that point beyond themselves to their own original narrative settings."[8]

What Hays is saying is that if we follow the allusion Jesus is making in Mark's Gospel to Psalm 22, we gain a more hope-filled perspective about the events that are occurring. With Psalm 22 in mind, Jesus is exclaiming from the cross, "We win in the end! I know it looks bleak now, but God is going to use this for victory." Rather than simply reading the words of Jesus as a cry of hopeless despair, the context of the psalm helps us to remember that Jesus understood that his death would be followed by his victorious resurrection.

By understanding what Jesus said, who Jesus was, and why Jesus did what he did, we can better understand what drove his followers to lead a revolution that would eventually transcend the sprawling Roman Empire and change the world. They had encountered a man who did things and spoke words unlike any ever seen or heard. They were compelled by their love for this man and felt they had no choice but to proclaim the good news of his life, death, and resurrection to anyone who would listen.

Their message was all about a man named Jesus. A man who was physically unassuming. A stonemason from a town famous for its zealots. A man who spent time among the lowly and dejected. A man who stood against the corrupt religious system of his day, while fulfilling every single word ever written about him in the Old Testament. He lived a life we couldn't live, and he died a death we should have died under the sentence of God's judgment. The agony and suffering of Jesus's cries to his Father on the cross are what make it possible for our own cries to be heard. However, ours are not cries of defeat, but words spoken in love to a Father who loves us as his very own. And for that we are eternally grateful for the one who died in our place.

Where Do We Go from Here?

Whenever I preach or teach about the things we've looked at in this book, insights that place Jesus back into the first-century context in which he lived, people always ask me afterward, "What books can I purchase to learn more about this?" There are many ministries devoted to recovering the Jewishness of Jesus and helping us find the Jesus we have forgotten over the centuries. There have been countless books written on the Hebraic background of Jesus and our reading of the scriptures, and there have been many teachings filmed in Israel trying to give Western Christians a culturally sensitive understanding of the land, the Messiah, and the people of God.

There is a broad movement today sometimes called the Jewish roots movement that has garnered interest in some circles and has begun publishing more scholarly works. Much of what I have learned has come from attending seminars and reading resources produced by those in this movement. Over the years, I have listened to teachings on this topic in an attempt to satisfy an insatiable desire to learn as much as I can about the first-century Jewish rabbi named Jesus.

Before I would venture to recommend additional resources, however, as a pastor I need to offer you a warning. Some of the material accessible to us today that comes from this movement is based on conjecture and speculation. This means that we cannot just take what we read and hear as if it is verifiably true. We must learn how to "eat the meat and spit out the bones," as the late Dwight Pryor once said to me. In their own resources on this topic, authors Lois Tverberg and Ann Spangler offer additional guidance for those wanting further study into the Jewish background to Jesus and the Bible:

> It is also important to treat the sources you read with caution. Traditional Jewish sources, by definition, do not assume that Jesus is the Messiah. Heated debate has gone on for 2,000 years between Jews and Christians, and both sides have reacted by distancing themselves from each other. Just as Christianity has ignored and distanced itself from its Jewish background, Judaism has sometimes done the same, downplaying earlier practices and beliefs that led large numbers of first century Jews to believe in Jesus as the Messiah.[1]

With these warnings in mind, I want to also encourage you to avoid pitting traditional Bible teachings against insights that you might read, especially if they offer a radically new or novel way of understanding who Jesus was and what he came to accomplish. Throughout this book I have sought to present insights that confirm and support the Jesus that the church has always followed and proclaimed, even if this means that some of the ways that we see Jesus and understand him are seen in a fresh light through these cultural insights. In the end, however, we cannot treat cultural background on par with the scriptures. We must wisely use the insights of historical research and cultural study to aid us, even as we resolve to trust the Bible as the sole authority for shaping our faith and practice.

Prayerfully, I've included the material in this book to challenge you to reconsider some of the details about Jesus and his life that you may have been taught for years that have been altered from their original, biblical context. By placing Jesus back into the context from which he came, we are able to see more clearly the miracles he performed, the lessons he taught, and the mission he fulfilled.

Ultimately, the goal of this knowledge is not to fill your head with useless facts, but to instill in you a hunger to read and study God's Word. In particular, I hope that you begin to see how we cannot truly grasp the message of the New Testament without an understanding of the Old, as the two complement one another and only make sense when they are studied together.

A Bible Reading Plan for Busy Believers

Knowing Jesus in a deeper and more personal way will come through spending time reading both the Old and New Testaments. The more we know of Jesus as the God of the Jewish people foreshadowed in messianic expectation, the more our love for him will grow as we encounter him on the pages of the New Testament. And as we grow to understand him more through God's Word, we will love him more, and he will manifest more of himself to us. Greater love for Jesus begins with a deeper knowledge of God's Word.

Reading through the entire Bible in a year can be a daunting task because many Christians don't know where to begin, what to read, or how to study. When I was a new believer, I utilized the "OPRA" technique for reading the Bible: I would randomly *Open* the Bible, *Point* to a passage, *Read* the verse, and try to figure out a way to *Apply* it to my life. Thankfully, I didn't land on the scripture that says, "He [speaking of Judas Iscariot] went and hanged himself" (Matthew 27:5). Reading random scriptures will not provide solid biblical growth any more than eating random foods out of your pantry will provide solid physical growth. An effective reading plan is required.

My wife, Kandi, and I have developed a reading plan called "Foundations: A Bible Reading Plan for Busy Believers" or F260. The F260 is a 260-day reading plan that highlights the foundational passages of scripture that every disciple should know. If you follow this plan, you will read through the entire Bible—even if you don't read *every verse* of the Bible. (We also have books for teens [Foundations for Teens] and children [Foundations for Kids] that coincide with the adult plan.)

The plan is a great place to begin, manageable for anyone who has never read the Bible in its entirety. You read one to two chapters a day for five days each week, with an allowance for weekends off. The two off-days a week are built in so you may catch up on days when you're unable to read. With a traditional reading plan of four to five chapters every day, unread chapters can begin to pile up, forcing us to skip entire sections to get back on schedule. It reduces Bible reading to a system of box-checking instead of a time to hear from God and to reflect on what you've read for that day. To help you get stated, I've included a copy of the F260 reading plan in the appendix.

Recommended Resources as You Begin

Finally, I'd like to point you in the direction of some additional resources. As mentioned earlier, not all of these hold to evangelical perspectives on Jesus, nor are they equally helpful. I include them here for those who are ready to engage in further study, but I would encourage you to first begin with a thorough study of the Bible and to ground yourself in the basics of Christian doctrine—what Christians everywhere have always believed and taught. My hope is that as you study the Bible and learn more about the cultural background of the scriptures you will come to know Jesus more closely.

Books

Bivin, David, *Understanding the Difficult Words of Jesus: New Insights From a Hebraic Perspective* (Fallon, MO: Treasure House Publishing, 1994).

Bivin, David, *New Light on the Difficult Words of Jesus: Insights from His Jewish Context* (Holland, MI: En-Gedi Resource Center, 2009).

Boman, Thorleif, *Hebrew Thought Compared with Greek*, Norton Library (New York: W.W. Norton, 1970).

Bonhoeffer, Dietrich, *Life Together* (New York: Harper & Row, 1954).

Edersheim, Alfred, *The Life and Times of Jesus the Messiah* (Peabody, MA: Hendrickson, 1993).

Feinberg Vamosh, Miriam, *Food at the Time of the Bible: From Adam's Apple to the Last Supper* (Nashville, TN: Abingdon, 2004).

Fleming, James W., *The Jewish Background of Jesus* (LaGrange, GA: Biblical Resources, 2004).

Flusser, David, *Jesus* (Grand Rapids: Manges Press, 1997).

Flusser, David, *The Sage from Galilee: Rediscovering Jesus' Genius* (Grand Rapids: Eerdmans, 2007).

Fruchtenbaum, Arnold, *Yeshua: The Life of the Messiah from a Messianic Jewish Perspective*, vol. 1 (San Antonio, TX: Ariel Ministries, 2016).

Gallaty, Robby, *Rediscovering Discipleship: Making Jesus' Final Words Our First Work* (Grand Rapids: Zondervan, 2015).

Guild, William, *Moses Unveiled: Or Those Figures Which Served Unto the Pattern and Shadow of Heavenly Things* (Edinburgh, Scotland: Andrew Shortrede, 1839).

Hays, Richard B., *Echoes of Scripture in the Gospels* (Waco, TX: Baylor University Press, 2016).

Hicks, John Mark, *Come to the Table* (Orange, CA: New Leaf Books, 2002).

Kermode, Frank, *The Genesis of Secrecy: On the Interpretation of Narrative* (Cambridge, MA: Harvard University Press, 1979).

Lancaster, D. Thomas, *Torah Club: Restoration: Returning the Torah of Moses to the Disciples of Jesus* (Marshfield, MO: First Fruits of Zion, 2005).

Lancaster, D. Thomas, *Torah Club: Chronicles of the Messiah* (Marshfield, MO: First Fruits of Zion, 2014).

Lancaster, D. Thomas, *Torah Club: Shadows of the Messiah* (Marshfield, MO: First Fruits of Zion, 2014).

Lancaster, D. Thomas, *Torah Club: Unrolling the Scroll* (Marshfield, MO: First Fruits of Zion, 2014).

Liebi, Roger, *The Messiah in the Temple* (Dusseldorf, Germany: Christlicher Medien Vertrieb, 2003), 290.

Meier, John P., *A Marginal Jew: Rethinking the Historical Jesus*, Anchor Yale Bible Reference Library (New York: Doubleday, 1994).

Phillips, John, *Exploring the Gospel of Matthew: An Expository Commentary*, The John Phillips Commentary Series (Grand Rapids: Kregel, 2005).

Pitre, Brant James, *Jesus the Bridegroom: The Greatest Love Story Ever Told* (New York: Image, 2014).

Pryor, Dwight, *Behold the Man* (Dayton, OH: Center for Judaic Christian Studies, 2008).

Safrai, Shmuel, et al., "Education and the Study of the Torah," in *Compendia Rerum Iudaicarum Ad Novum Testamentum*, section 1, vol. 2, *The Jewish People in the First Century: Historical Geography, Political History, Social, Cultural and Religious Life and Institutions* (Philadelphia: Fortress Press; Assen, Netherlands: Van

Gorcum, 1974–76).

Spangler, Ann, and Lois Tverberg, *Sitting at the Feet of Rabbi Jesus: How the Jewishness of Jesus Can Transform Your Faith* (Grand Rapids: Zondervan, 2009).

Stern, David H., *Jewish New Testament Commentary: A Companion Volume to the Jewish New Testament*, electronic ed. (Clarksville, MD: Jewish New Testament Publications, 1996).

Tripp, C. V., *Joseph, Jesus, and the Jewish People: A Gospel Tract Hidden in the Torah* (Enumclaw, WA: Redemption Press, 2015).

Tverberg, Lois, *Listening to the Language of the Bible* (Holland, MI: En-Gedi Resource Center, 2004).

Tverberg, Lois, *Walking in the Dust of Rabbi Jesus: How the Jewish Words of Jesus Can Change Your Life* (Grand Rapids: Zondervan, 2011).

Wiersbe, Warren W., *Be Obedient: Learning the Secret of Living by Faith* (Colorado Springs, CO: David C. Cook, 2010).

Wilson, Marvin, *Our Father Abraham: Jewish Roots of the Christian Faith* (Grand Rapids: Eerdmans, 1989).

Wright, Tom, *The Original Jesus: The Life and Vision of a Revolutionary* (Grand Rapids: Eerdmans, 1997).

Young, Brad, *Jesus the Jewish Theologian* (Grand Rapids: Baker Academic, 2011).

Websites

http://jcstudies.org/

http://www. ariel.org/

http://www.biblicalresources.net/

http://ffoz.org/

http://www.jerusalemperspective.com/

http://www.jewsandchristiansjourney.com/

http://www.ourrabbijesus.com/

https://www.thattheworldmayknow.com/

http://engediresourcecenter.com/

F-260
READING PLAN

WEEK 1 ☐
Genesis 1 -2
Genesis 3-4
Genesis 6-7
Genesis 8-9
Job 1-2

Memory Verses:
Genesis 1:27
Hebrews 11:7

WEEK 2 ☐
Job 38-39
Job 40-42
Genesis 11-12
Genesis 15
Genesis 16-17

Memory Verses:
Hebrews 11:6
Hebrews 11:8-10

WEEK 3 ☐
Genesis 18-19
Genesis 20-21
Genesis 22
Genesis 24
Genesis 25:19-34; 26

Memory Verses:
Romans 4:20-22
Hebrews 11:17-19

WEEK 4 ☐
Genesis 27-28
Genesis 29-30:24
Genesis 31-32
Genesis 33; 35
Genesis 37

Memory Verses:
2 Corinthians 10:12
1 John 3:18

WEEK 5 ☐
Genesis 39-40
Genesis 41
Genesis 42-43
Genesis 44-45
Genesis 46-47

Memory Verses:
Romans 8:28-30
Ephesians 3:20-21

WEEK 6 ☐
Genesis 48-49
Genesis 50 – Exodus 1
Exodus 2-3
Exodus 4-5
Exodus 6-7

Memory Verses:
Genesis 50:20
Hebrews 11:24-26

WEEK 7 ☐
Exodus 8-9
Exodus 10-11
Exodus 12
Exodus 13:17-14
Exodus 16-17

Memory Verses:
John 1:29
Hebrews 9:22

WEEK 8 ☐
Exodus 19-20
Exodus 24-25
Exodus 26-27
Exodus 28-29
Exodus 30-31

Memory Verses:
Exodus 20:1-3
Galatians 5:14

WEEK 9 ☐
Exodus 32-33
Exodus 34-36:1
Exodus 40
Leviticus 8-9
Leviticus 16-17

Memory Verses:
Exodus 33:16
Matthew 22:37-39

WEEK 10 ☐
Leviticus 23
Leviticus 26
Numbers 11-12
Numbers 13-14
Numbers 16-17

Memory Verses:
Leviticus 26:13
Deuteronomy 31:7-8

WEEK 11 ☐
Numbers 20; 27:12-23
Numbers 34-35
Deuteronomy 1-2
Deuteronomy 3-4
Deuteronomy 6-7

Memory Verses:
Deuteronomy 4:7
Deuteronomy 6: 4-9

WEEK 12 ☐
Deuteronomy 8-9
Deuteronomy 30-31
Deuteronomy 32:48-52; 34
Joshua 1-2
Joshua 3-4

Memory Verses:
Joshua 1:8-9
Psalm 1:1-2

WEEK 13   ☐
Joshua 5:10-15; 6
Joshua 7-8
Joshua 23-24
Judges 2-3
Judges 4

Memory Verses:
Joshua 24:14-15
Judges 2:12

WEEK 14   ☐
Judges 6-7
Judges 13-14
Judges 15-16
Ruth 1-2
Ruth 3-4

Memory Verses:
Psalm 19:14
Galatians 4:4-5

WEEK 15   ☐
1 Samuel 1-2
1 Samuel 3; 8
1 Samuel 9-10
1 Samuel 13-14
1 Samuel 15-16

Memory Verses:
1 Samuel 15:22
1 Samuel 16:7

WEEK 16   ☐
1 Samuel 17-18
1 Samuel 19-20
1 Samuel 21-22
Psalm 22; 1 Samuel 24-25:1
1 Samuel 28; 31

Memory Verses:
1 Samuel 17:46-47
2 Timothy 4:17a

WEEK 17   ☐
2 Samuel 1; 2:1-7
2 Samuel 3:1; 5; Psalm 23
2 Samuel 6-7
Psalm 18; 2 Samuel 9
2 Samuel 11-12

Memory Verses:
Psalm 23:1-3
Psalm 51:10-13

WEEK 18   ☐
Psalm 51
2 Samuel 24; Psalm 24
Psalms 1; 19
Psalms 103; 119:1-48
Psalms 119:49-128

Memory Verses:
Psalm 1:1-7
Psalm 119:7-11

WEEK 19   ☐
Psalms 119:129-176; 139
Psalms 148-150
1 Kings 2
1 Kings 3; 6
1 Kings 8; 9:1-9

Memory Verses:
Psalm 139:1-3
Psalm 139:15-16

WEEK 20   ☐
Proverbs 1-2
Proverbs 3-4
Proverbs 16-18
Proverbs 31
1 Kings 11-12

Memory Verses:
Proverbs 1:7
Proverbs 3:5-6

WEEK 21   ☐
1 Kings 16:29-34; 17
1 Kings 18-19
1 Kings 21-22
2 Kings 2
2 Kings 5; 6:1-23

Memory Verses:
Psalm 17:15
Psalm 63:1

WEEK 22   ☐
Jonah 1-2
Jonah 3-4
Hosea 1-3
Amos 1:1; 9
Joel 1-3

Memory Verses:
Psalm 16:11
John 11:25-26

WEEK 23   ☐
Isaiah 6; 9
Isaiah 44-45
Isaiah 52-53
Isaiah 65-66
Micah 1; 4:6-13; 5

Memory Verses:
Isaiah 53:5-6
1 Peter 2:23-24

WEEK 24   ☐
2 Kings 17-18
2 Kings 19-21
2 Kings 22-23
Jeremiah 1-3:5
Jeremiah 25; 29

Memory Verses:
Proverbs 29:18
Jeremiah 1:15

WEEK 25   ☐
Jeremiah 31:31-40; 32-33
Jeremiah 52; 2 Kings 24-25
Ezekiel 1:1-3; 36:16-38; 37
Daniel 1-2
Daniel 3-4

Memory Verses:
Ezekiel 36:26-27
Daniel 4:35

WEEK 26   ☐
Daniel 5-6
Daniel 9-10; 12
Ezra 1-2
Ezra 3-4
Ezra 5-6

Memory Verses:
Daniel 6:26-27
Daniel 9:19

WEEK 27 ☐
Zechariah 1:1-6; 2; 12
Ezra 7-8
Ezra 9-10
Esther 1-2
Esther 3-4

Memory Verses:
Zephaniah 3:17
1 Peter 3:15

WEEK 28 ☐
Esther 5-7
Esther 8-10
Nehemiah 1-2
Nehemiah 3-4
Nehemiah 5-6

Memory Verses:
Deuteronomy 29:29
Psalm 101:3-4

WEEK 29 ☐
Nehemiah 7-8
Nehemiah 9
Nehemiah 10
Nehemiah 11
Nehemiah 12

Memory Verses:
Nehemiah 6:9
Nehemiah 9:6

WEEK 30 ☐
Nehemiah 13
Malachi 1
Malachi 2
Malachi 3
Malachi 4

Memory Verses:
Psalm 51:17
Colossians 1:19-20

WEEK 31 ☐
Luke 1
Luke 2
Matthew 1-2
Mark 1
John 1

Memory Verses:
John 1:1-2
John 1:14

WEEK 32 ☐
Matthew 3-4
Matthew 5
Matthew 6
Matthew 7
Matthew 8

Memory Verses:
Matthew 5:16
Matthew 6:33

WEEK 33 ☐
Luke 9:10-62
Mark 9-10
Luke 12
John 3-4
Luke 14

Memory Verses:
Luke 14:26-27
Luke 14:33

WEEK 34 ☐
John 6
Matthew 19:16-30
Luke 15-16
Luke 17:11-37; 18
Mark 10

Memory Verses:
Mark 10:45
John 6:37

WEEK 35 ☐
John 11; Matthew 21:1-13
John 13
John 14-15
John 16
Matthew 24:1-31

Memory Verse:
John 13:34-35
John 15:4-5

WEEK 36 ☐
Matthew 24:32-51
John 17
Matthew 26:35-27:31
Matthew 27:32-66;
Luke 23:26-56
John 19

Memory Verses:
Luke 23:34
John 17:3

WEEK 37 ☐
Mark 16
Luke 24
John 20-21
Matthew 28
Acts 1

Memory Verses:
Matthew 28:18-20
Acts 1:8

WEEK 38 ☐
Acts 2-3
Acts 4-5
Acts 6
Acts 7
Acts 8-9

Memory Verse:
Acts 2:42
Acts 4:31

WEEK 39 ☐
Acts 10-11
Acts 12
Acts 13-14
James 1-2
James 3-5

Memory Verses:
James 1:2-4
James 2:17

WEEK 40 ☐
Acts 15-16
Galatians 1-3
Galatians 4-6
Acts 17-18:17
1 Thessalonians 1-2

Memory Verses:
Acts 17:11
Acts 17:24-25

WEEK 41 ☐
1 Thessalonians 3-5
2 Thessalonians 1-3
Acts 18:18-28; 19
1 Corinthians 1-2
1 Corinthians 3-4

Memory Verses:
1 Corinthians 1:18
1 Thessalonians 5:23-24

WEEK 42 ☐
1 Corinthians 5-6
1 Corinthians 7-8
1 Corinthians 9-10
1 Corinthians 11-12
1 Corinthians 13-14

Memory Verses:
1 Corinthians 10:13
1 Corinthians 13:13

WEEK 43 ☐
1 Corinthians 15-16
2 Corinthians 1-2
2 Corinthians 3-4
2 Corinthians 5-6
2 Corinthians 7-8

Memory Verses:
Romans 1:16-17
1 Corinthians 15:3-4

WEEK 44 ☐
2 Corinthians 9-10
2 Corinthians 11-13
Romans 1-2; Acts 20:1-3
Romans 3-4
Romans 5-6

Memory Verses:
Romans 5:1
2 Corinthians 10:4

WEEK 45 ☐
WEEK 45 (Nov 6)
Romans 7-8
Romans 9-10
Romans 11-12
Romans 13-14
Romans 15-16

Memory Verses:
Romans 8:1
Romans 12:1-2

WEEK 46 ☐
Acts 20-21
Acts 22-23
Acts 24-25
Acts 26-27
Acts 28

Memory Verses:
Acts 20:24
2 Corinthians 4:7-10

WEEK 47 ☐
Colossians 1-2
Colossians 3-4
Ephesians 1-2
Ephesians 3-4
Ephesians 5-6

Memory Verses:
Ephesians 2:8-10
Colossians 2:6-7

WEEK 48 ☐
Philippians 1-2
Philippians 3-4
Hebrews 1-2
Hebrews 3-4
Hebrews 5-6

Memory Verses:
Philippians 3:7-8
Hebrews 4:14-16

WEEK 49 ☐
Hebrews 7
Hebrews 8-9
Hebrews 10
Hebrews 11
Hebrews 12

Memory Verses:
Galatians 2:19-20
2 Corinthians 5:17

WEEK 50 ☐
1 Timothy 1-3
1 Timothy 4-6
2 Timothy 1-2
2 Timothy 3-4
1 Peter 1-2

Memory Verses:
2 Timothy 2:1-2
2 Timothy 2:15

WEEK 51 ☐
1 Peter 3-4
1 Peter 5; 2 Peter 1
2 Peter 2-3
1 John 1-3
1 John 4-5

Memory Verses:
1 Peter 2:11
1 John 4:10-11

WEEK 52 ☐
Revelation 1
Revelation 2-3
Revelation 4-5
Revelation 18-19
Revelation 20-22

Memory Verses:
Revelation 3:19
Revelation 21:3-4

Acknowledgments

I am thankful to God for the many people who worked alongside me to make this book a reality. I have benefited through the years from the ministries of Dwight A. Pryor, Arnold Fruchtenbaum, D. Thomas Lancaster, Ray Vander Laan, Lois Tverberg, Marvin Wilson, James Whitman, and Boaz Michael. The insights I gleaned through the years shaped the development and direction of this work.

I am grateful for the editorial insights of Lois Tverberg, who carefully offered comments from a Hebraic perspective to strengthen the material in the book. I've always appreciated your writing through the years and considered it a joy to talk by phone about your editorial comments. I also want to thank Hamilton Barber, who has been with me from the start to finish of this project. God has gifted you as a writer and as a Bible student. I am thankful for the men in my D-groups (discipleship groups of three to five people) who offered helpful comments: Chris, Mike, Allen, Jordan, Tommy, Austin, Andrew, Bobby, John, and Jason. I am indebted to my staff at Long Hollow who offered helpful insights as each of them read through the early manuscript.

Writing is a labor of love that requires extended time away from family to complete, which is why I am indebted to my wife, Kandi, for allowing me to research, develop, and write this book. She patiently leveraged time in our schedule for me to retreat. Her probing questions as we read through the unedited copy of the book were extremely helpful. My prayer is that God would use this contribution to the church as a means for growing my own boys closer to him through his Word. May they fall in love with Jesus the way I have.

Endnotes

Introduction

1. Pirkei Avot 5:22 [Online] http://www.sefaria.org/Pirkei_Avot.5?lang=en (accessed August 25, 2016). Pirkei Avot is translated in English as the *Chapters of the Fathers*. This collection of maxims and ethical teachings comprises a chapter of the Mishnah. The verse reads as follows:

   "He [Yehudah ben Teima] used to say: Five years [is the age] for [the study of] Scripture, Ten [is the age] for [the study of] Mishnah, Thirteen [is the age] for [observing] commandments, Fifteen [is the age] for [the study of] Talmud, Eighteen [is the age] for the [wedding] canopy, Twenty [is the age] for pursuit, Thirty [is the age] for [full] strength, Forty [is the age] for understanding, Fifty [is the age] for [giving] counsel, Sixty [is the age] for mature age, Seventy [is the age] for a hoary head, Eighty [is the age] for [superadded] strength, Ninety [is the age] for [a] bending [stature], One hundred, is [the age at which one is] as if dead, passed away, and ceased from the world."

2. Acts 1:15 reveals that there were around 120 disciples during that time.

3. Ann Spangler and Lois Tverberg, *Sitting at the Feet of Rabbi Jesus: How the Jewishness of Jesus Can Transform Your Faith* (Grand Rapids: Zondervan, 2009), 116.

4. Daniel Fuller, *The Unity of the Bible: Unfolding God's Plan for Humanity* (Grand Rapids: Zondervan, 1992), 29.

5. D. Thomas Lancaster, *Torah Club: Restoration: Returning the Torah of Moses to the Disciples of Jesus* (Marshfield, MO: First Fruits of Zion, 2005), 26–27.

6. Eusebius, *Life of Constantine*, 3.18–19.

7. Luther wrote a few books against the Jewish people entitled *Against the Sabbath Keepers*, *Against the Judaizers*, and *On the Jews and Their Lies*. In the final work, Luther denounced them completely by advocating for "burning down synagogues in every town and forcing Jews to convert or die."

8. Dwight Pryor, *Behold the Man* (Dayton, OH: Center for Judaic Christian Studies, 2008), 65.

9. John Phillips, *Exploring the Gospel of Matthew: An Expository Commentary*, The John Phillips Commentary Series (Grand Rapids: Kregel, 2005), 94.

10. Lancaster, *Restoration: Returning the Torah of Moses to the Disciples of Jesus*, 31–32.

11. Jesus quoted from Isaiah more than from any of the other prophets.

Chapter 1

1. D. Thomas Lancaster, *Torah Club: Chronicles of the Messiah* (Marshfield, MO: First Fruits of Zion, 2014), vi.

2. The Mishnah is a collection of 4,187 rules of dogma.

3. Brant James Pitre, *Jesus the Bridegroom: The Greatest Love Story Ever Told* (New York: Image, 2014), 172, Kindle.

4. Lancaster, *Chronicles of the Messiah*, xx.

5. Thorleif Boman, *Hebrew Thought Compared with Greek*, Norton Library (New York: W.W. Norton, 1970), 273.

6. Brad Young, *Jesus the Jewish Theologian* (Grand Rapids: Baker Academic, 2011), 273.

7. Ibid.

8. James W. Fleming, *The Difficult Sayings of Jesus* (LaGrange, GA: Biblical Resources, 2004), 57.

9. Boman, *Hebrew Thought Compared with Greek*, 74.

10. Robby Gallaty, *Rediscovering Discipleship: Making Jesus' Final Words Our First Work* (Grand Rapids: Zondervan, 2015), 44.

11. Boman, *Hebrew Thought Compared with Greek*, 74.

12. Ibid., 76.

13. Ray Vander Laan preached this at a Bible conference in Baton Rouge in 2007.

14. For a further explanation of this concept, see my *Rediscovering Discipleship*, 45.

15. A. S. Peake, ed., *The People and the Book* (Oxford: Clarendon Press, 1925), 353–82.

16. Dietrich Bonhoeffer, *Life Together* (New York: Harper & Row, 1954), 112.

17. Chagigah 9b at Sefaria, http://www.sefaria.org/Chagigah.9bil (accessed April 20, 2016).

18. Shmuel Safrai et al., "Education and the Study of the Torah," in *Compendia Rerum Iudaicarum Ad Novum Testamentum*. Section 1, vol. 2, *The Jewish People in the First Century: Historical Geography, Political History, Social, Cultural and Religious Life and Institutions* (Assen, Netherlands; Philadelphia: Van Gorcum, 1974–76), 945–70.

19. Sanhedrin, 99a at Sefaria, http://www.sefaria.org/Chagigah.9b (accessed April 20, 2016).

20. Marva J. Dawn, *Reaching Out Without Dumbing Down: A Theology of Worship for the Turn-of-the-Century Culture* (Grand Rapids: W. B. Eerdmans, 1995), 21.

21. Dave Browning, *Deliberate Simplicity* (Grand Rapids: Zondervan, 2009), Kindle.

22. Genesis 15:6 does use *he-emin*, which is the verb form of *emunah* that means "trusted, was faithful to" in reference to Abraham's commitment to God. However, the word *emunah* is not used until Exodus 17.

Chapter 2

1. We see how seriously God takes blood covenants and how greatly he abhors it when his people break them.

2. I first learned this concept from Ray Vander Laan at http://v2.followtherabbi .com/journey/israel/god-with-us1.

3. Leviticus 1:17 explains that the birds were to be left whole in order to preserve the intestines.

4. John Mark Hicks, *Come to the Table* (Orange, CA: New Leaf Books, 2002), 28. Although there is no biblical evidence, Hicks assumes the pieces were eaten by Abram after the ceremony as part of a covenantal meal of joy and celebration.

5. Ray Vander Laan, *Faith Lessons,* "Prophets and Kings," Film (Israel: Ray Vander Laan, 1996). Ray Vander Laan, "God With Us," That the World May Know (accessed July 22, 2016), https://www.thattheworldmayknow.com/god-with -us-article.

6. Matthew George Easton, *Easton's Bible Dictionary* (New York: Harper & Brothers, 1893).

7. C. Gilbert Romero, "Torch," ed. David Noel Freedman, Allen C. Myers, and Astrid B. Beck, *Eerdmans Dictionary of the Bible* (Grand Rapids: W. B. Eerdmans, 2000), 1321.

8. Easton, *Easton's Bible Dictionary.*

9. Rabbi Rashi is quoted on Genesis 15:10 in D. Thomas Lancaster, *Torah Club: Unrolling the Scroll* (Marshfield, MO: First Fruits of Zion, 2014), 56.

10. Lancaster, *Torah Club: Unrolling the Scroll,* 54.

11. Christopher T. Begg, "Rereading of the 'Animal Rite' of Genesis 15 in Early Jewish Narratives," *Catholic Biblical Quarterly* 50 (January 1988): 41.

12. See Mishnah, *Tamid* 3:7; Josephus, *Antiquities* 14.4.3; Philo, *Special Laws,* 1:169.

13. Vander Laan, *Faith Lessons,* "Prophets and Kings."

14. Flavius Josephus, "The Wars of the Jews," 6:423–427, in *The Works of Flavius Josephus* (London: Willoughby and Co., 1859), 749.

15. Ibid. The sacrifices offered during the Passover were "256,500," which "amounts to 2,700,200 persons that were pure and holy." Even if he embellished the number, the amount of people in Jerusalem during Passover is mindblowing.

16. *Pesahim* 5:1.

17. See Daniel M. Gurtner, "The Veil of the Temple in History and Legend," *Journal of the Evangelical Theological Society* 49, 1 (March 2006): 97–114.

18. See "The Basics of Kriah or Tearing a Piece of Clothing," My Jewish Learning, from *The Jewish Mourner's Handbook* (West Orange, NJ: Behrman House, 1992) http://www.myjewishlearning.com/article/the-basics-of-kriah-or-tearing-a-piece -of-clothing (accessed March 19, 2016).

19. Adapted from ibid. (accessed July 13, 2016).

20. Warren W. Wiersbe, *Be Obedient: Learning the Secret of Living by Faith* (Colorado Springs, CO: David C. Cook, 2010), 132.

21. Rabbi H. Freeman and Maurice Simon, *Midrash Rabbah* (London: Soncino Press, 1961), 493.

22. Josephus, *The Works of Flavius Josephus*, 19.

23. Lois Tverberg, *Walking in the Dust of Rabbi Jesus: How the Jewish Words of Jesus Can Change Your Life* (Grand Rapids: Zondervan, 2011), 19. This offering was called an *olah* or a whole burnt offering.

24. Donald Grey Barnhouse, *Genesis: A Devotional Exposition* (Grand Rapids: Ministry Resources Library, 1973), 203.

25. James Montgomery Boice, *Genesis: An Expositional Commentary* (Grand Rapids: Baker Books, 1998), 688.

26. Roger Liebi, *The Messiah in the Temple* (Dusseldorf, Germany: Christlicher Medien Vertrieb, 2003), 290.

27. C. V. Tripp, *Joseph, Jesus, and the Jewish People: A Gospel Tract Hidden in the Torah* (Enumclaw, WA: Redemption Press, 2015), 33.

28. *The Holy Bible: Authorized Version* (New York: American Bible Society, 1999), Genesis 41:45. The reference is found in Tripp, *Joseph, Jesus, and the Jewish People*, 40–43.

29. Flavius Josephus, *Antiquities of the Jews* (New York: Putnam, 1969), Book 2:6,§ 1.

30. Tripp, *Joseph, Jesus, and the Jewish People*, 40–43.

31. Some rabbinic traditions speak about two messiahs—a *mashiach ben David*, one who would be a glorious king like David, and a *mashiach ben Joseph*, one who would suffer like Joseph to save his family.

32. David Bivin originally pointed out that "prophet" was a messianic title referring to Deuteronomy 18:15. See "Prophet as a Messianic Title," www.jerusalemperspective.com.

33. Billy K. Smith and Franklin S. Page, *Amos, Obadiah, Jonah*, vol. 19B, The New American Commentary (Nashville, TN: Broadman & Holman, 1995), 26–27. Smith and Page note: "Amos used two other terms in 7:14 to explain what he was doing when God called him to prophesy to Israel (also see comments on that verse). Those terms are translated "shepherd" (*bôqēr*) and one who "took care of [*bôlēs*] sycamore-fig trees." *Bôqēr* designates a "herdsman," and *bôlēs* refers to one who scrapes or punctures or does something with sycamore-figs. T. J. Wright explored two possible meanings of the word *bôlēs*. He suggested that "one of the tasks of Amos was to nip the sycamore fruit in order to hasten ripening." His other suggestion was that "the concern of Amos with the sycamore was in providing fodder for those in his charge." An advantage of the latter meaning is the obvious connection between a shepherd's responsibility to feed the sheep and the possibility that the sycamore-fig provided one source of food. This latter side of his vocation would have required him to travel to lower elevations where the sycamore-fig grew.

34. J. Birney Dibble, "Why Should I Study the Old Testament?" *Enrichment Journal* (February 2011), http://enrichmentjournal.org/201102/201102_000_study_OT.htm.cfm.

Chapter 3

1. I bought the rights to these pictures years ago from Bible Places. http://www.bibleplaces.com.
2. James W. Fleming, Mishnah Sukkot 5.4)016. First Fruits of Zion, 2. From A Messianic Jewish Perspective, vol. 1 (San Antonio, TX: Ariel Ministries); *Turning Points in the Life of Jesus* (LaGrange, GA: Biblical Resources, 2004), 21.
3. Lancaster, *Chronicles of the Messiah*, 29.
4. J. C. Ryle, *Expository Thoughts on the Gospels.* https://www.monergism.com /the threshold/sdg/expository_web.html (accessed April 2, 2016).
5. Lancaster, *Chronicles of the Messiah*, 146.
6. James Strong, *Strong's Exhaustive Concordance of the Bible* (Peabody, MA: Hendrickson Publishers, 2009), https://www.blueletterbible.org/lang/lexicon/lexicon.cfm?t=kjv&strongs=g907 (accessed March 5, 2016).
7. Lancaster, *Chronicles of the Messiah*, 157.
8. See Dwight Pryor at www.jcstudies.org.
9. Richard B. Hays, *Echoes of Scripture in the Gospels* (Waco, TX: Baylor University Press, 2016), 251.
10. Dwight Pryor, *Unveiling the Kingdom*, vol. 6 (Dayton, OH: Judaic Christian Studies, 2013).
11. Joni Eareckson Tada, "God Permits What He Hates," *Joni and Friends*, May 15, 2013, http://www.joniandfriends.org/radio/5-minute/god-permits-what-he-hates1 (accessed April 3, 2016).

Chapter 4

1. Lancaster, *Chronicles of the Messiah*, 7–8.
2. Dwight Pryor, *The Shepherd of Israel*, audio version, www.jcstudies.org.
3. See Arnold Fruchtenbaum, *Yeshua: The Life of the Messiah from a Messianic Jewish Perspective*, vol. 1 (San Antonio, TX: Ariel Ministries, 2016), 410–12.
4. Alfred Edersheim, *The Life and Times of Jesus the Messiah* (Peabody, MA: Hendrickson, 1993), 611, http://www.ntslibrary.com/PDF%20Books/The%20Life%20and%20Times%20of%20Jesus%20the%20Messiah.pdf (accessed March 22, 2016).
5. Arnold Fruchtenbaum, *Messiah Yeshua, Divine Redeemer: Christology from a Messianic Jewish Perspective* (San Antonio, TX: Ariel Ministries, 2015), 28.
6. Charles L. Quarles, "Matthew," in *CSB Study Bible: Holman Christian Standard Bible* (Nashville, TN: Holman Bible Publishers, 2011), 1608.
7. D. A. Carson in Tremper Longman and David E. Garland, *The Expositor's Bible Commentary*, vol. 9 (Grand Rapids: Zondervan, 2010), 111.
8. David Wiley made me aware of the connection between Daniel and the magi.

9. Moses Maimonides, *Mishneh Torah, Hilkot Talmud Torah*, 1:8.

10. Saul Lieberman, *Hellenism in Jewish Palestine* (New York: Jewish Theological Seminary, 1962), 52.

11. Gallaty, *Rediscovering Discipleship*, 17.

12. Lancaster, *Chronicles of the Messiah*, 132.

13. Edersheim, *The Life and Times of Jesus the Messiah,* 171.

14. Pryor, *Behold the Man*, 25.

15. For a deeper look at this, examine several passages in Luke's Gospel: Luke 11:14ff.; 12:41ff.; 18:18ff.; 24:13ff.

16. Josephus, *Antiquities of the Jews*, 5:348/x.4.

17. Fruchtenbaum, *Life of the Messiah*, 44.

18. Dann Spader, *4 Chair Discipling: Growing a Movement of Disciple-Makers* (Chicago: Moody Publishers, 2014), 24.

19. Young, *Jesus the Jewish Theologian*, 24.

20. Lancaster, *Chronicles of the Messiah*, 132.

21. Mishnah, Avot 5:21. It's not by happenstance that Jesus began his earthly ministry at age thirty.

22. Mishnah, Avot 2:2.

23. See Mishnah, Avot 5.

24. Roland de Vaux, *Ancient Israel: Its Life and Institutions*, The Biblical Resource Series (Grand Rapids: W. B. Eerdmans, 1997), 104.

25. Lancaster, *Chronicles of the Messiah*, 184.

26. Johan Kemper, *Me'irat Enayim (Enlightenment of the Eyes)*, (Jerusalem, Israel, 1704), Rem. 11, v. 1. Kemper wrote a commentary on Matthew that emphasizes the unity of the Old and New Testaments.

27. *Midrash Koheleth Rabba: Ecclesiastes Rabba, Hebrew and English* (New York: P Shalom Pubns Publishers, 1989), 1:28.

28. See *Rediscovering Discipleship* for more of my thoughts on this connection.

29. Isaiah Horowitz and Miles Krassen, *The Generations of Adam* (New York: Paulist Press, 1996), 279. I also heard Dwight Pryor affirm this concept.

30. James W. Fleming, *The Jewish Background of Jesus* (LaGrange, GA: Biblical Resources, 2004), 11.

31. John Wesley, *Wesley's Notes on Psalms 118:22*, https://www.studylight.org/commentary/ psalms/118–22.html (accessed March 22, 2016).

32. Yechiel Tzvi Lichtenstein, *Commentary on the New Testament: The Holy Gospel According to Mattai* (Marshfield, MO: Vine of David, 2010), on Matthew 2:23.

33. Ray Vander Laan used this term at a Bible conference in Baton Rouge in 2007. He used this label to give a picture of the climate of the first century.

34. D. Thomas Lancaster, *Torah Club: Shadows of the Messiah* (Marshfield, MO: First Fruits of Zion, 2015), 283.

35. Spangler and Tverberg, *Sitting at the Feet of Rabbi Jesus*, 44.

36. The technique of connecting two different scriptures with the same key phrase or

word is called *gezera shava* as noted in T. Sanh. 7.11; Abot R. Nat. 37. Both texts utilize the same key word. Steven Notley first documented the Isaiah connection. See R. Steven Notley, "Jesus' Jewish Hermeneutical Method in the Nazareth Synagogue" in *Early Christian Literature and Intertextuality*, vol. 2: Exegetical Studies, ed. C. A. Evans and H. D. Zacharias (London: T&T Clark, 2009), 56.

37. Pryor, *Unveiling the Kingdom*, vol. 6, audio.

Chapter 5

1. Hays, *Echoes of Scripture in the Gospels*, 301.
2. Spangler and Tverberg, *Sitting at the Feet of Rabbi Jesus*, 44.
3. Dwight Pryor, *The Messiah and the Apostle* [Haverim study notes], 9 April 2007.
4. Lancaster, *Chronicles of the Messiah*, 158.
5. The Mishnah encouraged boys to be married by the age of eighteen.
6. Ray Vander Laan, *Faith Lessons,* "Life and Ministry of the Messiah," Film (Israel: Ray Vander Laan, 1996). Ray Vander Laan, "No Greater Love," That the World May Know, last modified 2016, https://www.thattheworldmayknow.com/nogreaterlove.
7. According to Dwight Pryor, the sycamore tree was synonymous with repentance in the first century. The tree he hung from was a picture of the response he would make. I first learned about this during an Israel study tour with Judaic Christian Studies in May 2007.
8. John P. Meier, *A Marginal Jew: Rethinking the Historical Jesus*, Anchor Yale Bible Reference Library (New York: Doubleday, 1994), 2:996, n. 118.
9. Hays, *Echoes of Scripture in the Gospels*, 72.
10. Ibid.
11. Ibid., 73.

Chapter 6

1. Some scholars are divided on whether it lasted seven or eight days. Regardless, Jesus stood up to speak on the final day of the feast.
2. Liebi, *The Messiah in the Temple*, 396. Liebi comments, "[The priest] went up the ramp, oriented towards the south, to the Altar and poured the water from the Pool of Siloam into the silver vessel which had been installed on the southern side of the Altar, near to its southwest corner."
3. David H. Stern, *Jewish New Testament Commentary: A Companion Volume to the Jewish New Testament*, electronic ed. (Clarksville, MD: Jewish New Testament Publications, 1996), John 7:37. Some believe the reason for joy during the Feast of Booths is because the Day of Atonement took place just five days before. During the festival, the nation confessed and received forgiveness from their transgressions, thus removing the guilt and shame associated with sin.
4. Roger D. Willmore, "Rivers of Living Water" (sermon), http://www.preaching.com/sermons/11557626/2 (accessed March 26, 2016).

5. I heard Ray Vander Laan reenact this encounter at the Feast of Tabernacle in Baton Rouge in 2007.

6. G. K. Beale and Mitchell Kim, *God Dwells Among Us: Expanding Eden to the Ends of the Earth*, 85 (Downers Grove, IL: InterVarsity Press, 2016), 85, Kindle.

7. Liebi, *The Messiah in the Temple*, 398.

8. Ibid., 400.

9. M. R. Vincent, *Word Studies in the New Testament* (Wilmington, DE: Associated Publishers and Authors, 1972), 103.

10. See Spangler and Tverberg, *Sitting at the Feet of Rabbi Jesus*, 180.

11. Lancaster, *Shadows of the Messiah*, 161.

12. Pryor, *Unveiling the Kingdom*, audio.

13. Dwight Pryor, *The Supreme Virtue*, audio, http://jcstudies.org.

14. Paraphrase of Genesis 3:8.

15. I'm paraphrasing something Dwight Pryor said in the *Unveiling the Kingdom* audio series.

16. Pryor, *Unveiling the Kingdom*, audio.

17. Song of Songs, Rabbah 1:2, https://www.jewishvirtuallibrary.org/jsource/judaica/ejud_0002_0019_0_18885.html (accessed April 3, 2016).

18. Arnold Fruchtenbaum, "Born Again," Ariel Ministries, http://www.ariel.org/qa/qbornag.htm.

19. Fruchtenbaum, *Messiah Yeshua, Divine Redeemer*, 62.

20. God ordered the destruction of the serpent in 2 Kings 18.

21. Terence E. Fretheim, "Commentary on Numbers 21:4–9," WorkingPreacher.org, 2008.

22. Terence E. Fretheim, *Exodus: Interpretation, A Bible Commentary for Teaching and Preaching* (Louisville, KY: John Knox Press, 1991), 172.

Chapter 7

1. Fruchtenbaum, *Yeshua: The Life of the Messiah from a Messianic Jewish Perspective*, vol. 1, 143–55.

2. Ibid. See also Arnold Fruchtenbaum, "The Life of the Messiah in His Jewish Context," from DVD series *Yeshua: The Life of the Messiah from a Jewish Perspective*, 46, 75.

3. See Mark 2:1–2.

4. Liebi, *The Messiah in the Temple*, 382.

5. Lancaster, *Chronicles of the Messiah*, 364.

6. I. Howard Marshall, *The Gospel of Luke*, New International Greek Testament Commentary (Grand Rapids: W. B. Eerdmans, 1978), 208.

7. Fruchtenbaum, *Yeshua: The Life of the Messiah from a Messianic Jewish Perspective*, vol. 1, 145–47.

8. *Babylonian Talmud*, Sanhedrin 98a.

9. Ibid., Sanhedrin 98b, emphasis mine.

10. Lancaster, *Shadows of the Messiah*, 502–3.

11. Arnold Fruchtenbaum, *The Three Messianic Miracles* (San Antonio, TX: Ariel Ministries, 1983), 14.

12. Moses' sister was healed before completion of the law, and Naaman was not an Israelite.

13. J. Dwight Pentecost, *The Words and Works of Jesus Christ: A Study of the Life of Christ* (Grand Rapids: Zondervan, 1981), 151.

14. Fruchtenbaum, *The Three Messianic Miracles*, 8–9.

15. Ibid., 10–12.

16. Fruchtenbaum, "The Life of the Messiah in His Jewish Context," 132.

17. Hays, *Echoes of Scripture in the Gospels*, 38.

18. Frank Kermode, *The Genesis of Secrecy: On the Interpretation of Narrative* (Cambridge, MA: Harvard University Press, 1979), 47.

19. Dwight Pryor, David Bivins, and Brad Young offer a different interpretation for Jesus teaching in parables from this juncture of his ministry. However, the text states when and why Jesus shifts.

20. *Genesis Rabbah* 63:6, http://www.sefaria.org/Bereishit_Rabbah.63.6?lang=bi (accessed September 19, 2016). This Rabbinical commentary on Genesis 25:22 cites the dispute between Jacob and Esau.

21. Fruchtenbaum, *The Three Messianic Miracles*, 18.

22. Ibid.

Chapter 8

1. Fleming, *Turning Points in the Life of Jesus*, 53.

2. Rabbi Jochanan, *Babylonian Talmud*, Megillah 31a. Dwight Pryor turned me on to this idea.

3. 1 Kings 9:13 (CSB) states, "Each man quickly took his garment and put it under Jehu on the bare steps. They blew the ram's horn and proclaimed, 'Jehu is king!'"

4. See Leviticus 23:33–40 for a detailed outline of the elements incorporated.

5. The Pharisees proved this in Matthew 22:41–42.

6. Liebi, *The Messiah in the Temple*, 79.

7. Fruchtenbaum, *The Life of the Messiah*, 58.

8. John MacArthur, "Nothing But Leaves," sermon at Grace Community Church, Sun Valley, CA, January 16, 2011, http://www.gty.org/resources/sermons/41–57/nothing-but-leaves?Term=judgement%20begins%20in%20the%20house?term=judgement%20begins%20in%20the%20house (accessed June 20, 2016).

9. Arnold Fruchtenbaum, *Feasts of Israel* (San Antonio, TX: Ariel Ministries, 1983), 8.

10. Lancaster, *Unrolling the Scroll*, 1301.

11. Robert Boyd, *World's Bible Handbook* (Iowa Falls, IA: World Bible Publishers, 1991), 122.

12. Fleming, *Turning Points in the Life of Jesus*, 60.

13. Pryor, *Behold the Man*, video.

14. Larry Largent, "Judas, Villain or Guest of Honor?," http://biblicalremains.com/judas-villain-or-guest-of-honor/ (accessed 20 December 2016).

15. Dwight Pryor revealed this concept to me at a Haverim Study in April 2007 in Dayton, OH.

Chapter 9

1. William Arndt, Frederick W. Danker, and Walter Bauer, *A Greek-English Lexicon of the New Testament and Other Early Christian Literature* (Chicago: University of Chicago Press, 2000), 63.

2. Mishnah Bava Kama 7.7, http://www.sefaria.org/Mishnah_Bava_Kamma?lang=en (accessed June 23, 2016).

3. See Josephus; The Artscroll Mishnah Sukkot 5.4; The Yom Kippur Machzor, 196 by Artscroll; *Jesus the Messiah* by Alfred Edersheim, 844; the Mishnayoth by Phillip Blackman; and Mishnah Sukkot 5.4.

4. Herbert Danby, *The Mishnah: Translated from the Hebrew with Introduction and Brief Explanatory Notes* (Peabody, MA: Hendrickson Publishers, 2011), Sukkah 5.4, Tamid 1.2, Yoma 1.8.

5. Marcus J. Borg and John Dominic Crossan, *The Last Week: A Day-by-Day Account of Jesus's Final Week in Jerusalem* (San Francisco: HarperOne, 2006), 2–4.

6. Francis Brown, Samuel Rolles Driver, and Charles Augustus Briggs, *Enhanced Brown-Driver-Briggs Hebrew and English Lexicon* (Oxford: Clarendon Press, 1977), 1069.

7. Merrill C. Tenney, *The Zondervan Encyclopedia of the Bible*, vol. 5 (Grand Rapids: Zondervan, 2009), THYATIRA, https://books.google.com/books/about/The_Zondervan_Encyclopedia_of_the_Bible.html?id=O6F9VYz74aUC (accessed June 24, 2016).

8. Hays, *Echoes of Scripture in the Gospels*, 85.

Conclusion

1. Spangler and Tverberg, *Sitting at the Feet of Rabbi Jesus*, Kindle.

Rediscovering Discipleship

Making Jesus' Final Words Our First Work

Robby Gallaty

Discipleship is the buzzword today. Many believers are contemplating in a fresh way what it means to take the Great Commission seriously. *Rediscovering Discipleship* takes the guesswork out of Christian maturity.

Based on insights gained from a decade of personally making disciples, author and pastor Robby Gallaty tackles the two hindrances that keep believers from getting involved in making disciples: ignorance and uncertainty. Since many believers have never been personally discipled, they have no model to guide them in discipling others. Their ignorance of the process fuels their uncertainty, which leaves them crippled from the start. With simple principles that are easy to apply, *Rediscovering Discipleship* provides readers with the tools to follow the Great Commission— to go and actually make disciples who multiply and make disciples.

Gallaty begins with a brief historical overview of the discipleship ministries of influential theologians, preachers, and pastors from years past, and then identifies roadblocks that hinder believers from becoming disciples before offering a step-by-step process for readers to immediately get started on the path to effective disciple making.

Available in stores and online!

ZONDERVAN®
.com